Manufacturing the Mathematical Child

Mathematics is a subject held in high esteem around the world, yet the teaching and learning of mathematics are rarely viewed as good enough, and many find the subject difficult to comprehend or engage with. In *Manufacturing the Mathematical Child*, Anna Llewellyn asks some difficult questions in order to determine why this is the case and to question who it is that we allow to succeed in mathematics, particularly within the context of neoliberalism, where education is a product of the market.

By looking at the various sites of production, Llewellyn examines the ways that key discursive spaces produce very different expectations of what it means to do mathematics and demonstrates that these place various homogenised expectations upon children. Arguing that these are not natural, but instead a reproduction of discursive norms, the book demonstrates why some people fit these standardised ways of being and others do not. Using England as a case study and referring to other international contexts, Llewellyn argues that there is a functionality found within certain educational policy discourses, and a romantic attachment to the natural child found within educational research, neither of which can match what happens in the messy classroom. As a result, it becomes evident that exclusion from mathematics is inevitable for many children.

Original and exciting, this book will be of great interest to academics, researchers, and postgraduate students within the fields of mathematics education, childhood studies, policy studies and Foucauldian or post-structural analysis.

Anna Llewellyn is an assistant professor in education at Durham University; her work examines constructions of childhood in education and society.

Routledge Research in Education

This series aims to present the latest research from right across the field of education. It is not confined to any particular area or school of thought and seeks to provide coverage of a broad range of topics, theories and issues from around the world.

Recent titles in the series include:

Politics and Pedagogy of Digital Participation
New Directions for Media Educators
Catherine Burwell

Blended Basic Language Courses
Design, Pedagogy, and Implementation
Hope M. Anderson

Latina Bilingual Education Teachers
Examining Structural Racism in Schools
Yukari Takimoto Amos

Questioning the Language of Improvement and Reform in Education
Reclaiming Meaning
Nicole Mockler and Susan Groundwater-Smith

Learning from Urban Immigrant Youth about Academic Literacies
Jie Y. Park

The Arts as Learning
Cultivating Landscapes of Democracy
Edited by Jay Hanes and Eleanor Weisman

Manufacturing the Mathematical Child
A Deconstruction of Dominant Spaces of Production and Governance
Anna Llewellyn

For a complete list of titles in this series, please visit www.routledge.com/Routledge-Research-in-Education/book-series/SE0393

Manufacturing the Mathematical Child

A Deconstruction of Dominant Spaces of Production and Governance

Anna Llewellyn

LONDON AND NEW YORK

First published 2018
by Routledge

2 Park Square, Milton Park, Abingdon, Oxfordshire OX14 4RN
52 Vanderbilt Avenue, New York, NY 10017

Routledge is an imprint of the Taylor & Francis Group, an informa business

First issued in paperback 2020

Copyright © 2018 Anna Llewellyn

The right of Anna Llewellyn to be identified as author of this work has been asserted by her in accordance with sections 77 and 78 of the Copyright, Designs and Patents Act 1988.

All rights reserved. No part of this book may be reprinted or reproduced or utilised in any form or by any electronic, mechanical, or other means, now known or hereafter invented, including photocopying and recording, or in any information storage or retrieval system, without permission in writing from the publishers.

Notice:
Product or corporate names may be trademarks or registered trademarks, and are used only for identification and explanation without intent to infringe.

British Library Cataloguing-in-Publication Data
A catalogue record for this book is available from the British Library

Library of Congress Cataloging-in-Publication Data
A catalog record for this book has been requested

ISBN: 978-1-138-29301-4 (hbk)
ISBN: 978-0-367-48783-6 (pbk)

Typeset in Galliard
by Apex CoVantage, LLC

Contents

Acknowledgements		vi
1	Introduction: stating the obvious: the context and the questions	1
2	Un-stating the obvious: theory to challenge norms	11
3	Un-stating the 'normal' and 'natural' child	37
4	Unpacking educational policy	65
5	Unpacking mathematics education research	89
6	Spaces of enactment	106
7	Messy bodies: what next?	128
	References	133
	Index	150

Acknowledgements

There are many people that have contributed to the thoughts and ideas in this book: the communities of Mathematics Education Society (MES), Mathematics and Contemporary Theory and the Disorder of Mathematics Education (DOME), in particular – thank you for debating with me and for allowing me a voice. Special thanks to Peter Gates for his support and encouragement and to Heather Mendick for her challenge and inspiration – I am eternally grateful.

1 Introduction

Stating the obvious: the context and the questions

Norms of mathematics education

It is a truth universally acknowledged that a child in education must be in want of a 'good' mathematics grade[1] – but why is this? Is it that mathematics is essential to a person's daily life, is it that mathematics is vital for the advancement of modern societies, or is it that achievement in mathematics is a clear signifier of individual success? Perhaps it is none of these in its entirety, but instead, this 'truth' operates through not what mathematics is or can be used for but through the power that mathematics occupies in society. I am suggesting that many of the 'truths' we associate with mathematics are fictitious, and instead, mathematics is only important because we construct it to be. I propose that mathematics as an integral part of schools and society is not factual but manmade.

The pursuit of a simplistic causal answer to these questions is something that permeates both education and mathematics: mathematics with its roots in absolutism – particularly for school mathematics. Whilst modern discourses of education also seek straightforward solutions to support systems, teachers, and students. The pursuit of 'what works' and what is generalisable is set up to offer causal, uncomplicated resolutions. Furthermore, both mathematics and education are invested in largely contestable truths. That mathematics and education are both incredibly important to a person and to society are some of those, and troubling these assumptions is very problematic. However, this is the starting point of this book, as it proposes silenced questions and asks why they are so difficult to consider.

For instance, imagine an education system where mathematics is a low-status subject – this is very hard to do – it jars against many taken-for-granted norms of education and society. Currently in the UK, mathematics teachers can earn £30,000 to train to teach. This is far in advance of many subjects, particularly the Arts. This incentive does link to the current shortage of mathematics teachers – however, these shortages are propagated by mathematics as a compulsory subject that is double weighted (alongside English) in Progress 8 – the most recent measure of success for compulsory English school students. Moreover, in the most recent UK budget, English schools are to be given extra money to encourage students to study mathematics; there is also money for mathematics specialist schools – not other subjects, just mathematics. The current UK chancellor Philip Hammond states that "knowledge of maths is key to the hi-tech, cutting-edge jobs in our digital economy" – this statement is worth consideration, but it is no way an incontestable truth, but it is presented as such. The digital economy may need programmers, but they would not need to have studied school mathematics. The digital economy also needs creative, artists, and managers. A society of technicist mathematicians yet no room for the Arts is highly problematic. Although perhaps governments can make such bold statements – as a society of mathematicians will never happen – it is always already a fictional promise and something that remains out of reach.

Some may think that I am forcing an unnecessary binary here, something which I am critical of elsewhere in this book – this is not my intention, and I do not wish to suggest you cannot be both mathematical and artistic. Historically, many great philosophers were also great mathematicians. However, within current society, when something is favoured – as mathematics is – it tends to take on quite a distinct and discrete life and meaning; furthermore, when schools have very limited funding, they will 'logically' chose to spend on the subject where students and teacher are held more accountable – it seems like the most straightforward solution.

These discourses of mathematics do not stop with the UK – the US has invested heavily in STEM (Science, Technology, Engineering and mathematics) subjects, with mathematics being seen as the core to these. The US (and many other countries) are concerned with their school performance in international measures such as the PISA (Programme for International Student Assessment) and the TIMMS (Trends in International mathematics and Science Study). These are measures comparing educational systems around the world; they are currently topped in mathematics by Far East countries and regions such as Shanghai. Again, we can ask why is measuring mathematics the best way to compare success – although for many this is difficult to consider.

This is my starting point for this book: that there are ways of doing and talking about mathematics that have become common sense and that we accept as the truth. Furthermore, these ways of speaking may actually do more harm than good. They restrict us by permitting certain ways of thinking. They limit the questions we can ask and the answers we are prepared to consider, for instance stating that mathematics is not a fundamental part of society is very problematic to hear and an impossible position for many to consider. But the point is that these truths do not exist in a vacuum outside of society – society and the people in it actively create and perpetuate them, and it is this society in which people experience mathematics. Furthermore, educational researchers of mathematics are absolutely complicit in this.

This leads me to another taken-for-granted truth, and one that is found more in mathematics education research, is that the best mathematics teaching involves active students who understand the mathematics. These classrooms are focused on 'why' questions, allow for discussion, and seek 'understanding' of mathematics. Influential reports on UK mathematics education contain this position:

> The fundamental issue for teachers is how better to develop students' mathematical understanding. Too often, students are expected to remember methods, rules and facts without grasping the underpinning concepts, making connections with earlier learning and other topics, and making sense of the mathematics so that they can use it independently.
> (Ofsted, 2008, p. 5)

> [M]athematics lessons in secondary schools are very often not about anything . . . There is excessive preoccupation with a sequence of skills and quite inadequate opportunity to see the skills emerging from the solution of problems.
> (Cockcroft, 1982, p. 462)

Hence, some of these ways of speaking are not only public discourses but are also actively enabled by authoritative figures such as government officials and educational researchers.

Whilst the preceding truths are not shared by all groups, where many of these disparate groups agree is that mathematics education is not really good enough and that there is always something schools, teachers and students can be doing better. Though to suggest this is a new 'truth' in mathematics education is problematic; poor results and "imperfect teaching" of mathematics were 'evident' around the time of the first UK education act in 1870:

> In arithmetic I regret to say worse results than ever before have been obtained – this is partly attributable, no doubt, to my having so framed my sums as to require rather more intelligence than before: the failures are almost invariably traceable to radically imperfect teaching.
> (HM inspectors, written in 1876, cited in Cockcroft, 1982, p. xii)

It is perhaps odd to think we have not fixed a 'problem' that was identified more than 100 years ago, particularly as the main concern of mathematics education research is to improve performance (Boero, 2008; discussed in Pais & Valero, 2011). And surely our current modern prosperous society should be on top of this – by design, we have exposed ourselves to an array of teaching ideas and research that are deemed to improve classroom and student outcomes. The preceding critiques by Ofsted and Cockcroft are very similar even though they were made 26 years apart – perhaps they are suggesting a solution that is impossible or asking the wrong questions. This highlights another concern this is exposed in this book: that the need for improvement is omnipresent in education, particularly in a high-stakes subject such as mathematics education.

However, what if there is no magical method of teaching and learning mathematics that works for every child? What if being good at mathematics was not seen as exceptional? What if mathematics was not viewed as important by society? These might seem quite fantastical questions, but by considering them we can begin to think differently about how we (and others) view mathematics education, how we (and others) view studying mathematics, and what we (and others) perceive those who do mathematics to be. All those questions are discussed in this book, as I attempt to unpack the norms that we find ourselves a part of and that I suggest simultaneously create and restrict what we can and cannot do within mathematics education. My suggestion is if we take off the blinkers, then we can begin to consider (a) are there different solutions to the questions we usually ask and (b) if we really should be asking those questions at all.

What is also clear, from preceding, is that our ways of thinking are often bounded by who we are, where we are, and the practices we are allowed to promote. The 'active' school student, who works in groups and queries the mathematics, is a culturally specific construction that is found in the UK (particularly in educational research) and other parts of the world, such as the US and Canada. China has a different model, where the education system is built on Confucian ways of being and the culture of respect and hard work. Here, teaching for student involvement is not excluded; however, it is thought that this can be best achieved through mastery of skills first, via the repetition of mathematical methods and cognising through listening. This pedagogy is often constructed as a passive, deficit model by Western writers, although work in cultural and language studies rightly questions this Othering and derisory, discursive positioning (Grimshaw, 2007). However, country boundaries are being eroded; with their students' success on the PISA, a version of Shanghai mastery mathematics has begun to permeate UK schools (discussed more in Chapter 4).

In stating the preceding, I am not saying that all teaching and learning in each of those countries follows those patterns; a country is not homogenous in its educational practices. However, I am saying that there are norms of practices within cultural contexts, and furthermore that we cannot consider what we do without considering these norms of culture and society. Too often, education initiatives and research are written about the disembodied school student who is bounded by cognition alone, Western education being dominated by psychological developmental narratives. Thus, I come to the topic of this book – 'Manufacturing the mathematical child'. With this title, I am suggesting that who is permitted to do mathematics is not natural, or merely cognitive (which are the dominant voices in education) but is produced by culture and society. Furthermore, these productions look quite different in various spaces – public, private, university schools, and so on. It is this representation of the child that enables some and disables others.

These versions of the mathematical child are built on and perpetuated by the 'truths' or norms of mathematics that are permitted by society. I suggest that these are often so invested in the good of mathematics, both to the individual and to society, that educationalists are blinkered in both the approach they can take and the conclusions they can make. For policy makers, mathematics is something that is easily measurable, and it is a maker of a prosperous society – it is difficult to say anything else. Logically, almost all educational researchers of mathematics are invested in the importance of the subject; their lives are dedicated to this premise. Moreover, there is often always funding opportunities in a society that both favours mathematics and suggests its practice in schools is not as good as it should be. These are some of the limits with which those who write about mathematics are faced – and mostly they are not acknowledged.

That we live in a society that privileges the funding of mathematics is part of a wider cultural system that favours data and assessment within education, part of which is connected to mathematics as an uncomplicated measure of achievement. Thus, another limit that education is currently facing, and one that underpins much of the discussion in this book, is that many societies operate within a system of measurability and accountability. In the next section I set the cultural scene more specifically by discussing the context that is currently permeating education within the UK, as well as wider society – that of neoliberalism.

The neoliberal culture of England and other parts of the world

The culture of the UK is currently caught up in a neoliberal performative agenda, where many parts of society are bounded by the privileging of measurement, accountability, and targets. Specifically, neoliberalism is a policy regime defined by "the progressive enlargement of the territory of the market" (du Gay, 1996, p. 56). England has been moving in that direction at least since the Conservative government of the 1980s (Newman, 2001), although neoliberalism is not constrained by national boundaries and "is affecting education in areas as diverse as Europe, the United States, South America and Australia (Grek, Lawna, Lingard, & Varjoc, 2009; Hultqvist & Dahlberg, 2001)" (Llewellyn & Mendick, 2011, p. 50):

> Neoliberalism is in the first instance a theory of political economic practices that proposes that human well-being can best be advanced by liberating individual entrepreneurial freedoms and skills within an institutional framework characterized by strong private property rights, free markets and free trade. The role of the state is to create and preserve an institutional framework appropriate to such practices.
> (Harvey, 2005, p. 2)

Hence, "the most basic feature of neoliberalism is the systematic use of state power to impose (financial) market imperatives, in a domestic process that is replicated internationally by 'globalisation'" (Saad-Filho & Johnston, 2005, p. 3). This rise in neoliberalism has seen significant reform in education throughout the world (Apple, 2003). And it is this reform that provides "the appearance that the state has taken responsibility for improving society and, therefore, increases the state's legitimacy" (Hursh, 2007, p. 18). This has significant implications for anyone involved in education. For instance, as I explore in this book, it is imperative that official discourses show that education is improving.

One way in which this is actualised in England is the shift towards the privatisation of the public sector or by the blurring of these boundaries between these previously distinct sectors. In education, this is evident through not only the introduction of private sponsors to run schools but also in the manner that schools are managed and monitored. For instance, at the time of writing, two of the most central education institutions in England are led by people with backgrounds in finance and economics – not education: the Office for Standards in Education, Children's Services and Skills (Ofsted)[2] being led by Amanda Spielman and the Department for Education (DfE)[3] by Justine Greening.

Significantly, the market has begun to drive general educational reform and policy (S. J. Ball, 1993a; Ozga, 2009; Whitty, Power, & Halpin, 1998). As such, terms such as *economy*, *efficiency*, and *measured outcomes* have entered both educational policy and discourses. Quality assurance and evaluation have become a method of governing (Grek et al., 2009), and "comparison for constant improvement against competition has come to be the standard by which public systems are judged" (Grek et al., 2009, p. 123). Hence, complex systems and processes become oversimplified into categories and data, for the purpose of 'value' judgement (S. J. Ball, 2003). This is evident in the widespread, normalised use of performance indicators, league tables, and student data. As such, education has become fabricated around these measurable statistics and is, in effect, "governing by numbers" (N. Rose, 1991) or 'educating by numbers'. Everyone, from nursery school student to professor of mathematics education, is a part of this performative agenda.

Within this neoliberal education system, surveillance is high as the public sector borrows management models of working from the private sector (S. J. Ball, 2003). Subjects become self-regulating (S. J. Ball, 2003, 2008) whilst management models create the appearance of autonomy both within policy and within classroom practice discourses (S. J. Ball, 1994). Thus, whilst teachers may follow the accepted best practice of mathematics education research and promote 'active' learning, they are not free within this; instead, it is the appearance of autonomy, as students are regulated and surveilled into a preferred way of being. But what if these students have different preferred ways of thinking and doing? What if teachers want to teach mathematics by mastering methods, as in China? What if they prefer to work individually? Is that wholly bad? There is no reason to suppose these suggestions limit or pacify school students. To suggest this is removing any agency from the individual. People are capable of being active and passive within the situations with which they are presented.

Whilst I have presented neoliberalism as a crucial part of current education initiatives in England, I am going to add a footnote here that at the time of writing, neoliberalism may be at a tipping point. With the recent Brexit and Trump victories in the UK and US, respectively, project neoliberalism may have failed or certainly may have failed to connect with the everyman. That being said, schools show no signs of slowing down with their investment in neoliberal ideas; similarly, universities in the UK seem to be taking onboard more of the practices of neoliberalism, with the recent TEF (Teacher Excellence and Students Outcomes Framework) being just one more example of measurement and the mass redundancies being another related to cost-efficiencies. The education discussed in this book, whether current or from previous governments, does sit within this agenda, and thus, neoliberalism provides the backdrop to the discussions. Whether discussing policy regimes, education research, or the opinion of teachers – every aspect is infiltrated by neoliberal performativity.

Thus, we have the context for my discussion (neoliberalism) and an idea that I will be dissecting taken-for-granted truths of mathematics education. For the rest of this introduction I explain the structure of the book, and how I have chosen to break down my discussion of 'Manufacturing of the mathematical child'.

Organisation of this book

As already mentioned, I am interested in norms, culture, and society, and how this creates what is possible for children studying mathematics. I am interested in exploring the different dominant stories that are told by various dominant groups that have a say in how education is both shaped and practiced; specifically, I discuss educational policy, mathematics education research and space of enactment via teachers.

It may already be clear from the language I use that I am influenced by particular ways of thinking about the world and people in it. I discuss this in Chapter 2, where I explore the purpose of using theory education and the ways it can help open 'alternative' stories about being and doing. These other positions are hard to find it education where success is often premised around what is most common and best for the majority. My assumption is that by looking at anything from the usually tread positions, we restrict ourselves to seeing certain results. My concern is that mathematics education (schooling, government, and research) is blinkered by the narrow positions, outlooks, and conventions that it tends to adopt. The particular theories I discuss in Chapter 2 are from the work of Michel Foucault. Foucault allows us to unpack norms and, more specifically, to critique the supremacy of reason, rationality, and progress (Foucault, 1970/2002), all of which are central to the production of mathematics education and the mathematical child. These discussions are helpful near the beginning of the book as they frame the majority of the discussion, and as mentioned I also argue for the importance of using theory. However, anyone prone to theory fatigue may want to skip this chapter and move straight to the discussions.

Chapter 3 moves on to discuss childhood. There are several points here that are worth highlighting, in the first instance that children are not an innocent category; instead, I draw on Edelman (2004) and Burman (2008a) to argue that they are the hope of a nation and hence can never simply be viewed as individuals, or within the present; they are bound to a futurity of the modern prosperous state. I follow Edelman's version of the Child, which refers to the symbolic representation of the child as opposed to the experiences of children. The second point concerns the construction of the child – specifically that the child commonly found in dominant educational narratives is a cognitive being and this often relies on a psychological development narrative, which is favoured in certain versions of education. However, the alternate argument is to draw on people like Walkerdine and contend that the very practices that claim to discover the child actually produce the child (Walkerdine, 1997, p. 61). Thus, the central argument, being that what we often view as natural, is instead created through systems, structures, and the production of dominant narratives. I discuss how this works to create the child of education and then, specifically, of mathematics education. This sets up the next few chapters of the book, which discuss how certain narratives are created within dominant domains that are responsible for producing knowledge.

The first site of analysis explored in Chapter 4 is educational policy; I suggest that we are currently within a time where not only is there significant investment in education from government but education also plays a role in the electability of a government – thus, government education policies are high-stakes. Specifically, I pay attention to the policies of the New Labour government, which were held up to be relatively progressive. Drawing on Foucault, I argue that we can better examine the present if we have a comprehension of the past. For New Labour my main argument is that the production of the mathematical child is concerned with functionality. I discuss how this enables and constrains possibilities for children. I move on to discuss education policies of the current Conservative government. I show that with the privatisation and academisation of many schools, and the move away from central government (in some ways), there are fewer educational policy documents. However, there are still messages about what the mathematical child should be. This is done on a bed of surveillance in terms of accountability yet with the appearance of pedagogical freedom. Also in this chapter I set the UK discussion in relation to policies from around the world.

Chapter 5 examines a different domain – that of mathematics education research. The first thing to point out is that mathematics education research is not, of course, a homogenous body – there are differences and variations. However, as discussed already there are certain things that are easier said, and certain things that are more easily heard. For instance, if I started saying that mathematics was overvalued in society, there would not be many people wanting to hear me speak or cite my work; it is not an accepted part of mathematics education research discourse. Thus, academia is concerned with producing certain types of knowledge, where the power of citation favours some knowledge and some bodies over others. This is a vitally important point to make as universities are often afforded unquestionable authority. Hence, mathematics education research is a crucial site to deconstruct. One of the truths I draw out that circulates within mathematics education research is that the child is predominantly an "active cognitive subject" (Valero, 2002, p. 542) who is often devoid of cultural, social context. This Child is produced through 'natural' cognitive development, more aligned to Rousseauian or psychological development, and hence offers a 'romantic' version of the child. I also discuss mathematics education research in relation to recent trends, particularly those associated with direct governance, 'impact', and large-scale data. This could be seen as a threat to the 'romantics' of mathematics education; however, I contend that a correct developmental path for the Child was a precursor to the overt surveillance and targets that are currently found in education in many parts of the world.

Chapter 6 draws on different sets of data to talk about the experience of teachers and people training to be teachers (whom I am calling pre-service). Within this I am not suggesting that any of these voices represent what a teaching body may think or how they may act. Drawing on Foucault, instead each voice explores individual stories looking for both cohesion and difference in how people interpret the world around them. Specifically, individual voices are discussed in relation to the dominant discourses explored in the previous two chapters – that of the functional and romantic Child of mathematics education. Do these different constructions from policy and educational research matter? How are they interpreted by actual teachers? I build on these discussions to explore whether these sites are still dominant within teacher discourse and education or whether teachers experience more fluid boundaries. Within New Labour years, training was led by the government; however, in the current English system, private companies can provide training, and there is also movement for teacher-led professional development. Furthermore, boundaries of knowledge transfer and production have arguably been smashed by the role of social media, particularly by sites such as Twitter. I imagine these as heterotopic spaces that play with traditional hegemonic boundaries, as well as with time, space, and place (thus, in addition, physical borders are more fluid).

Chapter 7 draws all these ideas together to suggest the various manifestation of the manufacturing of the mathematical child. Both the dominant versions of the mathematical child of educational policy and mathematics education research are largely homogenised cognitive subjects devoid of cultural, social context. The mathematical child of mathematics education research performs through natural activity, whereas the child of educational policy performs through functional performance. I suggest these are both produced, though one is deemed to be 'free' and the other is more viewed as constrained within a system. These discourses are disparate, but I also discuss how they do not acknowledge each other. The stories of the pre-service teachers demonstrate how these are impossible fictions to live up to. They also demonstrate how some people are easily excluded from mathematics. However, with the move away from centralised government within England and the fluid space of Twitter, there is a more recent blurring of discursive boundaries. Although the mathematical child still remains a cognitive body. I summarise what this means for England and make comparisons to other relevant countries. The final section of this book does what all education research is supposed to do, and it makes some implications, or I prefer to call these considerations, for teachers, education policy makers, educational researchers, and anyone doing mathematics. As you may have gathered, I have particular concerns over the homogenisation of children, the cognisation of the child, and the lack of self-reflection concerned with the production of knowledge.

So there you go, a book that is founded on the problems of assumptions and the value that is supposed when studying mathematics. Thus, before you partake on this it is worth considering what your own investments in mathematics education are: Do you believe in children discovering the mathematics? Do you believe in group work over individualised learning? Do you believe that mathematics is the most important subject in the curriculum? If so, why so? What assumptions have you made in taking these positions, and is it possible to suspend any? My suggestion is that by acknowledging our own investments, only then can we really begin to tackle the mathematical world of which we find ourselves a part.

Notes

1 This opening line is based on the opening line of Jane Austen's 1813 novel *Pride and Prejudice*.
2 Amanda Spielman has been HM chief inspector of education, children's services and skills for Ofsted since January 2017 (Adams and Weale, 2017). Adams, R. and Weale, S. 2017. New Ofsted Chief: 'I want everyone to see us as a force for improvement'. *The Guardian* https://www.theguardian.com/education/2017/jan/09/ofsted-chief-inspector-schools-amanda-spielman retrieved May 2017
3 Justine Greening was secretary of state for education from July 2016 until January 2018.

2 Un-stating the obvious
Theory to challenge norms

An interview for a promoted university lecturing post:

"We take a broad approach to Education in this department; our students as well as studying Education, also study a broad range of disciplines from the social sciences and the Arts – how would you ensure you met their research needs", asked the interviewer. "I would set up extra SPSS workshops", replied the candidate.

Introduction

The purpose of this chapter is to discuss ways in which someone may begin to unpack these very dominant 'truths' of mathematics and the mathematical child, how they can step outside the circles in which they operate. My starting point for this is to argue for the use of social theory, which in current research trends is often not viewed favorably. Thus, I begin by discussing the current context of educational research, what is privileged, and what opportunities and constraints this brings. The second part of this chapter explores the work of the particular theorist I use, Michel Foucault, and how his ideas influence the arguments in this book.

Why use theory in educational research

Over the last decade there has been a significant narrowing of what constitutes 'good' research in education; this is reflected in what is experienced on research programmes, what is privileged in academic writing, and what is preferred in academic funding. In many parts of the world (particularly the UK and the US) the movement in education is to privilege large data sets and quantifiable and objective results (Hamilton & Corbett-Whittier, 2013). This is demonstrated through the work of high-profile researchers (e.g. Gorard, 2013, 2014; Torgerson and Torgerson (2001), the funding of research projects (e.g. the EEF [Education, Endowment Foundation]), and the funding of quantitative research training programmes (discussed in Gorard, 2015). At the top of this tree of objectifiable 'excellence' are Randomised Control Trials (RCTs; championed by those such as Torgerson and Goldacre) that seek cause-and-effect relations; they are framed as the 'the Gold Standard of Education' (Oancea and Pring, 2008; Thomas, 2016). However, the privileging of RCTs as the best type of research creates hierarchical values around knowledge production. Specifically, the ways to both ascertain knowledge and what type of knowledge that is become extremely curtailed; consequently, *all* aspects of education can be reduced to a straightforward cause and effect, or the only questions worth asking are ones that are causal. Consequently, the implication is that all human interaction is reducible to this premise, and education can be framed by the pursuit and valuing of Gradgrind's[1] hard facts. There is no space for nuance, for grey areas for personable and individual stories, and there is no room for rich qualitative data.

Within this, it seems that education is framing itself as a Science. This reduces the human subjects to a carefully selected set of measurable variables, which I suggest they are not. What we are as humans is a complex and perhaps naïve question and not one that can be easily answered. Even if we were to cite 'hard' evidence, as Thomas (2016) shows, RCTs involve a huge amount of effort and money, and very few show any significant effect – thus, my *rational* conclusion is that humans in education do not work in simplistic causal ways; my affective response says the same – and I did not need hard data to tell me that.

However, it is a particular kind of science that is evident, one that is ignorant of RCTs' usage in medicine and the sciences; it is one that forgets other ways of experimenting or that science values singular case studies – those who study science are quite aware that there are many different ways, not the only way, to gain knowledge (discussed in Thomas, 2016). Hence, it is not *actual* science but, instead, is a fictionalised version that suits those who practise and promote it.

Within these pretentions to *science*, another hierarchy is produced, one that values *the study of science* more than the arts, the humanities, or the social sciences. This is evident through the closing of Arts faculties in universities around the world, the extra funding of STEM subjects, and the direct statements from government ministers and officials. Most recently Nicky Morgan[2] (2014) stated that "the subjects that keep young people's options open and unlock the door to all sorts of careers are the STEM subjects" (Morgan, 2014). This hierarchy is a 'truth' that diffuses this book and is *always already* inside the mathematical child.

Let me be clear here; it is not the method that I am against but the overvaluing of it. As Gary Thomas argues, there are perfectly reasonable questions that can be answered by RCTs, but there are perfectly interesting questions that cannot. For instance, we cannot comprehend the nuance and perpetuation of institutional racism or sexism, and very important, we cannot consider what it means to be the non-normative child that does not fit into mainstream and generalised discourse.

It is fair to say that trends in output are found elsewhere in the social sciences; sociology has certainly moved through the postmodern turn. Similarly, educational research is a product of and produces research trends. Importantly, this is not because, as modernity would suggest, we are constantly moving towards a greater *understanding*. Instead, academia creates and maintains these norms, standards, and practices, in which it operates, but moreover, the majority of academia is often ignorant of this – particularly within those research projects that claim to be objective. Consequently, some areas of research are privileged and some are excluded by academia's design. I have already mentioned how funding around large-scale quantitative research projects is openly preferenced – consequently, this style of research becomes normative, and it is these projects that are run and this type of knowledge that is produced. More and more academics choose to design these projects, thus maintaining its hierarchy. Within the neoliberal academy, there is pressure to publish and to find grants. There are not many academics who can choose to ignore this governance. Funding within the neoliberal academy aside, one of the most crucial and powerful aspects of academic production is citation, and that citation creates ways and forms of knowing. However, we are not all cited equally; some bodies are more easily referenced than others – the use of dead white men (of which I am guilty) is a common criticism. Indeed, Fevre and Bancroft's 2010 sociology study book *Dead White Men* attests to this. Of course, other excellent academics have made this point, Sara Ahmed (2013), in her Feminist Killjoy blog, states, "I would describe citation as a rather successful reproductive technology, a way of reproducing the world around certain bodies". In addition, there are movements (e.g. #FEAS) in the Gender and Education circle to cite more women, although I wish to be careful here of falling into the trap of 'white liberal feminism' which can exclude transgender and people of colour, and thus, I prefer Sara Ahmed's interpretation that takes a more intersectional approach to querying privilege. Furthermore, I want to query that this is something that resides more with new researchers or students who are told to read certain authors, or who may have studied specific curriculums. Many researchers cite who they know, not just what they have read, and those who are referenced are most often in powerful and privileged positions. It is a circular relationship that is difficult to contest, unless citation is disbanded or at the very least actively challenged, as #FEAS is doing.

Thus, the academy is responsible for creating the trends and the *facts* that are formed as a result. An alternative story, and one that would be peddled by many 'objective' researchers, is that they are seeking the *truth* and any narrowing of the field is as a result of this. Of course, truth is subjective – a *good* mathematics lesson for one student may not be for another, in spite of measurable results. But if these 'hard facts' are viewed as the incontestable truth, then they become difficult to challenge; particularly, if we only allow one version of knowledge we do not possess the broad range of academic language to critique it or to explore why. For instance, we cannot ask why some people do well at mathematics and others do not – we can merely note that they do. That, I suggest, is the place and value of theory, theory that allows us to step outside the biases and domains in which we are produced. I suggest that theory is as crucial as facts to education in the academy.

Primarily, I am concerned that whilst hard facts are positioned as dominant, theory becomes the inferior Other. As discussed earlier, the concern is for objective evidence, for results, and for impact; within this, a nuanced discussion of how and why is not often prioritised. As such, education takes on a rather instrumental approach, and as I argue throughout this book, so does our conception of the Child.

Furthermore, objective educational research itself is often viewed as apolitical; however, in line with Patel (2015), I suggest that it is imperative to view "educational research as a text that does work and as such it is never neutral but instead implicated with potential and unruliness to motivate disincentivize, and render invisible various realities" (Patel, 2015, p. 13). That education is viewed as a great enabler is a bold yet naive premise. Education is undoubtedly not neutral, from who decides what education is to who succeeds in it. As Battiste discusses in a narrative concerning decolonialisation of education, "education is a culturally and socially constructed institution for an imagined context with purposes defined by those who are privileged to be the deciders, and their work has not always been for the benefit of the masses" (Battiste, 2013, p. 159). Arguably, education was one of the first methods of colonising a country, and thus, children were the first recipients and products of this occupation. My concern with education – both school and university – is that it is often afforded a neutrality alongside authority, and that it may be about control and regulation and not emancipation and opportunity. Furthermore, educational research is at the apex of this constructed narrative.

For mathematics educational research particularly, we may elevate this further, mathematics being part of an absolutist narrative and much research similarly so: "For over two thousand years mathematics has been dominated by an absolutist paradigm, which views it as a body of infallible and objective truth, far removed from the affairs and values of humanity" (Ernest, 1991, p. xi). Perspectives such as Mathematical Platonism, the view that there are objects that are abstract, independent, and free of language and the human mind, seems to be quite prominent, and indeed, for some, the study of mathematics is the path to an objective truth (Plato, 375BC/2003). This view has been challenged by "a growing number of philosophers . . . [who] are affirming that mathematics is fallible, changing and like any other body of knowledge, the product of human inventiveness" (Ernest, 1991, p. xi). However, this latter account of mathematics is not always visible, particularly at school level. Instead, many narratives of mathematics fall very much into the binary camp – for instance, people are good or bad at mathematics; students should learn mathematics by rote or by discovery – many of these binaries are unpacked throughout this book.

The security of certainty can be appealing. As Ernest states, "if certainty is questioned, the outcome may be that human beings have no certain knowledge at all" (Ernest, 1991, p. xi), and for many that is a very vulnerable position, which can be especially troubling within a school context. The alternative position is offered by mathematics, where "mathematical reasoning presumes mastery of a discourse in which the universe is knowable and manipulable according to particular mathematical algorithms" (Walkerdine, 1990, p. 72). This description, of course, parallels dominant narratives of educational research. My argument is that objective and disembodied reasoning supports many of the issues found in mathematics education. For instance, this absolutist unquestioning nature of mathematics seems to support the position that doers of mathematics are naturally gifted. This is not a new assertion and can be read in Plato's ancient text:

> Those who have a natural talent for calculation are generally quick at every other kind of knowledge; and even the dull, if they have had an arithmetical training, although they may derive no other advantage from it, always become much quicker than they would otherwise have been.
> (Plato, 375BC/2003, p. 256)

Here, Plato disseminates common discourses of doers of mathematics that are still prevalent today that they are fast, naturally gifted, and held in high esteem (Mendick, 2006). This fiction of the 'naturally gifted' doer of mathematics helps perpetuate a myth of prestige around the subject and supports the production of the 'mathematician' as "a culturally and socially marked category of identity ... [that] has the power to impress, intimidate and alienate others" (Mendick, 2006, p. 7).

Hence, I suggest that for mathematics education research to do its job, it is imperative to break those normatives, to take off the blinkers, and to step outside the absolutist, objective narratives of which we find ourselves a part, and that is where I turn to theory.

When I talk of theory, I do not mean theory in the sense of scientific or explanatory theory (as discussed by Thomas, 2007), I mean theory that allows for a deconstruction and subsequent interpretation of the world and what happens in it. I mean theory often termed as social or critical theory. I mean theory that disrupts, that is offensive (MacLure, 2010). "The value of theory lies in its power to get in the way: to offend and interrupt. We need theory to block the reproduction of the bleeding obvious, and thereby, hopefully, open new possibilities for thinking and doing" (MacLure, 2010 p. 277). I mean theory that moves across and between disciples, that is not bounded by its origins or stature. I mean theory that allows us to ask, 'What am I a part of?' and 'What work does that do?'

Theory is, of course, not without is citation problems, and it not without trends – this is very problematic. As MacLure wrote in 2003,

> theory is linked to those funny 'turns' that are said to have befallen the disciplines as a result/cause of the 'crisis of representation' – the linguistic turn, the reflexive turn, the narrative turn, the postmodern turn ... they share the work of 'registering a new space 'for research and theorizing across the disciplines.
> (MacLure, 2003, p. 134)

MacLure herself has shifted her postmodern position and is currently part of the postmodern turn permeating education and social research. There is, of course, nothing wrong with this; I would not be a good theoretical researcher if I did not allow myself to be open to negotiating my personal position with theory.

However, for the purposes of this book, and where I currently sit theoretically, is firmly with poststructuralism and specifically the work of Michel Foucault. His work allows me to probe my own positioning in the world and in academia; moreover, his work allows me to challenge how the mathematical child is produced.

In this next sections I discuss his theories in more detail and depth.

Foucault, discourses, and a poststructural position

Introducing poststructuralism

Historically, poststructuralism may be viewed as a reaction to structuralism. Whilst both philosophies have some aspects in common, such as the decentring of text from dominant discourses, poststructuralism is more often viewed as a movement away from structuralism's rigid view of reasoning, language and of underlying 'truths'. Hence, I deliberately use the spelling *poststructuralism* in this book so that it is inscribed as its own position, rather than *post-structuralism*, where it is inscribed within a progressive relationship to structuralism. There are many areas of contestation about the term *poststructuralism* (particularly in relation to the term *postmodernism* and whether it is paradoxical to identify as a poststructuralist); however, there are some basic ideas that are mostly found. A key concept is that both structuralism and poststructuralism are critical responses to the Age of Enlightenment, an era where reason and the rational subject were legitimised (MacLure, 2003) and where education and childhood found prominence (discussed in more detail in the next chapter). As such, these theories are a key way to challenge normative discussions of Western childhood. Indeed, Foucault asserts reason and the rational subject to be the major arc of ongoing philosophical thought. He states,

> I think that the central issue of philosophy and critical thought since the eighteenth century has always been, still is, and will, I hope, remain the question: What is this Reason that we use? What are its historical effects? What are its limits, and what are its dangers? How can we exist as rational beings, fortunately committed to practicing a rationality that is unfortunately crisscrossed by intrinsic dangers?
>
> (Foucault, 1984, p. 249)

Hence, a critical question to consider is, 'What version of rationality and reason dominated during this period of Enlightenment and what version dominates now?' Or, more important, whose version was it, and as a consequence, who was included and who was excluded? These types of questions run throughout this book, as I attempt to show who does mathematics is not innocent and universal and that it is its own sociological and cultural construction, one where some succeed easier than others. Though to do this, I am, of course, engaging with apparently 'rational' arguments in order to present a coherent piece of academic work whilst simultaneously arguing against the over-reliance upon the rational.

This is one of the many paradoxes found within poststructural writing that I cannot avoid. However, I can attempt to navigate it, in part, by acknowledging it whilst I write.

In general, we can view poststructuralism as an attempt to question the reasoned mind and "escape the patriarchal paradigms of western thought" (Moi, 1988, p. 5). It is an endeavour to pull "ourselves free of the web" (Walkerdine, 1998a, p. 15) of rules that run through rationality. The themes and content of this book are of course, caught up in this web. In particular, education and mathematics education are shaped by rules and paradigms born of hegemonic times, many of which are unspoken and have come to be passed as common-sense truths (this is discussed further throughout this book, particularly in the next chapter). In this book, I attempt to both acknowledge and critique these webs, as I endeavour to move apart from them – if not completely free. Crucially, poststructuralism allows us to "think more about how we think" (Flax, 1987, p. 624), and consequently, we can avoid casually taking up common-sense assumptions, which are prominent in education as I have already discussed. In an educational world in which research tends towards homogeneity, rationality, and instrumentality, poststructuralism resists and contests – particularly that this is how education happens. Instead, poststructuralism allows for the mess and for the "daily struggle and muddle of education" (Donald, 1985, p. 242); in fact, it positively encourages it.

Introducing the work of Michel Foucault

As mentioned previously, this thesis is heavily reliant upon one particular theorist Michel Foucault. Many of his key concepts run explicitly and implicitly throughout. Indeed, I have already mentioned Foucault's critique of the hierarchy afforded to reason and rationality and the resulting difficulties of writing within rational argument. In the rest of this chapter, I discuss key aspects of Foucault's work whilst being aware of the paradoxes they inscribe. For example, in spite of being presented under distinct headings Foucault's categories should not be read as discrete constructs. Hence, at times, I explore how the notions overlap and contribute to each other. In addition, I struggle with the restrictions of using a linear narrative when ideas are not so. It suggests the direction of thought and writing is linear and progressive (Foucault, 1988), which, of course, it is not. Indeed, Foucault's work changed over time, and hence, what I set out in the following is only a fragment of his ideas. Furthermore, there are many areas of Foucault's work that I still negotiate. For example, how can you use a theorist who encourages you to pick and choose fragments of his work, who encourages fluidity, and who asks you to challenge grand narratives? Indeed, how do you use someone's work which questions the notion of truth and the authorship of language and specifically who questions the value of specifically referenced quotations (Foucault, 1980a)? This is, of course, true for all poststructuralism or postmodernism; Lyotard made the paradoxical observation that postmodernism is the master narratives of the end of master narratives (Lather, 1991; Morris,

1988). However, as Lather points out, "to write 'postmodern' is to simultaneously use and call into question a discourse, to both challenge and inscribe dominant meaning systems in ways that construct our own categories and frameworks as contingent, positioned, partial" (Lather, 1991, p. 1), and this is what I intend to do – "to write paradoxically aware of one's complicity in that which one critiques" (Lather, 1991, p. 10). In this sense, my writing should be uncomfortable and should provoke reaction and emotion.

At times my work steps outside of Foucault and is supplemented by reference to wider thinkers. Foucault said that "one should be able to read everything, to know all the institutions and all the practices" (Foucault, 1989i, p. 14). This is, of course, not at all possible, but it does encourage wider thought and referencing. Moreover, it helps us resist the urge to interpret his theories through a blinkered Foucauldian lens and instead to set them within a more extensive theoretical context. He reiterates this point throughout his work. For instance,

> [a]ll of my books . . . are, if you like, little tool-boxes. If people want to open them, or to use this sentence or that idea as a screwdriver or spanner to short-circuit, discredit or smash systems of power, including eventually those from which my books have emerged so much the better.
> (Foucault, 1975; cited in Patton & Meaghan, 1979, p. 115)

Furthermore, he states that "it's not up to me to establish users' rules" (Foucault, 1989e, p. 213). Thus, using Foucault is not about taking all his words verbatim or, indeed, using ad hoc quotations – I personally am not in favour of a pick 'n' mix approach to theory. For me, using Foucault is locating where I find meaning and being consistent in its application; however, it also involves remaining sceptical about the value of Foucault altogether as we consume and critique his ideas. As already mentioned, we should be careful of over-reliance on certain sources and critical of the power of citation.

Foucault's interpretation of critique is an important notion that runs through the book and more or less frames my work. I include a lengthy quotation where he makes this explicit:

> Criticism is no longer going to be practiced in the search for formal structures with universal value but, rather, as a historical investigation into the events that have led us to constitute ourselves and to recognize ourselves as subjects of what we are doing, thinking, saying. In that sense, this criticism is not transcendental, and its goal is not that of making a metaphysics possible: it is genealogical in its design and archaeological in its method. Archaeological – and not transcendental – in the sense that it will not seek to identify the universal structures of all knowledge [*connasissance*] or of all possible moral action, but will seek to treat the instances of discourses that articulate what we think, say, and do as so many historical events. And this critique will be genealogical in the sense that it will not deduce from the form of what we are what it is impossible for us to do and to know; but it will separate out, from

the contingency that has made us what we are, the possibility of no longer being, doing, or thinking what we are, do, or think.

(Foucault, 2003f, pp. 53–54)

Hence, Foucault does not look for a 'truth' but for what we perceive the truth to be and how it came to be constituted. He examines how knowledge comes to be but not from the perspective of historical accuracies but from the position that questions those readings of history. Thus, the questions become, 'How are we constituted into becoming who we are, and how are things constituted into becoming what they are? How do contingencies – not causes – shape the world around us and shape knowledge and truth? How are some things allowed to be, whilst others are not permitted? Moreover, how do events come together when we question the underlying value of rationality and reason?' Each of these ideas is explored in detail in the rest of this chapter. I begin with one of the most fundamental aspects of poststructural thought: that truth is a fiction created in time and context.

Truth and fictions

> I am quite aware that I have never written anything but fictions. I'm not saying for all that this is outside truth. It seems to me the possibility exists to make fiction work in truth, to induce effects of truth with a discourse of fiction, and to make it so that the discourse of truth creates, 'fabricates' something that does not yet exist, therefore 'fictionalizes'.
>
> –Foucault (1989e, p. 213)

For Foucault and poststructuralism, there is no singular truth, nothing that accurately describes the world; instead, there are ways of making sense of the world. These ways of making meaning differ in their status and their power to have effects in the world. Some will acquire the status of truths while others will be dismissed. In this book, I am concerned with the 'truths' found within mathematics education, society, and government that work to produce the mathematical child. My concern is to examine these as constituted truths of a time, rather than as universal Truths. My aim is to ask, " 'What's going on just now? What's happening to us? What is this world, this period, this precise moment in which we are living?' Or in other words: What are we?" (Foucault, 2003d, p. 133). It is these questions which allow for the examination of how we are constituted and what we think we are.

Truths are not absolute; instead, they are determined by time, culture, and context. For instance, 40 years ago many people would have thought that boys were better than girls at mathematics. Indeed, some people somewhere may still hold this opinion. How can this be damaging? Well, it may be that teachers holding such beliefs deliberately exclude girls from mathematics, or conversely, they may praise girls more, as they consider them to need more encouragement, which could exclude boys. Another gendered example is the notion that girls prefer pink. This can appear as a timeless, universal truth in the UK, the US, and other parts of the world. However, this is actually a modern concept that has only been around since the mid-20th century and is specific to certain parts of the world. But how can it be bad to think that girls prefer pink? Well, what if you are a boy who likes pink? Does that mean that there is something wrong with you and perhaps you are not a 'real' boy? So somewhere, and at some point, this 'truth' was created. I do not mean that someone sat down and thought, 'Hey, I know what would be good marketing, let's produce everything for girls in pink and for boys in blue'. Instead, I mean that through time and the use of language and practice, and in this case with the rise of consumerism for children (see the next chapter), we have come to accept something as having meaning. We have internally accepted it as the truth. Thus "reality is neither single nor regular" (Taylor, 2001, p. 12), for example the preferred colours for boys and girls in a remote village may be very different from those in the UK (though even these villagers are likely to have been impacted by the global media). Instead, we have to consider what we know, what we perceive to be the 'truth', and what we view as 'reality' within specific times and contexts. Moreover, we consider how 'truths' are constructed by the constraints around them. For instance, the girls who are thought of as 'poor' at mathematics are positioned as such by power relations that run throughout the social system. It is worth mentioning here another truth – that we even need to split sex and gender into the binary categories of boy and girl. Whilst I write, it seems that the world of popular culture is catching on to the need to break down both categories of sex and gender; however, whether that makes a breakthrough to education and research is another question – binaries can prove very attractive for comparative research projects.

Thus, my crucial point is that "truth is a thing of this world: it is produced only by virtue of multiple forms of constraint. And it induces regular effects of power" (Foucault, 1980c, p. 131), as I discuss in more depth later in this chapter. Thus, rather than seeing society as run by rational ideologies, society is instead constituted through various contingencies concerning truth and power within specific eras. Therefore, periods in history can present 'ideologies' (products of knowledge and power) that masquerade as the 'truth'. Specifically for Foucault, "each society has its regime of truth, its 'general politics' of truth that is, the types of discourse which it accepts and makes function as true" (Foucault, 1980c, p. 131). The argument that 'truth' and 'regimes of truth' are produced by power and discourses is explored in more depth in the following.

Discourses

In simple terms, discourses are permitted truths. In the first instance, this requires us to reconsider viewing language as fact and instead to consider "language as fragile and problematic and as *constituting* social reality rather than *reflecting* an already given reality" (Walshaw, 2007, p. 5). Discourse can have a variety of meanings, but in a Foucauldian sense, language is only part of what constitutes discourses; it has a broader and more encompassing meaning. Discourses

> are not, as one might expect, a mere intersection of things and words: an obscure web of things, and a manifest, visible, coloured chain of words . . . [discourses are] practices that systematically form the objects of which they speak. Of course, discourses are composed of signs; but what they do is more than use these signs to designate things. It is *more* that renders them irreducible to the language *(langue)* and to speech. It is this 'more' that we must reveal and describe.
> (Foucault, 1972/2002, pp. 53–54 original emphasis)

Thus, we can state that discourses create meaning, that they are constructive rather than descriptive, and that this is about the way we act towards something and about how it acts with us. Moreover, it is a fluid, two-way relationship; the subject is produced through and produces discourses (Walkerdine, 1997).

In addition, discourses are everywhere; they operate on many levels, within the social world and within disciplines. Earlier, I described a discourse of gender in relation to colour – that in general, society perceives gender through binaries and, specifically, in the UK and US, that boys prefer the colour blue and girls prefer pink. I argued that this discourse was specific to this regime, time, and context. Indeed, it can be seen as part of the consumerism and marketisation that has, over the past few decades, moved from adults to children and young people. From this, we can begin to appreciate how marketing companies and consumers have been part of this production. They add to a version of the truth where girls are conditioned to prefer pink and boys prefer blue, and this becomes a marker of their sex and gender. Pink signifies that they are 'real' girls.

The main point is that some discourses are more easily heard than others, and dominant discourses are taken up as the 'truth'; there is limited space for alternatives within the mainstream. For example, what would happen if schoolteachers acted like they did not want their students to do well in their assessments? This way of acting and speaking would not be permitted; instead, teachers may be ignored and/or branded abnormal or incompetent. A more pertinent example (explored in the introduction) is to suggest that mathematics education is not useful, which was the argument discussed recently by Pais (2013) at the conference 'Mathematics and Contemporary Theory'. Even here, within this supposed liberal academic space, resistance to this argument stemmed from the principle that Pais is saying something that this group of people did not want to hear. In their work, a lot of mathematics educationalists implicitly and explicitly refer to the usefulness of mathematics; as such, it is very difficult to comprehend another position. The same could be said for some of the arguments in this book, which I have presented over the last few years at various academic spaces. Whilst this has been well received in places, in one mathematics education faculty the ideas were condemned. Quite directly, I was told my work was offensive. Hence, quite

22   Un-stating the obvious

possibly, my work threatened the order and reason on which the academics that were present based their careers and work. I dared to challenge the normal discourses of mathematics education. Thus, discourses

> authorise what can and cannot be said they produce relations of power and communities of consent and dissent, and thus discursive boundaries are always being redrawn around what constitutes the desirable and the undesirable and around what it is that makes possible particular structures of intelligibility and unintelligibility.
>
> (Britzman, 2000, p. 36)

Moreover, we are often complicit in perpetuating discourses and in producing or maintaining boundaries; this is shown in the preceding examples from within the mathematics education community, and it is shown in the previous example of the relationship between gender and colour.

Consequently, as well as creating rules of inclusion "discourses are exclusionary: they *rule out* other ways of thinking, talking or acting" (MacLure, 2003, p. 178, original emphasis). Yet, the questions are, 'What enables some discourses to be taken up and accepted as normal, and what contributes to the marginalisation or resistance of other discourses?' For instance, why is the usefulness of mathematics, the story that is allowed to be heard? Or how has this story become dominant, and how are others excluded? This is particularly pertinent in education where discourses which focus on improvement are abundant; hence, most educational journal articles contain 'solutions' to educational (and societal) 'problems'. As such, the power of the journal article helps maintain certain particular discursive practices. However, this is an over-simplistic analysis and only part of the picture; discursive positioning is developed through many contingencies rather than being reliant on a simplistic cause and effect (Foucault, 1977/1991, 1978/1998, 2003f).

With this push for improvement, there are many different discourses in education. Many of these are referenced and/or explored in this book, ones that have already been mentioned are the usefulness of mathematics and the desire to improve education. Another that should be mentioned concerns the favouring of the psychological developmental child within education (Burman, 2008a; Henriques, Hollway, Urwin, Venn, & Walkerdine, 1998); this frames the central argument of this book. These and other key discourses are discussed in detail in the next chapter.

This does not mean that other types of talk do not occur; it means that these are the most acceptable discourses, and consequently, these are the ones that are more easily taken up as common-sense wisdom. It is this that creates regimes of truth and establishes what it is possible to know (Walshaw, 2007). It is this which gives voice to some, whilst silencing others. As such,

> discourses not only circumscribe what it is possible to say, know and do, but also establish what kind of person one is entitled/obliged to 'be'. It is

impossible, in other words, to speak without *speaking* as the kind of person who is invoked by one discourse or another. As Foucault [(1977/1991, p. 217)] put it, the individual is thus 'fabricated' into the social order. People are woven into, and woven out of, discourse.

(MacLure, 2003, p. 176 original emphasis)

Hence, everything we do and who we are are shaped by discourses; there is no discourse-free position – something which many academics and policy makers often neglect. Hence, I articulate the hidden discourses that shape our very way of practising mathematics education and the way they construct the mathematical child. There are webs of discourses that interweave, coalesce, and clash. Indeed, "it is this relationship among discourses, this inter-discursive framework or web, that we should try to analyze" (Foucault, 1989f, p. 163), as it is this conflict that creates opportunities for knowledge. The salient point is that "we should not 'burrow' into discourse looking for meanings. We should instead look for the external conditions of its existence, its appearance and its regularity" (Threadgold, 2000, p. 49). One way in which we do this is by examining power relations, which are explored in the next section.

Power

Fundamental to Foucault's work is the notion of power. Foucault argues that in designating what is 'normal' and what is the 'truth', "discourse transmits and produces power" (Foucault, 1978/1998, p. 101). Hence, power and discourses are part of the same production; as such, power circulates within all aspects of my analysis, although it is often hidden from plain view. However, discourses and power should not be viewed as dual concepts but instead can be viewed as a "three-dimensional constellation including discourse, knowledge, and power, . . . that is, both invaded and controlled, constituted as an object formulated in 'truth' and defined as an object, as the target of a possible knowledge" (Foucault, 1989f, p. 162). Hence, where we find permitted truths (discourses) we find power circulating and producing knowledge. Thus, for Foucault power and knowledge are inextricably linked. He states,

> We should admit rather that power produces knowledge (and not simply by encouraging it because it serves power or by applying it because it is useful); that power and knowledge directly imply one another; that there is no power relation without the correlative constitution of a field of knowledge, nor any knowledge that does not presuppose and constitute at the same time power relations.
>
> (Foucault, 1977/1991, p. 27)

This way of thinking is very different to many 'traditional' forms of knowledge, as it acknowledges how 'truths' (discourses) are constituted by power/knowledge relations and vice versa. For instance, as I explore in detail in the next chapter, this is shown in the psychological notion of the cognitive child, which appears as a 'truth' reasoned from an impartial standpoint. Foucault argues that it is this positioning of truths as impartial knowledge that can be dangerous (Foucault, 1977/1991, 1989i). Furthermore, he suggests the production of power/knowledge comes from systems and structures as opposed to belonging to individuals; again, this contrasts to 'traditional' Western reason that is often premised on individual thinkers. Thus, Foucault's power is found circulating within a system. It is a strategy rather than something which belongs to a dominant population:

> [Power] is a machine in which everyone is caught, those who exercise power as well as those who are subjected to it . . . Power is no longer substantially identified with a particular individual who possesses it or exercises it by right of birth. It becomes a machinery that no one controls. Obviously everyone in this machine occupies a different position; some are more important than others and enable those who occupy them to produce effects of supremacy, insuring a class domination to the extent that they dissociate political power from individual power.
>
> (Foucault, 1989c, p. 234)

As such, power/knowledge relations are omnipresent; specifically, "there are relations of power as fundamental as economic or discursive relations, that absolutely structure our lives." (Foucault, 1989h, p. 143). Power can be used to gain superiority, though it does not belong with that person; it circulates within the system.

To illustrate this, we can consider the construction of truths around standards in education and/or society. Specifically, through relations of power, governments impart their 'knowledge' of standards upon teachers, schools and the wider public, usually by "discourses of derision" (S. J. Ball, 2006; Kenway, 1990), "the destruction of the past" (Hobsbawm, 1994, p. 3) to enable the suggestion of a better future. "That is to say, power and knowledge are fused in the practices that comprise history" (S. J. Ball, 1994, p. 2) and the present. For example, governments often adopt a "discourse of myth" (Alexander, 2010, p. 25) where the past (e.g. supposed underachievement) is attacked to suit the political agenda of today (Alexander, 2010), hence (re)writing history. In simple terms, a government denounces the current or previous position in order to propagate its own position (for education and society). This also demonstrates that this government can deliver progress. It is, of course, much easier to promise improvements in something as subjective and manipulable as education, where something more tacit like reducing unemployment is far more complex, and thus far more difficult or risky to promise. However, these 'truths' are not sustained by a passive top-down model; instead, they are maintained by the way they act within systems and by the way they are taken up and reproduced by system and subjects. In this instance, teachers actively work to re-create these standards, and the permitted standards become discourses. Here, power can be thought of as a method of control through negotiation and surveillance rather than as wielding an authoritarian presence.

Hence, there is no oppressive position; instead, individuals "are always in the position of simultaneously undergoing and exercising this power" (Foucault, 1980d, p. 98). This is very different to a Marxist or juridical view of power, which Foucault vigorously critiqued. These versions of power are unidirectional and can be viewed as reductive. According to Foucault, a Marxist view of power is "conceived primarily in terms of the role it plays in the maintenance simultaneously of the relations of production and of a class domination which the development and specific forms of the forces of production have rendered possible" (Foucault, 1980d, pp. 88–89). It is important to note that Foucault does not deny there is class power but, rather, argues that power is not found in hierarchical structures, simply because they are hierarchical structures. The lack of reductionism within the reading of power relations is pertinent within education, as it allows us to work with the messiness of the practice of education and work with its complexities.

Power relations are not stable; instead, "power is constantly being transformed along with the productive forces" (Foucault, 1989c, p. 236). Consequently, individuals can shift their roles within this relation; they can "become powerful or powerless depending on the terms in which her/his subjectivity is constituted" (Walkerdine, 1990, p. 5). Therefore, "power is not something that is acquired, seized or shared, something that one holds on to or allows to slip away; power is exercised from innumerable points, in the interplay of nonegalitarian and mobile relations" (Foucault, 1978/1998, p. 94). "Power is 'capillary' in its operation" (Walshaw, 2007, p. 21), such that it flows through all levels of society and relations. Hence, power is not authoritarian. For Foucault, power

> traverses and produces things, it induces pleasure, forms knowledge, produces discourse. It needs to be considered as a productive network which runs through the whole social body, much more than as a negative instance whose function is repression . . . If power was never anything but repressive, if it never did anything but to say no, do you really think one would be brought to obey it?
>
> (Foucault, 1980c, p. 119)

Perhaps the simplest way to present this idea is to consider *power* as a verb rather than as a noun, such that it is something to be done rather than something that is or that someone has.

In summary, power is constituted through discourses; it is a positive, enabling, and a productive force. It "circulates within institutions and social bodies, producing subjects who exert a 'mutual 'hold' on one another" (MacLure, 2003, p. 49). Furthermore, "it is not possible for power to be exercised without knowledge, it is impossible for knowledge not to engender power" (Foucault, 1980b, p. 52). Thus, with power, there is knowledge, and the creation of knowledge is the thrust of this book, as I explore the 'truths' that are permitted. Finally "all relations of force imply a power relation . . . and each power relation can be referred to the political sphere of which it is a part, both as its effect and as its condition of possibility" (Foucault, 1989e, p. 211). Hence, this book seeks to highlight the power that runs through the political system of mathematics education. And by political, I mean not only the influence of government but also the political governance found in mathematics education research; this domain is particularly good at appearing impartial. Put simply, power is something which allows people to act in a certain way and encourages people to desire a certain way; neither of which is necessarily repressive. Consequently, where you find power you will find resistance to this power and you find new forms of knowledge or behaviour (Foucault, 1978/1998, 1980c). Thus, we can ask, what happens when different discourses are found in the classroom – what knowledges are produced? Emerging from this power/knowledge discourse relationship is the subject, both active and passive, which is explored in the next section.

'Man', the subject, and subjectivity

The poststructural "decentred self" (Walshaw, 2007, p. 5) is shaped by and shapes discourses. As power shifts and flows, it follows that the poststructural self is not fixed but instead is a fluid subject able to occupy different subject positions; it is a production of subjectivity and there is no true self to discover:

> Foucault, following Nietzsche, sees all views of human nature as the expression of contingent histories and social practices. Any particular theory of what a person ought to be like by nature is false, and has effects of constraining human possibilities and marginalizing those who fall outside the 'nature'.
> (Pickett, 1996, p. 452)

This position helps frame my argument concerning the mathematical child. Many discourses make implicit or explicit reference to the 'natural' child and that identity is more or less static. "Indeed, the presupposition of the individual as a unitary entity, a thinking, feeling machine which is self-directed as far as thought processes are concerned, is basic to a child-centred pedagogy and to developmental psychology" (Henriques et al., 1998, p. 102). Instead, I suggest that the child, explored in the next chapter, is not something to be discovered or engineered but instead is a discourse created within practices (Walkerdine, 1997, 1998b) and, as above, "has effects of constraining human possibilities and marginalizing those who fall outside the 'nature' ".

This is very different to the notion of the individual commonly found in psychological conceptions of humanity that seek to shape, classify, and regulate man. Foucault rigorously critiqued the human sciences, his "initial critique of human sciences is that they, like philosophy, are premised on an impossible attempt to reconcile irreconcilable poles and posit a constituting subject" (Best & Kellner, 1991, p. 42). He argued that "one has to dispense with the constituent subject, and to get rid of the subject itself, that's to say, to arrive at an analysis which can account for the constitution of the subject within a historical framework" (Foucault, 1980c, p. 117). This book contributes to this project, by arguing that the mathematical child is created by particular discourses within particular regimes of truth. This critique is particularly pertinent as the human sciences are currently popular in both general culture and educational discourses. This popularity propagates this discourse and encourages the fabrication of the subject around a 'real' self as something to identify with and aspire to. As such, the modern person can be drawn to essentialised discourses of the self that are aligned to psychological models. This fits well with the neoliberal landscape, where the autonomous and entrepreneurial figure is central and we are under the illusion that we govern ourselves (N. Rose, 1999a). For modern people this involves striving to make their lives meaningful and make sense of themselves: to see their lives as an ongoing project (N. Rose, 1999a). From a Foucauldian perspective, the modern person is "not the man who goes off to discover himself, his secrets and his hidden truth; he is the man who tries to invent himself" (Foucault, 2003f, p. 50). As Foucault would argue, we "govern (themselves and others) by the production of truth . . . the establishment of domains in which the practice of true and false can be made at once ordered and pertinent" (Foucault, 2003c, p. 252). Hence, we govern ourselves to accept fabricated fictions as the truth.

Thus Foucault argues that Man is a discursive construct (Foucault, 1970/2002), and moreover, Man is a modern invention perpetuated by the human sciences, or as Walkerdine puts it, "the subject was a fictional construct produced in those regimes of truth that claim to describe them" (Walkerdine, 1997, p. 61). From this perspective, the concern is not to determine what the person or subject is but what position the subject takes up within the available discourses and how this position demonstrates them as a 'legitimate' subject.

Specifically, the subject is located and locates itself in the discourses where it finds meaning and which we read through the absence and presence of signs.

For instance, school students may locate themselves as 'good' mathematics students; they may display this through the sign of 'confidence' (explored in a later section of this book). This 'confidence' may be presented through instances such as speaking up in class and/or answering questions quickly (Hardy, 2007). Outside of the mathematics classroom these students can adopt different roles and hence can perform to different fictions (Walkerdine, 1990, 1998a). For example, they can act as a 'troublemaker', 'coward', 'lad', or 'geek' – these positions are possible within a framework that views subjectivity as unstable. The point is that a person's self is not fixed; instead, the subject is capable of performing various roles at various times and, as such, takes on assorted relations to power. Moreover "there [is] no necessary coherence to the multiple sites in which subject-positions [are] produced, and . . . these positions might themselves be contradictory" (Henriques et al., 1998, p. 203).

It is important to note that, even though Foucault emphasises the discursive regime, the subject is not subjected to these roles from a position of all-obliterating domination. In his later work, Foucault argues that "technologies of the self" work alongside "technologies of domination" to position people in discourses. He states that technologies of the self

> permit individuals to effect by their own means, or with the help of others, a certain number of operations on their own bodies and souls, thoughts, conduct, and way of being, so as to transform themselves in order to attain a certain state of happiness, purity, wisdom, perfection or immortality.
> (Foucault, 2003e, p. 146)

Hence, subjects are not oppressed but instead have a constrained agency, with the capacity to be aware of their own actions, thoughts, and desires. Moreover, their positioning in discourses is not only determined by power and production within social mechanisms but also from "the possibility of self-determination and the choice of their own existence" (Foucault, 1989a, p. 452). Writing this book is an example of the self and agency. I am both subject to the disciplining machine of academia whilst I am also attempting to critique the fictitious relations on which much of academia is proposed. Hence, I am in conflict with the power that circulates in academic and mathematics education, of which I am also a part. As such, I am "keep[ing] watch over the excessive powers of political rationality" (Foucault, 2003d, p. 128) and, I am using "resistance as a chemical catalyst so as to bring to light power relations, locate their position, find out their point of application and the methods used" (Foucault, 2003d, p. 128). Hence, the subject is not predetermined but is produced through its actions within the social systems that are available. "In our involvement in a wide range of social practices, we will often be categorised quite differently from one context to another" (Walshaw, 2007, p. 100). Once again, we see that the self is neither stable nor coherent but fluid and messy – my central concern is there is little space for this narrative within general educational discourses which seek coherence, stability, and normative narratives – and are based on impact and evidence.

However, there are commentators, such as Sarup (1993), who argue that Foucault did not really have a theory of the subject. In fact, some researchers (such as Henriques et al., 1998; Walkerdine, 1997) turn to psychoanalysis and, in particular, to the poststructural psychoanalyst Lacan to explore subjectivity. Psychoanalysis is attractive to many as it offers a theorisation of how we resist change (Henriques et al., 1998); it also suggests connections between the social and the psychic, something which is outside of Foucault's work. I do not wish, or have space, to explore Lacan or psychoanalysis in depth. However, I do draw on people who have used these theories, in particular, to offer explanations of subjectivity within discourses.

In the next two sections I go on to explore how certain versions of the subject come to dominate, and how these are propagated through systems of governance and regulation. This idea of normalisation is a key concept for Foucault as I suggest that education (by design and practice) is a site of normative practice. Differing from psychoanalysis, this draws on the social and cultural rather than the 'psychic'.

Normalisation

An aspect of both power and discourse is that they install and propagate normalisation (Carabine, 2001), a process that encourages a specific version of the 'normal' that subsequently becomes taken for granted or 'natural' (Foucault, 1977/1991, 1978/1998). If we examine this through the gender examples discussed earlier, we find that 'normal' girls prefer pink and play with dolls, crafts, make-up, and so on whilst 'normal' boys prefer blue and play with construction toys, cars, and action heroes. This discursive positioning creates what is possible for both girls and boys, boys being active heroes whilst girls are often passive homemakers, a familiar gendered discourse (Walkerdine, 1990, 1998a; Walkerdine & Lucey, 1989). The key point is that there is nothing natural or inevitable about this perceived normality. Instead, this 'normal' is created within the axis of power/knowledge. Just as "the subject was a fictional construct produced in those regimes of truth that claim to describe them" (Walkerdine, 1997, p. 61), so is the 'normal'.

Normalisation is a key concept in this book, as I explore what is 'normal' and how the pursuit of the 'normal' happens within various educational contexts. It is, of course, a key concept for Foucault; he sees it as all pervading:

> The problem is: aren't all powers currently connected to one specific power, that of normalization? Aren't the powers of normalization the techniques of normalization, a kind of instrument found just about everywhere today, in the educational institution, the penal institution, in shops, factories and administrations, as a kind of general instrument, generally accepted because scientific, which makes possible the domination and subjection of individuals? In other words, psychiatry as a general instrument of subjection and normalization – that, in my view, is the problem.
>
> (Foucault, 1989h, pp. 139–140)

Hence, for Foucault, the role of psychiatry and psychology is problematic as, as noted in the preceding extract, he argues that "modern definitions of normalcy are invariably constructed by the human sciences." (Pickett, 1996, p. 453). In particular, the 'normal' child of human sciences, whom I specifically critique in the next chapter, is defined by developmental targets and criteria that he or she must achieve. I suggest that the specifications of the 'normal' mathematical school student are formed through comparison and reference to fabricated criteria. For instance, the school, the classroom, the teacher, and the students are all expected to reach 'normal' targets of attainment or exceed them. In addition, there are 'normal' ways of behaving in school – in the corridors, in the classroom, in the playground. Yet, the 'normal' student of the playground may not be the same as the 'normal' student of the classroom. Regardless, space and roles within the classroom/school are products of normalisation, and thus, permitted ways of being are created. Hence, many aspects of (Mathematics) education both inside and outside the classroom are constructed around a version of the normal, which I call the manufacturing of the mathematical child.

Walshaw (2007) argues that normalisation in schools is propagated by the covert and overt surveillance and supervision that circulate. She states that a school

> performs a normalising function – and does it admirably well, by the way; disciplining intellect through remedial classes and extension groups, setting/streaming, repeat testing and examination, and so on . . . Students every actions and interactions, and their understandings of their place in the school, are just some of the aspects of their place in the school, are just some of the aspects of their subjectivity that come under the constant gaze of teachers, principals, other students and so on. The gaze differentiates and compares. The tiniest deviation from normal practice is noticed.
>
> (p. 130)

Hence, the fictional normal educational environment and subject/actor become desirable, and any person or system that diverges from this is designated defective and undesirable. As mentioned earlier, these disparities are monitored through systems and structures such as judgement, comparison, tracking, and other instances of 'support' and surveillance. Thus, efforts are made through the self and systems to bring the deviance back into line, and the usual UK educational environment tends towards homogenisation. As Foucault states, normalisation is "another system of surveillance, another kind of control: an incessant visibility, a permanent classification of individuals, the creation of a hierarchy qualifying, establishing limits, and providing diagnostics. The norm becomes the criterion for evaluating individuals" (Foucault, 1989g, p. 197), which is an all-pervading feature of education.

Pickett (1996) notes that schools (and universities) are particularly problematic sites as "they transmit a conservative ideology masked as knowledge" (p. 455) and as the truth. Generally, we do not usually question what we are told by schools (and especially universities); instead, we expect them to be sites of professional expertise that offer opportunity and erudition. This is an attractive fiction to which many may want to adhere. Indeed, one persuasive aspect of normalisation is that it

> opens up membership to social entities that have a sense of cohesion about them . . . Education is one such social institution. It provides a perfect demonstration of how easy it is to be seduced by its emancipatory rhetoric. Membership to its services is through practices and understandings that measure up to the norms it sets.
>
> (Walshaw, 2007, p. 130)

Hence, normalisation can thrive in education, as we often aspire to improvement and/or liberation. Furthermore, the suggestion of a unified system to achieve this is very appealing.

Of course, the version of normalisation that is present depends on the regime of truth in which knowledge circulates. The present knowledge base in education in the UK and many other parts of the world is caught up in truths of neoliberalism. Normalisation functions in a particular way within neoliberalism. As we saw, neoliberalism normalises a particular model of selfhood as autonomous, psychological, and entrepreneurial (N. Rose, 1999a). Within this, subjects become self-surveilling as they seek self-improvement and pursuit of the normal (S. J. Ball, 2008). In schools "students learn to monitor their own being, and they do this by practices of self-regulating, ever mindful of the gaze of others" (Walshaw, 2007, p. 131). As Foucault's work shows surveillance and regulation are not unique to neoliberalism, but they have become central within our neoliberal system. Such social systems constrain not through the use of force but through the production of normalised subjects. This process is called governmentality and is the focus of the next section.

Governmentality

Explicitly, governmentality is the principle that governments or social systems constrain, not through the use of force but through the production of normalised subjects; thus, people are governed into practices of normalisation as opposed to being governed simply by authoritarian principles (Walkerdine, 1990). In the gender example discussed earlier, the demand that boys prefer blue or 'action' toys is not administered through dictatorship but instead is managed through surveillance, supervision, and the illusion of choice, specifically through the creation of a preferred normative choice. It is probably fair to say that the majority of people want their children to be normal – or to present as normal – and children themselves often want to be normal. Hence governmentality is not restricted to governments as "practices of the government are, on the one hand, multifarious and concern many kinds of people – the head of a family, the superior of a convent, the teacher or tutor of a child or student" (Foucault, 2003b, p. 233). Thus, governmentality applies to any social system rather than just to state politics. Moreover,

> studies of governmentality are not sociologies of rule. They are studies of a particular 'stratum' of knowing and acting. Of the emergence of particular 'regimes of truth' concerning the conduct of conduct, ways of speaking truth, persons authorized to speak truths, ways of enacting truths and the costs of so doing.
>
> (N. Rose, 1999b, p. 19)

In terms of this book, I am interested in the social systems that are found in the school, the classroom, government, universities, and social media. I am exploring who is allowed to speak and who and what is heard. In addition, I analyse how we come to know mathematics education and how this version of events is constructed as the truth. Specifically, I tell stories of how governments entice subjects into normalised patterns of behaviour and how this behaviour became positioned as good for everyone. Similarly, this principle applies to mathematics education research, where again a preferred way of being is produced. This is not achieved via tyranny or dictatorship but instead is accomplished through a covert and subversive manner of governing that breeds a specific acceptable version of the normal. Indeed, the role of the state, or the institution, is to create a regime of truth that demands this 'normal' behaviour (N. Rose, 1999a). Governmentality is a means of legitimatising, systemising, and regulating the use of power but one that is discursively produced as for the good of both the system and yourself. Hence, I am interested not only in how governmentality works in government but also in universities and the community of mathematics education research and explicitly how practices position themselves as factual. I investigate "how forms of rationality inscribe themselves in practices or systems of practices, and what role they play within them – because it's true that 'practices' don't exist without a certain regime of rationality" (Foucault, 2003c, p. 251).

Thus, this is a study of governmentality within several interconnected sites of power/knowledge. In particular, "the school and the university both perform the function of a technology of power . . . without, of course, resorting to physical restraint. They train people towards acceptable behaviour" (Walshaw, 2007, p. 102). For the university, it is vitally important that as a critical institution, we are aware of our own practices in the formation and maintenance of 'truths' (discussed in detail earlier in the chapter) Yet, there seems to be very limited questioning of the knowledge imparted and often a limited interrogation of the systems and strategies employed. Indeed, education establishments are most often positioned as places of universal good and are symbols of mastery of nature and society (Dale, 2001).

Governmentality is governing by tactics as opposed to governing by law (Foucault, 2003b). The tactics constitute a system where there is "enforced obedience to rules that are presumed to be for the public good" (Walshaw, 2007, p. 102). It is not about obeying the 'governors', but it is more about influencing the conduct of individuals and societies. Thus, "to govern humans is not to crush their capacity to act, but to acknowledge it and to utilise it for one's own objectives" (N. Rose, 1999b, p. 4). Within this, it is important to remember the role of (constrained) agency. For instance governmentality "also embraces the ways in which one might be urged and educated to bridle one's own passions, to control one's own instincts, to govern oneself" (N. Rose, 1999b, p. 3). This is coherent with the current regime of truth, neoliberalism, where subjects are concerned with self-regulation (S. J. Ball, 2003, 2008); within this, the subject has agency and is both passive and active:

> 'Governmentality' implies the relationship of the self to itself, and I intend this concept of 'governmentality' to cover the whole range of practices that constitute, define, organize, and instrumentalize the strategies that individuals in their freedom can use in dealing with each other.
> (Foucault, 2003a, p. 41)

Thus, governmentality is concerned with "maximising the forces of the population collectively and individually" (N. Rose, 1999b, p. 23). Hence, it is not limited to the individual but is concerned with using and normalising the population through power/knowledge relations. This is particularly pertinent within New Labour's version of neoliberalism, which is sometimes labelled as "neoliberalism with a human face . . . the third way" (Arestis & Sawyer, 2005, p. 177), which mediates between "collectivism and capitalism" (Wacquant, 1991, p. 63). It is governance which is rationally marketed as best for the consumer and for everyone; it is individualism with a collective social conscience, which can be very appealing and can draw on the image of education as liberation.

Biopower becomes important here, which includes "numerous and diverse techniques for achieving the subjugations of bodies and the control of populations" (Foucault, 1978/1998, p. 140), specifically that schools and universities are not sites of emancipation but instead work to control populations and bodies. These educational institutions are sites where constants surveillance and examination are used to discipline children in 'artificial terms' (Allen, 2014, 50).

Thus, in summary, like normalisation, governmentality takes on a specific purpose within neoliberalism. Power is thought to be decentred, and individuals are regulated through self-regulation. The role of the state, or the institution, is to create a regime of truth that demands this individuality (N. Rose, 1999a). It is not a dictatorship but a covert and subversive manner of governing that breeds a specific acceptable version of the normal. 'Freedom' is offered, but this is an illusion, and instead, people are governed through discourses of freedom, for example through notions such as the promise of enterprise, entrepreneurialism, and/or autonomy (N. Rose, 1999a).

The questions of how we examine governmentality and normalisation, how we take into account power/knowledge, and how we unpack discourses/truths are explored next.

Archaeology, genealogy, and deconstruction

Using the concepts discussed earlier, Foucault tended to talk about two 'methodologies' for analysis:

> 'Archaeology' would be the appropriate methodology of this analysis of local discursivities, and 'genealogy' would be the tactics whereby, on the basis of the descriptions of these local discursivities, the subjected knowledges which were thus released would be brought into play.
> (Foucault, 1980d, p. 85)

Hence, Foucault examined the conditions of possibility of social mechanisms, and particularly the emergence of accepted norms and practices, all done through the ideas discussed in this chapter. Hence, my analysis searchers for contingencies rather than causes; in addition, I take nothing as the 'truth' and instead examine the conditions that allow discourses to be positioned as such. I do this by using Foucault's readings on truth and power, on discourses and subjectivity, and on normalisation and governmentality, as tools of analysis. Hence, my analysis concerns decentring text, destabilising oppositions, and unpacking 'truths'.

Some poststructuralists would describe this as deconstruction, and there are times when I use this terminology. Hence, in the next part of this section, I visit the use of this word from a general and a Derridean perspective.

Derrida states that deconstruction

> is an analysis which tries to find out how . . . thinking works or does not work, to find the tensions, the contradictions, the heterogeneity within their own corpus . . . Deconstruction is not a method or some tool that you can apply to something from the outside. Deconstruction is something which happens and which happens inside.
>
> (Derrida, 1994 in Caputo, 1997, p. 9)

As this definition suggests, it is quite problematic to be too specific about what deconstruction is or indeed how to do it. The aim is to

> be essentially anti-essential and highly unconventional, not to let its eyes wax over at the thought of either unchanging essences or ageless traditions, but rather to advocate an in-ventionalistic incoming, to stay constantly on the lookout for something unforeseeable, something new.
>
> (Caputo, 1997, p. 42)

Thus, like all poststructural research, I attempt genealogy or deconstruction from the premise of non-essentialism, such that meanings are not there to be found but instead are shaped by and shape discourses/text. As Lather (1991) states, "deconstruction includes a Foucauldian awareness of the oppressive role of ostensibly liberating forms of discourse" (p. 13). The aim is to not take anything as given and to question everything – to apply a close reading of the text. Moreover, "deconstruction is made of: not the mixture but the tension between memory, fidelity, the preservation of something that has been given to us, and, at the same time, heterogeneity, something absolutely new, and a break" (Derrida, 1994 in Caputo, 1997, p. 6). Thus, it should lack uniformity and take from old and new. However, it is not an attack on everything that has been; "deconstruction . . . is always an attempt to open it up, not bash it or knock it senseless" (Caputo, 1997, p. 74), which again parallels a Foucauldian analysis, which through genealogy examines how histories create present-day regimes of truth. Thus, in the later part of the book I very much signal past governments and past educational research as enablers of present discourses of the mathematical child.

The other aspect of deconstruction that is commonly referenced to Derrida concerns the Other and the positioning of binary oppositions. This is by no means exclusive to Derrida; the idea of the Other is commonly found within psychoanalytical frameworks of analysis, and discussion of culture (for example in the classic work by Edward Said). Some of my analysis draws from this; in addition, I frequently refer to researchers who have used both Derrida's reading of deconstruction and psychoanalysis. Derrida contends that text is composed of dualisms and that these "binary oppositions are one of the key ways in which meaning and knowledge are produced" (MacLure, 2003, p. 10). Thus, they exist only in relation to each other and are value laden, for example us and them, black and white. boy and girl. "According to Derrida (1998), this oppositional logic reflects a form of 'metaphysical' thinking that has been practised by Western philosophy from Plato onwards, and which he called 'logocentrism'" (MacLure, 2003, p. 10). One term is established as more important, and more valuable, to the detriment to the other:

> Relations of difference and opposition, and the epistemic, 'violence' that they effect, can be found everywhere – from the minutiae of in-group academic skirmishes . . . to the fundamentals of philosophy. They are of course everywhere to be found in the discourses of education.
> (MacLure, 2003, pp. 10–11)

These "simple [binary] claims are more effective than complicated ones" (Buckingham, 2011, p. 7). They allow us to work out who are the 'goodies' and who are the 'baddies', (Buckingham, 2011) which is a familiar cultural trope. Alexander terms these oppositions as "discourses of dichotomy" and agrees that they are prominent within education (Alexander, 2010, p. 21) and that thus restrict educational possibilities.

Derrida contends that identity is formed from the difference represented in these dualisms, and by the wider context of reference to that meaning. Thus, identity is dependent on excluding the Other. This difference is how meaning is produced:

> Identity is not the self-identity of a thing, this glass, for instance, this microphone, but implies a difference within identity. That is, the identity of a culture is a way of being different from itself; a culture is different from itself; language is different from itself; the person is different from itself.
> (Derrida in Caputo, 1997, p. 13)

Doing deconstruction (or genealogy) involves acknowledging and highlighting these oppositions, their presence, and their interplay. It is an attempt to destabilise hierarchies, taken-for-granted notions, and Western thought; it can be thought of "as a project of resistance to the institutionalized forgetting that takes place when matters attain the status of common sense, in educational policy, pedagogy and research itself" (MacLure, 2003, p. 179). Thus, deconstruction and genealogy are attempts to unpack relations and disrupt unifying truths and hegemonic grand narratives and that is how they are used in this thesis.

Concluding remarks

The aim of this chapter was twofold – first, to argue for the use of social theory in educational research and writing, and second, to introduce the work of Michel Foucault and how it has influenced this book. Thus, I am setting up the tools of analysis I use and my epistemological position. Specifically, I drew out ideas of discourses as permitted truths and power as capillary. "Power invents, power creates, power produces" (Foucault, 1989f, p. 158); thus, power is not destructive but constructive. Power produces meaning and discourses that are found within social systems. This book examines power relations within systems to explore what can and cannot be said and what are produced as permitted truths. In particular, I explore these in key social institutions within mathematics education, (Mathematics education research, education policy, the classroom, and social media); they are institutions that, I argue, are complicit in normalisation through the process of governmentality and biopower. That is, they both permit and restrict until there is a preferred version of being that can be perceived as natural or inevitable. This is not done through authoritarian procedures but instead through tactical governance and agency. Within this, subjects are both passive and active and capable of taking up multiple subject positions. I explore this positioning, and unpack, or deconstruct, common sense taken-for-granted truths of mathematics education, my aim being to take apart what we know and what we perceive to be 'truth'. To do this, I focus on various aspects of mathematics education that allow me to talk about one of the hidden, normalised, and intensely governed objects of current mathematics education – the mathematical child – who I argue is a fundamental part of the modernity. I begin this exploration in the next chapter, where I discuss normative discourses of the Child.

Notes

1 Thomas Gradgrind is a character from Charles Dickens's 1854 novel *Hard Times*.
2 Nicky Morgan was secretary of state for education in England from July 2014 to July 2016.

3 Un-stating the 'normal' and 'natural' child

Heard in passing in an education department:

"They don't do childcare right – they don't focus on the developmental model"

(De)Constructing childhood

Introduction

This chapter moves on from theory to examine discourses of childhood. Thus, I am using Foucault's theories to seek out the systems and structures which turn certain constructions of childhood into everyday common thought and practice. In particular, I contest the current concept of childhood in UK mathematics education, which is predominantly influenced by a 'natural', developmental version of the child. This is supported by child psychology and, as I argue, reinforced by our neoliberal society. First, I introduce the child by discussing why the concept/construct of childhood is so appealing. In doing this I am showing that Western culture heavily invests in the image of the child as symbol of the past and as holder of the future. I then unpack childhood as a construct, by examining how it can be culturally and socially constituted around laws and education. Next, I examine different discourses of childhood and of the child, arguing that these are never neutral, in spite of appearing so. Finally, I bring together these discourses, highlighting those that are dominant in the current regime of truth. From this, we should see that there are questions about constructions of the child that may cause conflict in practice, as explored in part two of this chapter.

The appeal of childhood

There is a certain fascination with childhood. The image of the child represents many things a society may strive towards. The child can be, and has been, used to signify innocence and a purity that adults cannot obtain, the child being yet to encounter the 'troubles' that 'taint' adults. Edelman (2004) states that "the Child has come to embody for us the telos of the social order and come to be seen as the one for whom that order is held in perpetual trust" (p. 11). Hence, the image of the child is entrusted with upholding society – present, past, and, above all, future. The child is then far broader than its relation to its family; the child belongs to and represents society; "children are everybody's concern and . . . they constitute an investment in the future in terms of the reproduction of social order" (James et al., 1998, p. 15). The 'universal' child offers innocence and hope to people and to society.

Burman (2008a) further argues that discourses of childhood help us correct past mistakes as well as make sense of ourselves; "they are part of the cultural narratives that define who we are, why we are the way we are and where we are going" (Burman, 2008a, p. 67). However, our images and recollections of childhood are, of course, always retrospective. As such, they tend to draw on romantic constructions of the past (Burman, 2008a) and can encourage memories of a golden age, where events were much better, regardless as to how they were at the time (W. Brown, 2001; Kenway & Bullen, 2001). For example, in their laments of the 'loss' of childhood, Winn (1983), refers to a "golden age of innocence", and Postman discusses "turn[ing] back the clock" (1982/1994) to a time when adults were in control and society was better. The chastising of 'children today' as less than what adults remember is a common refrain.

Thus, the child is symbolic of an almost untenable position, of being both a reminder of the past and a holder of the future. The child requests that we look in both these directions at once. Hence, analysing the present child is problematic, especially with regard to temporality and discourses of progress. This concern is rarely mentioned, yet it is always already present within studies and the governance of childhood.

Specifically, the present child is someone that we once were, and adults that will one day be. "On to the child we heap the thwarted longings of decaying societies and try to figure something better. It is a hard burden for children to carry. Surely they should be their own future, not ours" (Burman, 2008b, p. 171). Between this and successive neoliberal governments, it is perhaps no surprise that in the UK, "childhood is the most intensively governed sector of personal existence" (N. Rose, 1999a, p. 123), with children having a "prominent place in the policy and practices of legal, welfare, medical, and educational institutions" (James & Prout, 1997, p. 1).

As mentioned earlier, the loss of childhood has troubled many in modern societies, and "the notion that children are growing up deprived of childhood has become a staple theme in popular psychology" (Buckingham, 2000, p. 21). A common argument is that childhood is being rushed, as children move quickly into traditionally adult domains (e.g. Elkind, 2007/1981). However, many of these authors (such as Elkind, 2007/1981; Kline, 1995; Postman, 1982/1994; Winn, 1983) tend to treat children as a passive, homogenous mass with no agency and/or place their own value judgements on the situation. For example, in his critique of how he sees cartoons replacing classic literature, and

> as in a great deal of Marxist cultural critique, Kline paradoxically takes the position of the 'old bourgeoisie' in his attack on the new ruling ethos . . .

His contrast . . . is suffused with value judgements which are never explained nor justified.

(Buckingham, 2000, p. 160)

Of course, as discussed in the previous chapter, power and agency are more complicated than this, and the principle that anyone is in a value-free position is a myth. In the 1980s, Elkind, Kline, and Postman were concerned with the television infiltrating its way into children's home and lives. In the present day, many similar concerns are raised about the internet, that children are exposed to adult domains and experience, that adults no longer have control over what children have access to – indeed that children grow up too soon. This raises several points for contestation: first, that, as mentioned, there tends to be a romanticisation of the past; second, that within this construction there is a specified path of development that children are supposed to ascribe to – thus maintaining a discrete distinction between the adult and the child; third that adults have the say over what is right for children – within this, there are clearly designated adult and clearly designated children's spaces. This last point, in particular, is maintained throughout wider society. We live in an adult society, where judgements are most often made about children from adult perspectives. Space and voice are adult domains; arguably the internet is one space that queries this and disrupts the power and the discursive norms that beset children and young people and where children and young people are marginalised (discussed more in Chapter 6).

In summary, the key point is that childhood is not universal, and it is not innocent, and as I shall explore in the book, I suggest it is dangerous to read it so. Instead, it is a sign constituted within discourses, and discourses are not without context and power:

[A]ny description of children – and hence any invocation of the idea of childhood – cannot be neutral. On the contrary, any such discussion is inevitably informed by an *ideology* of childhood – that is, a set of meanings which serve to rationalize, to sustain or to challenge existing relationships of power between adults and children, and indeed between adults themselves.

(Buckingham, 2000, p. 11)

Furthermore, these descriptions are norms are not constrained to Western audiences:

Global norms about who children are and what childhoods should be are circulating through international law, global media, and transnational NGOs . . . These global norms of childhood . . . do not map onto most, perhaps any, children's experiences of the world.

(Wells, 2015 p. 203)

Hence, conceptions of the child are fraught with power relations, as well as being social and cultural context dependent. However, this may not be obvious, as the image of the child is usually presented as innocent, harmless, and universal. Crucially, how we define the child, is often dependent upon what the child is expected to do, and as Buckingham alludes, the child "cannot be imagined except in relation to a conception of adult" (Jenks, 2005, p. 3); childhood becomes in relation to difference and to the marked boundaries created by reference to its Other. Thus, it is always a minority category, and it is always about what children are not or what they are to become and not what they presently are.

Defining childhood

How society decides if someone is a child or adult has valued over time and context. Currently there are various rules of governance that ascribe the age of an adult around the world. In the UK for instance, you can have heterosexual sexual intercourse at 16, but you need to be 18 to drink alcohol, serve on a jury, or vote in a government election. If we take the voting age as a sign of adulthood, 18 seems to be the most popular age in many parts of the world, though it can be as young as 16 (e.g. in Brazil, Austria, Isle of Man, and for the recent Scottish referendum on independence) or as old as 21 (e.g. in Fiji, Philippines). However, for the majority of countries this age limit has been lowered from 21 within the last 50 years, suggesting again how ideas of childhood shift; the UK changed in 1970. The timescale of compulsory education is similarly problematic, (and it is worth mentioning that not everywhere in the world has access to education for everyone); however, in the UK it seems to be moving in the opposite direction to voting law. Currently, compulsory education in England is from 5 to 18 (this has been raised from 16 in 2013 and was increased to 18 in 2015; DfE, 2013, 2014). It had been set at 16 since 1972. From this, we cannot argue that conceptions of childhood have become shorter or longer. However, it does show that the length of childhood and the type of actions one expects of adults, and of children, are not static but, as discussed earlier, are part of the cultural production of the time. Indeed, there are times when these laws would not have ascribed adulthood. For instance, in the UK women could not legally vote before 1918 (although then this voting was restricted to women older than 30 who met certain criteria). In addition, in the 19th and early 20th centuries, children were expected to work by society and by their parents. My own great grandfather's mother doctored his birth certificate to enable him to 'legally' work down the coal mines a year early – at age 10 instead of waiting until age 11.

Thus, how childhood is defined varies throughout history; moreover, we cannot examine childhood without constituting it within the epoch of the time. For instance, is the current increase in the age of compulsory education about rights to education or social control and a way of manipulating youth unemployment statistics? Moreover, in using these forms of governance to discuss childhood, I am not making the assertion that voting or compulsory education defines the time span of being a child. Instead, I am suggesting that these are markers that contribute towards the construct that we recognise as childhood. Some of these markers are more profound than others; for instance, sexuality is one aspect of childhood that, for many, is very problematic – it is the one where 'natural' development is not viewed positively:

> Sexuality, perhaps more than any other, helps define and uphold the fragile distinction between adulthood and childhood; it is an area where 'maturity' in a child is frequently perceived as a problem to be dealt with . . . rather than a normal part of development to be encouraged or praised.
>
> (Monk, 2009, p. 183)

The age of criminal responsibility is similarly troublesome – currently in England and Wales it is 10, in Scotland 8 – between these ages and 18, children are dealt with in special youth courts; thus, they have responsibility but not adult responsibility. Perhaps it is this law that represents a threat to childhood. These children represent a threat to the image of childhood as innocent and in need of protection, as they refuse to remain childlike.

There are, of course, other markers and specifically when we begin to consider what childhood is. These laws constitute childhood as different from adults and restricted in terms of agency. However, we can also examine childlike behaviours within their specific cultural context, such as examining childhood through toys or games or children's television. I explore this next, primarily through the work of Ariès (1962/1996).

Ariès was one of the earliest and most prominent thinkers to question the biological basis of childhood. Mostly drawing on French (and some English) examples, he documented how children have become (re)defined through social and cultural history (Aries, 1962/1996). His detailed account examines how the 'concept' of childhood as a distinct place starts around the 16th century, becoming part of common awareness around the time of the Enlightenment. Indeed, Postman (1982/1994) makes a clear causal link between the emergence of childhood and the invention of the printing press in the 15th century. This has been fervently contested by Luke (1989) on the point of accuracy; furthermore, as mentioned previously, Postman's work depends on a homogenous concept of the child, and a Foucauldian approach, which I adopt, suggests that the development of childhood is more dependent on a range of contingencies rather than a single cause. To illustrate his points, Ariès examines the child through its representation in relation to various concepts and constructs with regard to its distinction from the adult. For instance, he uses examples from 17th-century portraiture to illustrate children being portrayed within their 'own right'; he shows how prior to this they were depicted as miniature versions of adults. Before this era, Ariès argues that the child was not perceived with great importance, although this did not mean that the child was not cared for. Hence, rather than lacking a concept of childhood, previous societies lacked a concept of childhood with which we are currently familiar (Archard, 1993). This is not necessarily temporally progressive; indeed, in ancient times there seemed to be more familiar depictions of the child. For instance, the ancient Greeks believed children should be educated, though they did not share modern developmental views of child nurturance (Postman,

1982/1994), which I discuss later in this chapter. For instance, in relation to educating the child, Plato has a far more direct form of ensuring a child's development. He states that "if he [*sic*] obeys, well and good; if not, he is straightened by threats and blows, like a piece of bent or warped wood" (Plato, 380BC/2009, p. 44).

As a result of his choices of example, critics of Ariès state that his analysis is wholly dependent on the French middle/upper class (Buckingham, 2000). This, of course, does not devalue Ariès's contributions but should keep us mindful about comparisons to other countries and contexts and, furthermore, that his ideas may be another example of middle-class male Western privilege. As Wyness states,

> modern sentiments regarding childhood had a limited impact on the poorer sector of society until well into the nineteenth century. . . . [and] Ariès' construct of childhood really only applies to boys; girls were excluded from schooling throughout most of the modernising period, continually expected from an early age to have domestic responsibilities (Gittens, 1998).
>
> (2012, p. 16)

This again allows us to highlight the problems with the singular category child, when experiences are anything but homogenous.

As Jenks (2005) points out, the idea of an emerging rather than a pre-existing childhood is much easier to understand if we consider modern conceptions such as the toddler, or the teenager which came to prominence in the post-war era. Along with these categories comes teenage music, teenage fashion, teenage culture – in fact, these are all markers of what is a product of, yet also produces, the conception of teenager. More recently we have another classification – the 'tween', a preadolescent, which seems to have risen within the current consumer-driven, high-marketing era (Buckingham, 2011). These constituted subcategories of childhood add to the dissemination of a normalised and governed version of the child.

As illustrated by the ancient Greeks, one of the key ways in which this development can be supported is education; as such, the child needed to become in the correct manner.

Education as shaping childhood

One of the key Enlightenment thinkers responsible for the interest in the needs of children was Rousseau (Robertson, 1976). He is often "credited with inventing the modern notion of childhood as a distinct period of human life with [a] particular need for stimulation and education" (Burman, 2008a, p. 73). But Rousseau and education are not a cause in relation to the effect; it is far more complex than this. In a Foucauldian reading of contingencies,

> the modern conception of childhood arose as a result of a complex network of interrelationships between ideology, government, pedagogy, and

technology, each of which tended to reinforce the others; and as a result, it developed in different ways, and at different rates, in different national contexts.

(Buckingham, 2000, p. 37)

Education is problematic as it is always already viewed alongside freedom, emancipation, and opportunity. Indeed, the right to an education is defined by United Nations Educational, Scientific and Cultural Organization (UNESCO) as a Universal Human Right (UNESCO, 2000) and universal primary education was defined as a United Nations (UN) Millennium Goal (UN, 2013). However, education is also a structured form of discipline and governance, and thus, education is always already concerned with shaping children into the correct kind of adult:

> As the child became an object of pleasure he or she also became an object of discipline: a creature in need of education; someone who needed watching. That with the invention of schooling came our modern sense of the long childhood . . . Children would begin to be schooled for adulthood . . . Once you invent the child you need something – like a school or family – to contain it.
>
> (Phillips in his introduction to Ariès, 1962/1996, pp. 7–8)

Hence, one reason why the compulsory schooling period in many countries has been extended may be the need to exert control over a longer period. Indeed, there are often concerns in the UK about the summer break when children are left to 'run wild' through the streets. Another reason, of course, may be that this is the easiest way for a government to impact youth unemployment figures. It is far easier to keep them in school than to create employment opportunities.

Burman (2008a) advances the suggestion of societal control and states that "the process of schooling demanded a state of ignorance in return for advancement of opportunities for a limited few" (p. 75). Specifically, with compulsory schooling, the factory child moved from breadwinner to dependent, and the working-class family was programmed to remain in poverty. As such, education moves from the architect of equity, that it is often claimed to be (Hendrick, 1997), to the architect of inequity and inequality.

Moreover, modern conceptions of education prioritise certain versions of adulthood over others, signifying the correct pathways for children. Specifically, a learned professional, such as a doctor or accountant, is held in higher esteem than someone who is a skilled labourer. Indeed, there have been other versions of schooling throughout history, for instance schools in medieval times were "a sort of technical school for the instruction of clerics, young and old" (Ariès, 1962/1996 p. 317); thus, many different people – adults and children were welcomed. This is in sharp contrast to modern society where school is primary a place to contain children.

Perhaps the most critical argument is that when education became for the masses, children (as a whole) become more visible, and the normalisation of childhood, as a distinct period and development and specific governance, was perpetuated. Ariès argues that this was propagated by the construction of the school class, which intensifies and formalises a relation between age and stage. This construction is very powerful, perhaps more so than the previously discussed examples of adolescents and tweens which are less formal and more fluid. Not only is the construction tighter, but 'the class' is also validated by the authority and knowledge afforded from an educational institution and the governance and discipline that circulates with specific age groups. Thus, the class, as much as the school, helps shape the identity and perception of the modern school student. Specifically (and in many education systems around the world) "the child changes his [*sic*] age every year at the same time as he changes his class" (Ariès, 1962/1996, p. 172). The child is subject to, and subject of, a new curriculum, often a new teacher, and new classroom expectations. "The result is a striking differentiation between age groups that are really quite close together" (Ariès, 1962/1996, p. 172), yet this is rarely questioned. Consequently, there is homogenisation around small age groups and differences within ages are often overlooked, whereas differences between these constructed age groups are amplified (Ariès, 1962/1996). That is the case within the majority of UK schools:

> Today the class, the constituent cell of the school structure, presents certain precise characteristics which are entirely familiar: it corresponds to a stage in the progressive acquisition of knowledge (to a curriculum), to an average age from which every attempt is made not to depart, to a physical, spatial unit, for each age group and subject group has its special premises (and the very word 'class' denotes both the container and the contents), and to a period of time, an annual period end at the end of which the class's complement changes.
>
> (Ariès, 1962/1996, pp. 171–172)

As such, the class is both "container and contents" (Ariès, 1962/1996, pp. 171–172). It is the curriculum, the pedagogy, and the culture; it is the boundaries and the borders, the discipline and the governance. It both creates and restricts its physical space and discursive space, confining and shaping those within and those without. Thus, there is a constructed relation between age and stage. However, it was not until the 19th century that the class became explicitly related to age, and largely that is the way it has stayed (Ariès, 1962/1996). Previously, if classes existed they were more often formed around 'development', than age – this can still be found in some parts of the world. With the 'age and stage' class, standard rates of development gain authority and become normalised. Those standard students are normal; the above and, more crucially, the below, are culturally marked as defective.

Thus, in summary, childhood has the appearance of naturalness and universality, although it is a culturally, socially, and politically constructed category, which has in the last few centuries gained legitimacy through its association with education; this is propagated by the container of the class and arguably differentiates norms of childhood, and the apparent homogenisation of childhood even further. Next, I move to examine contemporary debates within the field of childhood studies. These shape the current regime of truth around childhood and the child in school, and I suggest contribute to the manufacturing of the mathematical child. I begin by discussing the postmodern child of the current context.

The (post)modern consumer child

As mentioned previously the loss or 'death of childhood' has troubled many in academia and society (such as Elkind, 2007/1981; Kline, 1995; Postman, 1982/1994; Winn, 1983). For example, these scholars may argue that children's access to televisions and to the internet has enabled the destruction of traditional boundaries, that would have kept children 'in their place'. Hence, there is more fluidity between the previously distinct categories of the adult and the child. However, as argued previously, this is not a loss of childhood but a redefining of socially, culturally, and politically constructed boundaries. Specifically, the modern child is arguably produced by "consumer culture and media culture" (Kenway & Bullen, 2001, p. 2); within this, children have gained economic power within their 'own right' (Buckingham, 2000). This is part of a wider discourse of neoliberalism, where the autonomous individual is sought and marketisation drives many aspects of society. In particular, Western children are explicitly advertised to through overt and covert means. For instance, the creation of television, film, and popular music tie-ins to merchandise has ensured that "children's leisure has become inexorably tied up with the 'consumer revolution' of the post-war period" (Buckingham, 2000, p. 72). Within this, there are often two polarised views of the child. Either children are innocent, ingénues powerless to resist the evil of advertising and popular culture, as stated by some of those who bemoan the 'death of childhood', or children are savvy consumers, making active and rational choices, from those proposed by the marketers. "Either we believe in the power of consumers, or in the power of the market; either consumers are autonomous, or they are enslaved" (Buckingham, 2011, p. 33). Though as discussed in the previous chapter, a Foucauldian reading of power, takes power to be both enabling and restricting. Drawing on Buckingham (2011) and Cook and Kaiser (2004), in this context, and Walkerdine (1990, 1998a) and Davies (2003) in a wider educational context, I propose a position between these unnecessary extremes and between the model of 'goodies and baddies'. Instead, children are active (and passive) agents capable of negotiating multiple subject positions within multiple contexts.

This consumer production does not stop with the child; indeed, parents and teachers are consumers too. In particular, children are increasingly surveilled by their parents, who are themselves influenced by the increased emphasis on 'good parenting' and the marketisation of appropriate educational experiences at home (Buckingham, 2011). This is part of the wider resurgence of the human sciences and, in particular, the popularity of psychological development in popular culture. Within this, there is a 'real' parent/child that the 'real' autonomous individual can train themself towards. Of course, this can propagate essentialised discourses of the subject. However, it is clear that these developmental opportunities are not found equally across all children. These ways of being are invariably connected to the middle class (Buckingham, 2000, 2011):

> Childhood, then, certainly is changing. Children's lives are both more institutionalized and privatized, and less stable and secure, than they were thirty years ago. The boundaries between children and adults have been eroded in some areas, but strongly reinforced and extended in others. Children have been empowered, both politically and economically; but they have also been subjected to increasing adult surveillance and control. And the inequalities between rich and poor have grown exponentially.
>
> (Buckingham, 2000, pp. 78–79)

Sociologists James, Jenks, and Prout (1998) state that the location of agency with the child can be traced to the rise in the popularity of childhood studies in sociology. The poststructural child draws comparisons to some sociological theories, in that the child is socially constructed; it is not universal, and it has agency. However, the poststructural subject is messy and identity is fluid. The child is shaped by and shapes discourses as the poststructural child negotiates positions within those discourses (Davies, 2003; Henriques et al., 1998). Ariès's work is part of the wider network of interest in the child as social. The socially constructed child came to prominence around the 1970s "when the dominating philosophical paradigm shifted from a dogmatic materialism to an idealism inspired by the works of Husserl and Heidegger" (James et al., 1998, p. 26). This is a hermeneutic model of childhood, such that it is one bound by the child's interpretation.

However, in spite of the awareness in childhood studies of the social and of the poststructural child, including multiple identities and agency, "the study of childhood is typically the province of psychology . . . [where] the primary interest is in *internal* mental processes" (Buckingham, 2011, p. 49), and certainly this is the dominant voice in education. Some of these perspectives have included conceptions of the social, such as Vygotsky who contended that development was the "conversion of social relations into mental functions" (Vygotsky, 1981, p. 165). However, many, including the most popular views drawn from Piaget, are based solely on cognition, where the mind is viewed as distinct from the body. Piaget, with his cognitive theory of development, is considered the most influential theorist within English education (James et al., 1998). Indeed, it has influenced some interpretations of the consumer child which envisage the child gradually becoming more rational and informed with each passing age and stage of development (e.g. McNeal, 2007). Piaget's work is part of a wider field of developmental psychology which gained popularity in the 1960s and 1970s and maintains huge influence in the classroom (Burman, 2008a; James et al., 1998). Hence, within education, and popular culture, this 'natural' child development is normalised; it becomes part of common discourse; it's not only the most popular voice but is also often the only story that is allowed to be heard.

In the next section I go into more depth and detail about Piaget's naturally developing child. However, I begin by exploring Rousseau's natural child. As argued earlier, Rousseau is one of the earliest theorists to explore childhood. Traces of his ideas can be found in many examples of educational theory and in Piaget's work. My aim is to provide the background to the principles and ideas that are still part of common discourse in education and that contribute to the normalisation of the natural child and child development. These sit in contrast to the messy fluid child of poststructuralism that I have presented above.

Rousseau's child – the natural child

As mentioned, the Enlightenment, and, in particular, Rousseau, gave rise to the idea that the child required education and this would fix/shape the child. Within this, a specific version of the child emerged, one which is still highly influential in education today (James et al., 1998).

Rousseau's principle thesis was that man in/as a 'state of nature' breeds innocence and consequently brings liberty; he states that "nothing is so gentle as man in his primitive state" (Rousseau, 1755/2007, p. 67). He viewed traits such as morality and goodness as innate and hence placed precedence on the 'natural man' without the corruption from the 'evils of society'. Moreover, Rousseau argued that all men should seek this freedom. In contrast, he stated that "woman is specially made for man's delight" (Rousseau, 1763/2007, p. 336); they were the passive to men's active, which kept the state of the 'natural' order. Hence, his 'natural' freedoms for men were very much constructed around hierarchical binaries and an essentialised order – man's freedom was founded on woman's confinement. Rousseau is clear that for this to be achievable, "all that we need . . . is the gift of education" (Rousseau, 1763/1884, p. 6, 1763/2007, p. 12). However, education was seen as broader than the classroom it "comes to us from nature, from men or from things" (Rousseau, 1763/1884, p. 6, 1763/2007, p. 12). For Rousseau learning to respond to nature and learning to 'control' responses were the pinnacle of his perfect, educated, natural man, and it is this that Rousseau argued brought freedom and allowed for man to live a good and moral life even within the constraints of an immoral society.

Thus, in contrast to some classic educationalists/philosophers such as Plato, Rousseau did not see the pursuit of knowledge as the ultimate goal of man. Rousseau's Child was a reasoned man:

> The noblest work in education is to make a reasoning man, and we expect to train a young child by making him reason! This is beginning at the end; this is making an instrument of a result. If children understood how to reason they would not need to be educated.
>
> (Rousseau, 1763/1884, p. 256)

However, this reasoning was seen as analogous to character development, which he suggested was achieved through practical experience and not reading.

Rousseau's primary thesis on education was written in *Emile, or on Education* (Rousseau, 1763/1884, 1763/2007). In it, he documents appropriate interventions for each stage of a male child's (Emile's) life; for instance, emotion and sentiment are left until the child is a teenager; thus, there is the assumption of 'natural' child development. However, Rousseau's teacher was also a key part of this process. Specifically, the teacher was a solitary tutor who supported by covertly guiding the child without his or her knowledge. According to Rousseau, this 'allowed' the child to respond to nature naturally, without the intervention of others. Of course, just because the teacher's mediation was not explicit or authoritarian does not mean it did not happen; arguably, it is these hidden forms of governance that are more problematic through their masquerade.

Hence for Rousseau, education should be concerned with covertly facilitating man's constructed experiences within the immediate environment. As such, many of his philosophies can be found in the principles of progressive education (Darling, 1994; James et al., 1998), as can the influence of theorists, such as Pestalozzi, Froebel, Dewey, and Kilpatrick (Darling, 1994), who drew on Rousseau's ideas. Indeed, Rousseau drew on the writings of another influential theorist, John Locke. Specifically, Locke's (1693/1932) version of child development was also based on reason. However, Locke's child was less innocent and less idealised. Locke's child was not defined by innate goodness but was a child who could develop through exposure to experience and reason. Hence, Locke's account combines some aspects of Rousseau's with a more empiricist and perhaps conservative account of childhood education (James et al., 1998; Postman, 1982/1994).

There are many issues with Rousseau's interpretation of childhood and education. In the first instance, even the apparently free are products of discourse, including discourses of freedom itself. As I have argued, whilst we live under apparent freedom, we are, in fact, governed through freedom (N. Rose, 1999a). Rousseau's child, though left to his or her own devices, is governed specifically through the structured interactions with his or her tutor, which are tailored around constructed stages in the child's life. Though more covert than authoritarianism, this form of governance is still concerned with producing a specific version of the child that is found within certain discourses. Furthermore, as children are products of discourses which are products of the regime of truth which is cultural and specific – there is no innate child to discover or 'develop'. Instead, I suggest that Rousseau ignores the cultural situation of his own work; *Emile, or on Education*, was focused on a middle-class French boy around the time of the French Revolution. This is not to suggest that these 'truths' are homogenous for all similar identities; however, these 'truths' for Emile are most probably not the truths for others around the world. Moreover, Emile's freedom is only possible alongside Sophie's confinement, further verifying the myth of freedom as autonomous and equitable.

In the next section I explore one of the most influential theorists within education, who took the basis of Rousseau's work but applied a more 'scientific' approach to the study of childhood, Jean Piaget. As such, I continue unpacking natural child development, which, I argue, is the basis for the construction of the mathematical child within mathematics education research.

The normal, developed, psychological child – Piaget

Development psychology has emerged over the last century, though its influences date back several hundred years, including to the Enlightenment and Rousseau. A key principle is that the mind is distinct from the body; this gendered binary can be viewed as one amongst many that underlie Western thinking (Lloyd, 1993). In this instance, a cognitive model of normal child development is produced, and most important, this development is both "natural and inevitable" (Burman, 2008a, p. 69), and leads to maturation (James et al., 1998). Hence "developmental psychology capitalizes . . . on two everyday assumptions: first, that children are natural rather than social phenomena, and secondly, that part of this naturalness extends to the inevitable process of their maturation" (James et al., 1998, p. 17). This is heavily laden with assumed hierarchies and linear temporalities; "developmentalism implies that the movement from childhood to adulthood involves a linear progression from the simple to the complex and from the irrational to the rational" (Kenway & Bullen, 2001, p. 3), all of which assume a mass homogeneity of children and adults. Specifically, this normal developing child is a natural inquirer, a problem solver, and is 'free' to make decisions. In addition, this child is actively engaged, develops from his or her experiences, and produces his or her own knowledge. Thus, the psychological model of child development can be viewed as a commitment to science, rationality, and reason (Burman, 2008a). "The developmental trajectory of children's thinking follows the 'up the hill' model of science and progress (Rorty, 1980): a hierarchical model of 'cognitive structures' emerges whereby a more mature logic arises from and supersedes earlier and less adequate structures" (Burman, 2008a, p. 252). There are obvious comparisons to Rousseau's child and to the human sciences that Foucault critiques, which was discussed in the previous chapter.

As mentioned, arguably the most influential thinker in this movement was Piaget (James et al., 1998), who depicted the child as a "budding scientist systematically encountering problems . . . and learning by discovery and activity (Piaget, 1957)" (Burman, 2008a, p. 251). For Piaget, as for Rousseau, science, rationality, and reason could overcome the immorality of humanity. He states that "science is one of the finest examples of the adaptation of the human mind. It is the victory of mind over matter" (Piaget, 1933, p. 7). Again, this is similar to Rousseau's Enlightenment Child and suggests that the preferred or 'natural' child within is stronger than the society outside. However, in contrast to Rousseau, Piaget's child does not develop into anything, but rather, there is a specific child that is the epitome of maturation and intelligence (James et al., 1998). In addition, Piaget wrote about child development and not about men and boys as superior to women and girls, as Rousseau did.

Where Piaget stands out, is that he is largely responsible for popularising the view that children think differently to adults (Burman, 2008a). He states,

> Education, for most people, means trying to lead the child to resemble the typical adult of his society . . . for me, education means making creators, even if there aren't many of them, even if one's creations are limited by comparison with those of others.
>
> (Piaget, 1980, p. 132)

Hence, Piaget, along with his colleague Inhelder (Piaget & Inhelder, 1969/2000), developed a model of children's thinking as deliberately distinct from adults' thinking. Specifically, he devised a theory of growth that specified clear relations between age and stage that would develop through experience. Within this, cognitive thinking begins at the 'sensorimotor stage', where behaviours concern basic motor responses, and culminates in a 'formal operational stage', where high levels of abstract reasoning should occur (Piaget & Inhelder, 1969/2000). These stages of development are hierarchical, temporal, and constructed as normative, though Piaget did not expect everyone to reach the later formal stage; from the earlier quotation, it is clear to see the model is not inclusive of all children. This constructivist model provides a contrast to behaviourism that proposed that a person's behaviour has no relation to internal thought, for example see Watson (1913), Skinner (1938, 1974), Guthrie (1933; discussed in Driscoll, 1994); these were popular at a time prior to Piaget's work.

Piaget never explicitly set out a model for teaching, he was more concerned with the child developing autonomy, and learning through discovery. Thus, teachers and educators have interpreted Piagetian-style teaching as facilitating the activity of the child (Driscoll, 1994) usually through the use of problem-solving or creative tasks (L. Smith, 2001), which I discuss more in the second half of this chapter. Piaget's work and ideas are one of, if not the most, influential in Western education.

Piaget's critics cite his approach to research as flawed, which was largely based on observing and experimenting with his own children (L. Smith, 2001). In addition, some have questioned the explicit and exclusive structure of the stages, as other observations of children have shown that children can move between stages or apply thought in a different stage within localised situations (Driscoll, 1994). Furthermore, Piaget is often criticised for removing the social from the child (and the child from the social). More significantly, and as argued in this book, we can dispute any claim that is reported as a universal truth (Burman & Parker, 1993). For instance, these truths are solely based on Western, and specifically European, culture:

> Developmental psychology's commitment to a view of children and child development as fixed, unilinear and timeless is not only ethnocentric and

culture-blind in its unwitting reflection of parochial preoccupations and consequent devaluation of differing patternings, but is also in danger of failing to recognise changes in the organisation of childhood subjectivity and agency.
(Burman, 2008a, p. 82)

Thus, the psychological cognitive child is not a universal child, but a white, middle-class Western child removed of his or her cultural and sociopolitical context. Furthermore, this child is not a reflection of society but is actively negotiated within cultural contexts. Hence, rather than assume that Piaget describes childhood, we can examine how psychology produces childhood within the social structures where it is found. Here, "the child is a sign created within discursive practices" (Walkerdine, 1997, p. 61), and more specifically "'the child' is deferred in relation to certain developmental accomplishments"; importantly, the very practices that claim to discover the child actually produce the child (Walkerdine, 1997, p. 61). Similar critiques can be found in Burman (1992, 2008a, 2008b), Burman and Parker (1993), Henriques et al. (1998), Walkerdine (1998a) and Walkerdine and Lucey (1989). Thus,

> [d]evelopment psychology was made possible by the clinic and the nursery school . . . They thus simultaneously allowed for standardisation and for normalisation . . . It thus not only presented a picture of what was normal for children of such an age, but also enabled the normality of any child to be assessed by comparison with this norm.
> (N. Rose, 1999a, pp. 145–146)

Hence, developmental psychology produces and is produced by comparisons to the normative, and the normal child becomes the desire of education, and everyone else is constructed as defective; "it is the normalisation of development that makes abnormality possible, and vice versa" (Burman, 2008a, pp. 20–21). It is this version of the child that has come to dominate current perceptions of the child in education. This is within the neoliberal context of the human sciences that facilitate the fabricated subject (N. Rose, 1999a); it is within the child as a product of consumer and market discourses. Hence, the "will to know" (Foucault, 1978/1998) may cohere to the psychological child. The simpler categories of the psychological child offer a logical and achievable model that fits into the current system. Hence, this 'developing' child is the 'real' child, and anything removed from this is Othered. However, what happens in these spaces of conflict in relation to educational practice is what is explored in detail in Chapter 6. I begin mapping these spaces in the rest of this chapter.

(De)Constructing childhood in mathematics education

In Chapters 4 to 7 of this book, I examine how the mathematical child is constructed around norms of mathematics education. Specifically, though rather simplistically "Mathematics education is devoted to the study of how students learn and how teachers teach" (Clarke et al., 2004, p. 1). Hence, in this next section, I discuss some norms of mathematics education, particularly in relation to preferred learning and teaching pedagogies, whilst relating this to constructions of the mathematical child using ideas already discussed in the first half of this chapter.

Mathematics education: pedagogies, mathematics, and the mathematical child

As already discussed, perhaps the most influential thinker in education was Piaget, and the most influential movement within education, and mathematics education, comes from developmental psychology. Indeed, writing in 1994, Lerman notes that the "mathematics education community has always been influenced by developments in educational psychology, and in that community Piaget's work was still dominant" (p. 42), privileging the cognition of the mathematical child. This slightly dated remark remains relevant today with the marketisation of education, and the current popularity of the human sciences.

Specifically, under neoliberalism, governmentality the principle that social systems restrict the subject through normalisation, is in the ascendance. Hence we live under the illusion of freedom, but instead we are governed through this apparent freedom (Foucault, 1977/1991, 1978/1998; N. Rose, 1999a).

> The human sciences have actually made it possible to exercise political, moral, organizational, even personal authority in ways compatible with liberal notions of freedom and autonomy of individuals and ideas about liberal limits on the scope of legitimate political intervention . . . these new forms of regulation do not crush subjectivity. They actually fabricate subjects . . . capable of bearing the burdens of liberty.
> (N. Rose, 1999a, p. viii)

Consequently the modern person strives to make their lives meaningful and make sense of themselves (N. Rose, 1999a). As such they can become drawn into normalising essentialised discourses of the self; this applies to researchers, teachers, and students. Even those who specify that they are 'finding themselves', which is a popular trope in the human sciences, are arguably 'inventing' themselves around specific models of selfhood. The point is that education is a crucial part of this production, conjuring an emancipatory narrative where redemption can be sought by both the individual and society. Moreover, the child being a symbol of both. However, this is the autonomy that Foucault critiques. Specifically, "in their development the human sciences lead to the disappearance of man rather than his [*sic*] apotheosis" (Foucault, 1989d, p. 16). As discussed in the previous chapter, Foucault and poststructuralism "dis-assembles the humanist subject – the thinking, self-aware, truth-seeking individual ('man') who is able to master both 'his' own internal passions and the physical world around him, through the exercise of reason" (MacLure, 2003, p. 175). Instead, poststructuralists, and I, argue that the notion of autonomy is a fabricated myth and that the humanist subject is a fiction acting through discourses (Walkerdine, 1990). Hence, the popularity of developmental psychology in mathematics education is paralleled by the rise of the individual within neoliberalism and the governance of individuals through the promise and positioning of autonomy (N. Rose, 1999a). We are in a society concerned with progressive versions of the self, and similarly, these markers can be found running through discourses of the mathematical child.

Piaget and developmental psychology have been extremely influential on mathematics education, particularly with regards to the proposed manner of learning and teaching. This, as mentioned, is in spite of Piaget not specifically addressing teachers and teaching. In mathematics education, we may crudely split mathematics pedagogy into two principal philosophical domains and two resulting pedagogies: 'progressive' also known as reform, open, nontraditional, and student-/child-centred – which has its roots in developmental psychology – and 'traditional', also known as closed, teacher-led, and subject-centred, which can have its roots in behaviourism. Several scholars warn against propagating these false binaries (including Alexander, 1994, 2010; Pring, 1989); however, in mathematics education these polarised ways of being in the classroom seem to hold resilient positions. This is evident in the UK, and around Europe, but is also reflected in the 'Math Wars' found in the US, where proponents of reform and traditional mathematics education fiercely advocate each position and corresponding curricula. Indeed, "there is evidence that the two sides of these math wars are not attending to the points made by the other side" (Davison, Mitchell, & Montana, 2008, p. 143). Thus, I am presenting these philosophical pedagogies as a polarity; however, I do not believe this to be 'real'. My argument is concerned with exposing the tendency to strongly advocate one position over another and create a dualism, in this case to promote progressive or traditional education. As discussed by Alexander (2010), these discourses of dichotomy are prevalent within education and limit possibilities. Opinions are restricted to these binaries, discussion is focused around extremes, and consequently, the creation of new knowledge is constrained. Furthermore, people are positioned into feuding from mythical fixed locations. This tendency towards tunnel vision is common within political and educational discourses, where strong principles as statements of worth are required. However, I suggest these mathematics pedagogies are products of sociopolitical discourse and forms of governance, each producing a preferred version of the mathematical child.

As mentioned, progressive education has its foundations in educational reformers such as Rousseau (see Rousseau, 1763/1884), Dewey (see e.g. Dewey, 1902/1956; Dewey, 1916), and/or development psychologists such as Piaget (see e.g. Piaget & Garcia, 1989, or Piaget & Inhelder, 1969/2000). As such (and as discussed in the previous section), the basis of progressive education is that the child is positioned as free, and knowledge is produced through experience. Thus, the progressive child is thought to be predisposed to education and development, which is seen as both natural and inevitable. Specifically for progressive education or "child-centred pedagogy, 'the child' is deferred in relation to certain developmental accomplishments" (Walkerdine, 1997, p. 61), for example Piagetian stages, where the child learns in 'logical' developmental blocks.

Within mathematics education, progressive education is often produced as synonymous with constructivism. In simple terms, and similarly to progressive education, constructivism is the perspective that human beings construct their own knowledge of the world (Wood, 1998). There are, of course, variants of constructivism: radical, progressive, conservative and reactionary (Phillips, 2000), and/or individual/cognitive (often linked to Piaget) and social (linked to Vygotsky; Sjoberg, 2007), and there are differences between these. However, my concern here is not with these minutiae but instead is focused on how the broad definition of constructivism is taken up and used as a dominant discourse within mathematics education pedagogy and what this means for the mathematical child. Within this domain, the term *constructivism* is often used as an umbrella term when referring to any child-centred learning or teaching, inquiry, or discovery-based activities (Sjoberg, 2007); as such, I also use it as broadly and may refer to it as constructivism or progressive mathematics education.

Fosnot (2013), an eminent writer/researcher on constructivism, describes the constructivist pedagogical perspective in more detail:

> A constructivist view of learning suggests an approach to teaching that gives learners the opportunity for concrete, contextually meaningful experience . . . the classroom in this model is seen as a mini-society, a community of learners engage in activity, discourse, interpretation, justification and reflection . . . what the teacher knows begins to dissipate as teachers assume more of a facilitator's role and learners take on more ownership of the ideas. Indeed, autonomy, mutual reciprocity of social relations, and empowerment become the goals.
>
> (p. preface)

From this, the constructivist thinker produces the constructivist child as a problem-solver, a negotiator, and an interrogator; the child is very much ready to learn, and is a natural active agent. Hence, "the notion of the active creative child, building her or his own concepts, was offered a theoretical rationale by constructivism, which argued that learning is something that children can only do for themselves" (Lerman, 1994, p. 41). Moreover, the teacher is thought to be in a less authoritarian role, as they are the facilitators of this experience. They are not the holders of greater knowledge but are tools to enable the experience that helps the child produce his or her own knowledge. Similarly, Simon (1995), in a frequently cited article, proposes the following four principles for a constructivist mathematics pedagogy. He particularly highlights the switch from teacher to student-driven learning, stating that the teacher's knowledge should also be challenged:

1   Students' thinking/understanding is taken seriously and given a central place in the design and implementation of instruction;

2 The teacher's knowledge evolves simultaneously with the growth in the students' knowledge;
3 Planning for instruction is seen as including the generation of a hypothetical learning trajectory;
4 The continually changing knowledge of the teacher creates continual change in the teacher's hypothetical learning trajectory. (Simon, 1995, p. abstract).

This constructivist pedagogy usually involves the mathematical child in solving problems, discovering patterns, questioning methods, and exploring possibilities; thus, there is an overall emphasis on reflective inquiry (Handal, 2003). Moreover, this perspective can draw from a fallibilist or a quasi-empiricist (Ernest, 1991; Lerman, 1983, 1990) perspective on mathematics; such that mathematics is a human activity, to be contested and continuously reconstructed.

As noted, the self-governing of the child and the non-dictatorial role of the teacher, can both be questioned. The progressive/constructivist child is a product of covert surveillance that masquerades as freedom. The classroom is not without rules, and the teacher is not without governance; they have a role, to facilitate a specific kind of development that they define. For example, Walkerdine (1998a) describes a teacher who feels unable to reprimand boys in her class concerning their aggressive sexual language towards her. The teacher has determined it is part of the boys' 'natural' development. The notion that 'boys will be boys' is hugely problematic, as it makes normal sexual harassment and violence.

In the preferred scenario, this mathematical child is naturally intrinsically motivated, naturally curious, and naturally predisposed to education. Thus, it assumes that intrinsic motivation, inquisition, and curiosity are real. However, if the natural is not evident, the teacher's role is to produce it; thus "the behaviours [of the child] do not precede the practice precisely because their specificity is produced in these practices" (Walkerdine, 1990, p. 138). And mathematical child is not natural but is a production of discourses of progressive education, and developmental psychology (Burman, 1992, 2008a; Burman & Parker, 1993; Henriques et al., 1998; Walkerdine, 1997, 1998a; Walkerdine & Lucey, 1989). Additionally, "the cognitive model of the infant as problem solver mirrors that of the assembly worker, with research privileging those activities and products which will enhance performance" (Burman, 2008a, p. 43). Thus, constructivism/progressive education is always already focused on development, more so than the here and now. It is future orientated despite the focus on 'free' play. Attention is given to what the child will become rather than with what the child is now (Burman, 2008a), which as discussed in a familiar narrative of childhood studies. Of course, this is hugely problematic as children are never allowed to be within the present. It is a specific kind of development and anyone who does not follow this is defective (Walkerdine, 1990). Hence, a specific kind of mathematical child is privileged – who presents the required production

Traditional education is often positioned as the complete contrast to this. Transmission models tend to be based on direct instruction, where learning occurs through the transference of knowledge from a teacher ('master') to a student (novice). Hence, they follow a more behaviourist model of learning (e.g. see Watson (1913), Skinner (1938, 1974), Guthrie (1933; discussed in Driscoll, 1994), or indeed may be influenced by a more Lockean (1693/1932) view of childhood, where "the child is an unformed person who through literacy, education, reason, self-control, and shame may be made into a civilised adult" (Postman, 1982/1994, p. 59). In mathematics pedagogy this may be through the repetition of standardised questions and practice or through the modelling of methods and solutions.

Hence, traditional mathematics education values recognised methods and techniques for doing mathematics. Also, the focus may be on 'the basics', before moving onto more 'complex' tasks, thus suggesting a fixed, hierarchical narrative for learning mathematics. The emphasis is on the teacher as the holder of absolute knowledge, often supported by discourses of absolute mathematics, which have connections to Platonism and/or Logicism and/or Euclidism (Ernest, 1991; Lerman, 1990), all of which suggest that there are mathematical objects that are abstract, independent, and free of language and the human mind. This position of mathematics as an absolute truth is prevailing: "For over two thousand years mathematics has been dominated by an absolutist paradigm, which views it as a body of infallible and objective truth, far removed from the affairs and values of humanity" (Ernest, 1991, p. xi). The security of certainty, particularly of mathematics, can be appealing. As Ernest states, "if its [Mathematics] certainty is questioned, the outcome may be that human beings have no certain knowledge at all" (Ernest, 1991, p. xi), and for many, that is a very vulnerable position, which can be especially troubling within a school context. Instead, "mathematical reasoning presumes mastery of a discourse in which the universe is knowable and manipulable according to particular mathematical algorithms" (Walkerdine, 1990, p. 72). Placing the same structures around the mathematical child and pedagogy may appear the 'logical' approach. It may even suggest that future society is similarly certain.

The dominance of absolute mathematics is not shared by all in mathematics education research. In the majority of mathematics education research, and educational research, in general, traditional pedagogies and learning are often positioned as a deficit model; a few prominent examples of research include Von Glasersfeld (1991) Schoenfeld (1992, 2002), and Boaler (1997b, 2002). These works are highly referenced, which demonstrates that these works are the acceptable face of mathematics education research, they are what is allowed to be said and heard. More often than not, those advocating a constructivism/progressive education are positioned as the "good guys", and those advocating traditional education are the "bad guys" (Sjoberg, 2007, p. 1) in a familiar and simplistic cultural trope. This is also evident in classifications such as Bloom's (1956) taxonomy – where knowledge is seen as the lowest classification, and hence the lowest form of intelligence – and Skemp's (1976) relational and instrumental understanding – the latter positioned as an inferior form of knowing. As such the mathematical child of traditional education is very much positioned as inferior.

Dewey (1902/1956), a reformist, argued that if education relied solely on 'traditional' education, where the emphasis is on factual recall and transmission of knowledge,

> the child is simply the immature being who is to be matured; he [sic] is the superficial being who is to be deepened; his is narrow experience which is to be widened. It is his to receive, to accept. His part is fulfilled when he is ductile and docile.
>
> (p. 8)

Hence, a critique of traditional education is that it does not value the child or indeed that it underestimates the capacity of the child. Other critics, such as Schoenfeld (1992), state that it "trivialises mathematics" (p. 335) and that teaching mathematics as disconnected facts is "impoverished" (p. 335). Another argument is that it adds to inequity, marginalising certain groups of mathematics' students (Boaler, 1997b; Schoenfeld, 2002). Yet Dewey's earlier remark demonstrates how advocating one position such as progressive education is reliant on attacking the Other.

However, what both progressive and traditional pedagogies tend to ignore is individual agency and the positioning of the subject, with regard to both the student and the teacher. As discussed, the child is neither active nor passive in either situation but instead is capable of both these positions. For example if you believe, as constructivists do, that children create their meaning of the world, following methods in a mathematics classroom will not prevent them doing so; working through a method does not deny agency. Neither of these positions is free from regulatory discourse, each suggesting a preferred way of being, where the preferred teacher works towards the preferred student. In addition, both these positions are rather simplistic in advocating a one way is best for all in mathematics education and learning. As such, the mathematical child is similarly positioned as homogenous, one version of a child that prefers this pedagogical discourse. What is ignored is that one student's favourite classroom is another student's nightmare. One person's freedom is another's confinement.

Moreover, as these discourses are positioned against each other, they propagate and fabricate each other, often with little acknowledgement of the importance of the Other. Instead of restricting ourselves to these binaries there are many positions between that are not so extreme (Davison et al., 2008). For instance, in a well-cited article, Raymond (1997) has five classifications of mathematics pedagogies: Traditional, Primary Traditional, Even Mix of Traditional/Nontraditional, Primary Nontraditional, and Nontraditional. These can be viewed as graded classifications of the divide between the extremes of traditional and progressive/nontraditional mathematics education. However, we can question how far this is helpful, as it is a spectrum that is anchored by the 'real' pedagogies (which is a similar argument to one made by Wilchins (2004) about 'real' genders). Raymond's work explicitly draws on Ernest's (1991) five classifications of mathematical "educational ideologies": industrial trainer, technological pragmatist, old humanist, progressive educator, and public educator. The progressive mathematics education I have described earlier is similar to Ernest's progressive educator and public educator. Traditional mathematics education would be the industrial trainer at its most extreme but may also be the old humanist or the technological pragmatist. Each of his classifications specifies a preferred pedagogy, but each is broader, in that Ernest also identifies a "political ideology; view of mathematics; theory of society; theory of the child; theory of ability; mathematical aims; theory of learning; theory of teaching mathematics; theory of resources; theory of assessment in mathematics; theory of social diversity" (pp. 138–139). This neat classification demonstrates how theories of teaching mathematics are embedded with theories of the mathematical child, even if this is not acknowledged – which I suggest it is not. For many it is normal to talk about the mathematics and the teaching, but the child is not written and, as such, is an unacknowledged by-product.

Ernest's classifications further demonstrate that mathematical pedagogies should not be viewed as objective and isolated from the epistemologies of the educators; moreover, mathematics pedagogies cannot be removed from cultural, social, or political context. Hence, the focus within certain parts of the world on progressive and traditional pedagogies is not a natural position of worldwide, timeless, mathematics education – in spite of many illusions that this position exists; instead, it is a cultural production of the time and context. These pedagogies are what is allowed to be said and heard.

In spite of the seemingly fixed appearance of these classifications, Ernest suggests that in practice, perspectives are often mixed. Raymond does not dispute the fixed classification (though as stated, we could argue that her classifications are a mixing of the two 'real' binaries, traditional and nontraditional/progressive), but she does contend that there are inconsistencies between teachers' beliefs about mathematics pedagogies and their practices. Instead, she argues that there may be a stronger link between teachers' beliefs concerning mathematics content (e.g. absolutist or fallibilist) and their actual practice. However, a poststructural position complicates these categories and this assumption. Soriede (2007; who, in a Norwegian context, where there was not the same neoliberal agenda) examines in detail the different discourses available to contemporary teachers. She states that conceptions of teaching are related to identity, and in particular, identity construction "occurs through the identification by the individual with particular subject positions within discourses" (Weedon, 1997, p. 112). However "there are no simple, one-dimensional and causal explanations or predictions to why teachers are positioned within some identities as others are rejected" (Soriede, 2007, p. 70). Thus, it is too simplistic to say that teachers believe that mathematics is fixed and hence pedagogy and/or the mathematical child are similarly so. Moreover, Zembylas (2003) "challenge[s] the assumption that there is a singular 'teacher self' and an essential 'teacher identity' as implied in popular cultural myths about teaching" (p. 214). As previously discussed, the poststructural self is not fixed; however, the common identity of a teacher may be most often aligned to the normalised discourse of the time; there are, of course, many spaces for resistance and agency. Thus (and paraphrasing Zembylas), it is not a question of who but of what, how, and when.

Hence, there are more positions than progressive and traditional pedagogies within mathematics education, some of which (such as Mastery mathematics) I will come back to in later chapters. Certainly, a teacher's positioning within this is more complex than our assumptions suggest. However, my focus on this progressive/traditional dualism comes as it is the binary that has dominated and still governs the mathematics education landscape. Thus, in the next section, I draw on documents that are designed to shape the practice of school teachers to explain how the English education system has flip-flopped between advocating these positions for mathematics pedagogy.

Mathematics pedagogy in UK classrooms: pedagogies in practice, the teacher, and the mathematical child

The debate over the 'best' pedagogy to use in the mathematics classroom is a recurrent discussion within mathematics education. More often than not this is framed around necessary and expected improvement and progress, of grades, education, and/or society. Whilst "the current [New Labour] preoccupation with education is most obviously manifested in the emphasis on 'standards and achievement'" (Buckingham & Scanlon, 2003, p. 3), mathematics seems to have always sought this improvement. In particular, this discourse of derision is evident from around the time of the first education act in 1870, as I showed in Chapter 1 when I quoted the government inspector's ascription of poor arithmetic to "radically imperfect teaching". Similar critiques abound in recent reports on mathematics education (Ofsted, 2008; A. Smith, 2004; Williams, 2008). Hence, the 'incompetence' of mathematics teachers is a relatively static discourse within education and within this the failure of the mathematical child to develop fully.

Alongside this, the importance of mathematics is well documented. In the UK, it is expected that every person should achieve at least a grade C at General Certificate of Secondary Education (GCSE) – which was recently remodelled to level 5. Furthermore, research cites a link between gaining an A level in mathematics and entrance to Russell group universities, even for subjects with no mathematical content (Dilnot & Boliver, 2017). Thus, along with the subject English, in UK schools mathematics occupies a 'privileged' position; it is one of the core, compulsory subjects, and one that has a high-status achievement level for the 'normal' student. For instance, Alexander observes that throughout compulsory education in England, education is concerned with "reading, writing, number and little else" (Alexander, 2010, p. 5). Of course, I query that this is a real cause and effect and instead suggest that mathematics itself is not important; mathematics is instead a cultural marker; it is not so much what mathematics is but what it represents.

However, although studying mathematics (or at least number) has always been important, and the teaching and learning subjected to derision, one way the discourse has shifted is with regard to the type of pedagogy that is advocated. Specifically, the pedagogy of mathematics education seems to follow cyclical patterns of dominance; hence, and following Foucault, we can question the notion of linear progress and a teleological approach to history. In particular, and as introduced in the previous section, this dichotomy/divide between the pedagogy associated with transmission and the pedagogy associated with exploratory mathematics has become one of the major and normalised discourses of mathematics education. Within this, different versions of the mathematical child appear, though this is not always foregrounded in the discussions.

As discussed throughout this chapter, Piaget is perhaps the most influential theorist in education, and his ideas are found within progressive education. "During the 1960s this work by Piaget and his colleagues was at the peak of its influence. It was very widely known and widely accepted" (Donaldson, 1978, p. 34), both in mathematics education research, as previously discussed, and in official reports on primary education. The 'Plowden report' (Central Advisory Council for Education, 1967a, 1967b; the first report on general primary education since 'Hadow's' (Hadow & Great Britain. Board of Education. Consultative Committee on the Primary School, 1931) was a particularly influential document that drew largely on Piaget and progressive education. This is evident through chapter titles such as "the children, their growth and development". Plowden emphasised the virtues of discovery teaching and of developing understanding. Consequently, at this time, the former became a marker of proficiency for mathematics teachers and the latter became a marker of proficiency for people doing mathematics. Subsequently, during the late 1960s and 1970s, guidance on teaching mathematics (and general primary education) was predominantly 'child-centred'. This direction can be seen as part of the wider liberal and progressive political thought that gained prominence during this time.

Within this, a specific kind of discourse of the teacher came to prominence, which still holds some influence today. In particular, Woods and Jeffrey (2002) argue that the discourse of the primary school teacher of the 1970s and 1980s was strongly influenced by progressivism and in particular the Plowden report (1967). As such, humanism and vocationalism were key to teachers' roles and identities. Specifically,

> [t]his set of values centres around holism, person-centredness, and warm and caring relationships . . . Teachers see children in holistic terms. Basic to this outlook is the child as person. They base their notion of 'good teaching' on child-centred principles, core features of which are full and harmonious development of the child, a focus on the individual learner rather than the whole class, an emphasis on activity and discovery, curriculum integration, and environmentally based learning (Sugrue, 1998). Teachers place a high priority on feelings in teaching and learning, and on making emotional connections with knowledge and with children (Woods & Jeffrey, 1996) . . . The Plowden primary teacher . . . feels that teaching is a vocation.
> (Woods & Jeffrey, 2002, pp. 92–93)

This discourse of primary teaching as nurturing (Coffey & Delamont, 2000) or primary teaching as a "culture of care" (Nias, 1999, p. 66), also draws from older and wider maternal discourses (Griffin, 1997). For instance, Walkerdine highlights that the 'Hadow Report' (Hadow & Great Britain. Board of Education. Consultative Committee on the Primary School, 1931) states that women go into teaching "to amplify their capacities for maternal nurturance" (Walkerdine, 1990, p. 22). As such primary school teaching was positioned as a "feminised semi-profession" (Acker, 1989) and as 'natural' women's work. "Like mothering, caring for young children in schools is regularly regarded as a natural sphere for women, making monetary incentives or public tributes unnecessary" (Acker, 1999, p. 4). Walkerdine also shows how the conflict between emotional and rational discourses can leave women caught in an impossible fiction. Particularly, that with the teacher as 'guide', "the servicing labour of women makes the child, the natural child, possible" (Walkerdine, 1990, p. 24). Consequently, "women teachers became caught, trapped inside a concept of nurturance which held them responsible for the freeing of each little individual, and therefore for the management of an idealist dream, an impossible fiction" (Walkerdine, 1990, p. 19). This is particularly true within progressive pedagogies. Walkerdine continues, arguing that this process of normalising the rational is done in a covertly rather than an overtly disciplinary manner (see also Walkerdine & Lucey, 1989). Hence, the illusion is of the child as "originator of its actions. The autonomous child is the empowered child, the child potentially ready to take its place in a democracy . . . [This] is an illusion, an elaborate charade" (Walkerdine & Lucey, 1989, p. 25). Thus, Foucauldian surveillance is present, with both students and teacher; although, as was apparent in the last section, it masquerades under the notion of natural development of, or what is best for, the child.

However, time and governments alter, and consequently so do political discourses. In a political backlash to progressive education in England, the then Conservative government of the late 1970s and 1980s implemented an agenda that valued 'traditional' education. On the whole, this saw rote and routine and traditional values return to the majority of mathematics classrooms. To enable this transition to occur, the government created conditions in which returning to basics becomes the 'choice' of the public; as Ball notes, "education policies construct the 'problems' they address and, thus, the solutions they propose" (S. J. Ball, 2008, p. 94), and "people think of schooling as the major institution by which to improve society" (Popkewitz, 1988, p. 78); furthermore, and as I have mentioned before, it is easier to make changes and thus promises in education rather than propose to effect unemployment rates. Thus, the government created stories around the failure of progressive classrooms, linking this to failings in wider society. One example concerns the then prime minister Margaret Thatcher, who opposed progressive mathematics education; mockingly, she stated that "children who need to be able to count and multiply are learning anti-racist mathematics – whatever that may be" (quoted in Epstein, 1995, p. 64). "Here we have quite explicitly the notion that education (though the action of teachers) is inherently subversive" (Epstein, 1995, p. 65) and, in this instance, could contest the principles of traditional education and the values of 'innocent' children, children whom we should protect as individuals who cannot protect themselves and as they are the future of society.

In this instance, Thatcher's comment is one of many that perpetuates a discourse to become a truth – that progressive mathematics is not appropriate or good mathematics education and, simultaneously, that there is a certain type of mathematics (and society) – both traditional, that is correct. We can see in this statement that this traditional agenda can be viewed as a neo-conservative ideology, as "neo-conservative cultural restorationism ties together education, the family and the state with the past" (S. J. Ball, Kenny, & Gardiner, 1990, p. 5). Moreover, one of the 'aims' of a "'back to basics' curriculum . . . it is argued, is to reproduce gender, racial, and class distinctions in society" (Popkewitz & Brennan, 1997, p. 302). Hence, these events could be viewed as the neo-conservative government seeking more 'control', not just over classrooms but over the direction of the people and society. However, it is important to remember that whilst these discourses are dominant, they would not have been taken up by everyone; teachers, students, and schools still have agency and would still negotiate subject positions. For instance, Alexander (2010) argues that traditional values were never really absent from the classroom. As such the 'actual' picture is more complex than simple binaries and my over-simplification suggests.

The 1980s saw the appearance of an influential report on mathematics education in the UK – mathematics *Counts: The Cockcroft Report* (1982). This report was produced under a neo-conservative government and could be viewed as a reaction to their ideology – a form of resistance. In particular, it criticised mathematics lessons for being irrelevant to students' lives and for being dominated by rote learning. It states "Mathematics lessons in secondary schools are very often not about anything . . . There is excessive preoccupation with a sequence of skills and quite inadequate opportunity to see the skills emerging from the solution of problems" (Cockcroft, 1982, p. 462). Hence, the Cockcroft Report was seen as favouring problem-solving. Many in mathematics education (teaching and research) reference it as such (e.g. Holton, Anderson, Thomas, & Fletcher, 1999; Watt, 2005), and/or make links to constructivism (e.g. Romberg, 1997). At the very least, the Cockcroft Report legitimised progressive approaches, such that it was "'official' recognition of problem solving and investigation" (M. Rose, 2000, p. 31).

However, the advice given in the Cockcroft Report was for a range of pedagogies in the classroom; one of the most quoted paragraphs of the report states,

Mathematics teaching at all levels should include opportunities for:

- exposition by the teacher;
- discussion between teacher and students and between students themselves;
- appropriate practical work;
- consolidation and practice of fundamental skills and routines;

- problem solving, including the application of mathematics to everyday situations;
- investigational work. (Cockcroft, 1982, p. 71)

Thus, the focus not only is on investigations, discussion, and problem-solving but also includes teacher-led activities and the practice of routines. So how has it come to be that the former is elevated and the latter is seen as secondary? According to Orton and Frobisher, originally writing in 1996, teacher explanation is commonly found in classrooms, whereas problem-solving is often neglected, or not done well:

> This [extract] still stands as the best short statement of advice available. The suggestion has also been made frequently, both before and after the introduction of the NC, that mathematics teachers as a whole have been traditionally good at exposition, and at teaching aimed at consolidation and practice of skills and routines, but much less good at the other four elements of the Cockcroft report.
> (Orton & Frobisher, 2005, p. 9)

The implication is that the absence of problem-solving and discovery learning, as advocated by Cockcroft, leads to unsatisfactory learning of mathematics. This message is (re)produced, and explanation is constructed as an inferior aspect of the mathematics classroom. Furthermore, teachers in this instance are subjugated through "discourses of derision" – they are not good enough. Similarly, the mathematical child is produced in this vein and with these expectations.

Another shift in education in England was seen in 1988 as the National Curriculum, a prescriptive document that legislated what content had to be taught, was introduced. Thus began an era of overt political regulation of classrooms and schools. In the run-up to the 1992 general election, the same Conservative government implemented another 'back-to-basics' agenda, launching an attack on progressive styles of teaching (Alexander, 2010) and its role in holding back standards. In mathematics, a government Numeracy Task Force was instigated, which was the forerunner for what would become the National Numeracy Strategy, which became a key part of the New Labour government agenda. Alongside this, mathematics education research very much promotes child-centred/progressive/constructivist pedagogy as its gold standard of education (which is discussed in detail in Chapter 5). The specifics of the New Labour (1997–2010) and the Conservative (2015–present) and Conservative–Liberal Democrat (2010–2015) are discussed in the next chapter.

Concluding remarks

In summary, within mathematics education, a strong discourse is that the results and the teaching are often not good enough, though this is part of the wider discourse of education that is concerned with improvement (Dale, 2001; Mendick,

2011) and the wider neoliberal discourses concerned with self-improvement. However, in educational policies and official discourses, what has varied is the type of pedagogy that has been condemned, and the type that has been championed. Specifically, the advocation of 'traditional' or 'progressive' styles of teaching has switched positions throughout the last 50 years. This demonstrates how education has taken on an increasingly political function and specifically how it has become a tool to be held responsible for the creation of a 'good' society. In addition, it shows how the mathematical child should not be viewed only as cognitive and individual but as part of the cultural production of the time.

4 Unpacking educational policy

Our top priority was, is and always will be education, education, education.
—Blair (1996)

Mathematical knowledge is the most precious gift an education can bestow.
—Gove (2011)

Introduction

When Tony Blair[1] named education as his government's highest priority he was doing several things. In the first instance, he was signifying his intentions to invest in education and to improve it under his government's mould; of course, as stated, gaining data to verify you have improved education is a more straightforward task than improving crime or unemployment rates. Second, Blair's investment signalled to parents/voters that he was investing in their highest priority – their children. Third, he was signaling his investment in society, as children and education both literally and symbolically represent the future. However, in singling out education, Blair also elevated the public's awareness and expectations that should arise from education. Thus, the public becomes invested in what should be addressed and what should be achieved.

This chapter takes that idea and subsequently contends that education policy is currently a dominant space in educational discourse; the narratives of a child's experiences in UK schools are very much shaped by the decisions that are made by those in government, and over the past 20 years children have been exposed to an inordinate amount of policy and educational shifts that dictate and facilitate children's life choices and who they are expected to become.

Thus, this chapter examines the multitude of educational policy documents from the last 20 years in England, and specifically asks, what kind of mathematical child is produced. Here, the merit is not only in questioning what was produced within that period (e.g. the New Labour era) but also in examining the recent past allows us to more deeply consider the contingencies that shape the present and the possible future (Foucault, 2003g). We can only answer who we are, if we consider how we have come to be. Thus, I begin by focusing on Tony Blair's

New Labour where I suggest education became the dominant narrative that is still found and influential today.

In particular, I contend that the New Labour years (1997–2010) were a site of extreme governance within English education, where "education, education, education" (Blair, 1996), and particularly mathematics education, were positioned as a priority of neoliberal government; for example through the introduction of the National Numeracy Strategy.

Setting the New Labour scene

In 1997, when Tony Blair's New Labour government came to power, education was positioned as one of its highest priorities. Specifically, the expectation was on students, teachers, and schools to 'achieve' to a new 'high' standard. The 'raising standards for every child' (Estelle Morris in DfEE, 2001, p. 3) agenda is at first glance an incontestable notion. Everyone is in favour of a better education system. However, it is a common fiction of education that it is universal – instead, I suggest that education does not have shared values and is not equitable to all. To argue this, I start by asking what these standards are and who they are for; moreover, I suggest these standards are very much a social, cultural, and political construction.

Specifically, New Labour's government was very much part of the neoliberal agenda and the marketisation of education. These policies and practices were arguably supported by their Conservative predecessors who paved the way with similar rhetoric. Throughout the New Labour era, the discourse of education for education's sake largely disappeared from state schools, and instead, "education is now seen as a crucial factor in ensuring economic productivity and competitiveness in the context of 'informational capitalism'" (S. J. Ball, 2008, p. 1), mathematics education being vital in that role as tied to progress of the individual and society. Hence, "learning is re-rendered as a 'cost-effective policy outcomes'; [and] achievement is a set of 'productivity targets'" (S. J. Ball, 2003, p. 218). Crucially, performativity is used as a method of legitimising education (S. J. Ball, 1994):

> Performativity is a technology, a culture and a mode of regulation that employs judgements, comparisons and displays as means of incentive, control, attrition and change – based on rewards and sanctions (both material and symbolic). The performances (of individual subjects or organisations) serve as measures of productivity or output, or displays of 'quality' or 'moments' of promotion or inspection. As such, they stand for, encapsulate or represent the worth, quality or value of an individual or organization within a field of judgement.
>
> (S. J. Ball, 2003, p. 216)

Thus, the teacher, the school, and the student were remodelled around marketisation, performativity, and autonomy. There were targets to be met by all and consequences for not aligning to the norms. For schools being marked as inadequate could mean being closed or moved towards privatisation; for teachers it may mean not passing threshold[2]; for students it can mark out their future path. For all, it means not being correct, not being good enough, and for individuals this is very problematic in terms of constructing one's own identity.

Within neoliberalism the self is always already concerned with self-improvement. More important, if this fails, it is the self that is solely responsible. That is the trick of neoliberalism and governmentality: that we are under the illusion that we govern ourselves, and instead, we are governed through this promise of freedom (Rose, 1999a, 1999b).

Within this performative agenda New Labour's key reforms consisted of funding, training and a multitude of resources and policies that were written for the government by private companies. This is reflective of the neoliberal shift towards the privatisation of the public sector or, at the very least, the blurring of these previously distinct boundaries. This is also evident within the operation of the school, from the private sponsored money to the management and accountability of staff and students. Significantly, marketisation had begun to drive general educational reform and educational policy (S. J. Ball, 1993a; Ozga, 2009; Whitty et al., 1998).

Within neoliberalism, the private sector influences models of working in the public sector. In particular, the management of the self becomes a priority. Subjects self-surveil and self-regulate as they work towards a preferred way of being under the illusion of autonomy (S. J. Ball, 1994, 2003, 2006, 2008). This requires an investment in self-improvement via notions of the "productive self" (N. Rose, 1999a, p. 103).

New Labour's policies could be described as "neoliberalism with a human face . . . the third way" (Arestis and Sawyer, 2005, p. 177). They encompassed broad and inclusive agendas such as *Every Child Matters* (DfES, 2003a) and the 'child-friendly' *The Children's Plan* (DCFS, 2007a), thus rhetorically advocating a 'whole-child' approach to education. Their key policy reform was the *National Strategy* framework, which contained a wide range of documentation, some of which alluded to inclusion, for example 'Aiming High: Raising the Achievement of Minority Ethnic Pupils' (DfES, 2003b). However, alongside these recommendations, there were two dominant functional initiatives that cemented their position at the top of the primary school arena. The *National Literacy* and *National Numeracy Strategy* were initially introduced separately, but in 2006 became a joint initiative. Part of the strategies required schools to allocate a dedicated hour of time to both subject every day, another aspect advocated three-part structured lessons, and specific advice was given on what each section should entail. Furthermore, these standards in Literacy and Numeracy were to be measured and thus monitored through the collection of national 'comparative' statistics. Hence, in primary schools of the New Labour era, literacy and numeracy were given maximum importance and high status – they were the gold standard of education for schools, teachers, and students. Thus, alongside Alexander, I suggest that New Labour "was less about enshrining 'excellence', 'enjoyment' 'breadth' and 'balance' [as they suggest] than more about embedding the literacy and numeracy strategies through new frameworks" (Alexander, 2004, p. 36); it was still overt governance of functionality in spite of allusions to equality and inclusion. It was opportunity constructed around neoliberal tropes such as the self and hard work (Llewellyn & Mendick, 2011).

Secondary schools similarly were exposed to their own version of the Strategy and a specific *Framework for Teaching mathematics*. The National Numeracy Strategy (NNS) and the Framework for Teaching mathematics (FTM) (DfEE, 1999) were positioned as fundamental in guiding teachers of mathematics on the subject content to be covered, the pedagogy to be used, and the nature of students' learning. Specifically, both frameworks pedagogy dictated that mathematics classes were teacher-led, fast-paced, and had short-term targets; as such, it seemed that teaching and learning for understanding, so central to progressive pedagogies, had taken a back seat.

In the next two sections I interrogate this premise in more detail, by unpacking both general New Labour documentation and then mathematics-specific policy documentation. I argue that New Labour overriding production of the mathematics child is concerned with functionality.

As previously, I 'selected the policy documents partly systematically and partly eclectically, borrowing from cultural studies approaches (du Gay, Hall, Janes, Mackay, & Negus et al., 1997)' (Llewellyn and Mendick, 2011, p. 50). This echoes Foucauldian studies that examine both normatives and disruption to those normatives.

The functional child within New Labour documentation

The functional child of New Labour is produced in various ways. I have already discussed how the language and discourse of education take on a performative function, moving away Plowden's nurturing educational landscape to something more akin to business. The shift is from the personal to the general, from care to the consumer, from nurturance to accountability (Woods & Jeffrey, 2002, p. 97). As Ball points out, much of the normative education language changed, and terms more common in business were now part of the educational narrative. Arguably, education takes on a functional performance.

This functionally is further demonstrated through the privileging of skills within the curriculum and documentation. For example, in 2001 the Department for Education and Employment (DfEE) became the Department for Education and Skills (DfES). New Labour stated that "every young person, not just some, now needs good skills and qualifications" (Ed Balls[3] in DCFS, 2009a, p. 2), and "to prosper in the 21st century competitive global economy, Britain must transform the knowledge and skills of its population" (DfEE, 2001, p. 5). In these quotations we can read that New Labour is appealing to everyone, but the appeal is of functional skills and performative markers qualifications; furthermore, New Labour is evoking a relationship between progress of the self and progress of the nation, reiterated by Brown in his statement "we have got to upgrade our skills" (Gordon Brown, cited in Gillies, 2008, p. 686) and in further documentation: "The success of our children at school is crucial to the economic health and social cohesion of the country" (DfEE, 2001, p. 5) and success can "secure the future success of our country and society" (DCSF, 2009, pp. 2, 5, 15).

These statements highlight a concern discussed earlier – that children's futures belong to society and not themselves. It further demonstrates how problematic discourses of education are, in that both the child and education are tasked with securing the future prosperity of a nation – that is a huge burden and one that is surely too much for individual children. So within New Labour discourse we can see the illusion of individualism, but instead, there is an overriding management of the population as whole, and a need for normalcy. This is indicative of Foucault's (1978/1998) biopower that works to control and regulate populations.

There are many other examples of the promise of individuality; for instance New Labour initiated the *Every Child Matters* agenda, which included the maths specific document *Every Child Counts*. This had similarities to George Bush's *No Child Left Behind* Act in the US that became more positively phrased as *Every Student Succeeds* Act under Barack Obama. The language of these initiatives suggests that everyone is included, and everyone has the right to succeed; however, in spite of the illusions to individuality, these generic brandings instead propose that everyone is the same – and, of course, they are not. Every child is expected to make the same levels of progress within society; they are expected to function as automata.

Normalised expectations of progress are a key part of New Labour's educational discourse – progress of both the individual and the state. As Mendick states,

> [w]ithin their [New Labour's] policies, progress figures as an unproblematic good . . . we see the conflation of national and individual progress, and the binding of these to discourses of economic competition and individual potential . . . there is an explicit linking of these discourses to a concept of history as linear and teleological.
>
> (Mendick, 2011, p. 50)

As such, progress of the individual, the school, and the state needs to be overtly measurable and visible. For the school perspective, league tables become direct ways of governing the population; they are markers of perceived success and failure; they are signifiers of conformity. They are the manner in which governments hold schools accountable to the public and to the consumer. Under New Labour "school performance tables will be more useful, showing the rate of progress pupils have made as well as their absolute levels of achievement" (DfEE, 1997, p. 6). They will "focus more on the progress made between different stages" (DfEE, 1997, p. 26). This assumes that rates of progress are universal and uniform between and within children, both of which are impossible fictions. Furthermore, the term *rate of progress* implies that progress should be fast; this is reiterated in the statement "a pupil taught by one of the most effective teachers will typically learn at twice the speed of one taught by one of the least effective" (H. M. Government, 2009, p. 51).

First, New Labour's *National Numeracy Strategy* broke down an already-objective structured mathematics curriculum into micro objectives. Thus, targets and levels became the language of the classroom and what each normal student is programmed to achieve.

Writing with Heather Mendick, we argued that

> '[l]evelling' captures even more clearly the compulsion to progress. Levelling, like quality, blurs several meanings, including: making flat, knocking down, and placing on the same level. To understand it in this context, it is helpful to know something about the organisation of compulsory schooling in England. Since 1988 this has been structured around four Key Stages (KS):
>
> KS1: ages 5–7
> KS2: ages 7–11
> KS3: ages 11–14
> KS4: ages 14–16
>
> KS1 and KS2 constitute primary schooling, and KS3 and KS4 secondary schooling. Each KS ends with compulsory national tests in mathematics and English, the results of which are widely published in national and local newspapers, websites etc. National expectations are set for each KS. Pupils are expected to reach level 2 of the National Curriculum at KS1 and level 4 at KS2. Time-demarcated targets are set for the proportion of pupils attaining the expected levels. In addition, expectations are set around the quantity of progress (two levels) required across each KS. As indicated in the Ofsted [(2008)] report, this can be micromanaged to produce expected levels of 'progress' in every lesson.
>
> (Llewellyn & Mendick, 2011, pp. 52–53)

Many schools have broken down each level into three sub-levels, adding even more structure and measurement. Hence, levelling is authenticated by overt surveillance on a micro and macro level, by Ofsted (mentioned earlier) and with the publication of school results and league tables. New Labour's justification is that "the rigorous use of target-setting has led to high standards and consistent year-on-year increases in the proportion of pupils who reach or exceed national expectations" (DfEE, 2001, p. 10). However, this is a cause-and-effect assumption that is contestable. An alternative argument is that pupils are better at achieving targets as teachers are better at test preparation (M. Brown, Askew, Millet, & Rhodes, 2003). Teachers are part of the marketisation of education, and it is not a system that is comparable year on year, in spite of the way data are operated by governments.

For this version of progress to be possible a particular version of the mathematical child is required. Specifically, teachers are tasked with "ensur[ing] that children progress through the levels expected for their age" (DCSF, p. 2009b). As before, this relies on the construction that students are programmed to move at linear rates and through these predetermined levels at the optimum speed. They are products fit for conversion (Llewellyn & Mendick, 2011); they are becoming governed into becoming a functional mathematical child.

This message is echoed within the publications *Increasing Pupils' Rates of Progress in mathematics* (DfES, 2004) and the *Making Good Progress* series (DCSF, 2007b, 2009b; DfES, 2007). These documents contain guidance on teaching and learning in mathematics; however, they are framed around the markers of progress. For instance, they state "the focus . . . is to increase rates of progress for pupils in mathematics by refining and developing planning, teaching and learning" (DfES, 2004, p. 5), and

> [i]n many schools pupils improve on average by one and a half levels in mathematics through Key Stage 3. In some schools pupils improve on average by two levels through Key Stage 3. Nationally we need to ensure that this becomes more commonly the case in all schools.
>
> (DfES, 2004, p. 5)

The overriding message is that students are required to conform as part of the system; they are expected to behave a certain way; they are not esoteric or individual; they are instead a functional child of educational policy. This is "another system of surveillance, another kind of control . . . The norm becomes the criterion for evaluating individuals" (Foucault, 1989g, p. 197).

By New Labour's third term in government this surveillance and discursive construction had become more explicit, which is shown in the *Making Good Progress* series of publications. For example there are sections titled, "obstacles to progress in KS2 for all slow moving pupils starting at Levels 2 & 3", "obstacles hindering progression from level 2 to 4" (DCFS, 2008b, p. 2) and "actions to support progression from Level 3 to Level 5" (DCFS, 2008b, p. 3). Hence, there are a further breakdown and examination of what is means to achieve normality, and that anything aside from this is both abnormal and defective. The surveilling and the governing of this 'normal functional progress' in pursuit of the 'normal functional mathematical' child is further demonstrated through micro managing the pupils outside their presence. This is discussed in the following extract:

> Holding pupil progress meetings can help to maintain and sustain improvement. These meetings allow children's progress to be discussed and ways of helping children to overcome existing barriers can be planned . . . The meetings also provide opportunity to identify children whose progress has recently stalled or slowed, and those children who no longer require support – a time to review membership of the focus groups. Schools are increasingly holding pupil progress meetings for the class teacher and senior leadership team, including the mathematics subject leader.
>
> (DCSF, 2009b, p. 24)

In the preceding the pupil/mathematical child is capable of "stalling" as a machine, a product that fits, or not, into the projected production line. The mathematical child is a "target" to be prodded and probed by authorities, without their presence or opinion. There are many more extracts that exemplify this positioning of the mathematical child as functional machine. For instance "the progress of . . . pupils needs to be tracked on a regular basis and obstacles to progress identified and addressed" (DCSF, 2009c, p. 26), and teachers are asked to "track progress and to tell pupils how they can do better" (DCSF, 2007a, p. 64). Here, the responsibility of monitoring seems to be placed on the teacher, with the students as passive recipients; the teacher is mostly charged with keeping normalisation on track, which is an overt simplification of the situation, which is common with government policies and documentation which assert authority with their clean lines (Curtis, 2006).

The pursuit of the 'normal' is further demonstrated by "droid diagrams" that appear in the *Making Good Progress* series of documents (Llewellyn & Mendick, 2011). This is a pictogram type illustration which uses colour-coded icons as a representation of national progress in comparison to expected levels. In these diagrams:

> the normal is defined in comparison to the other as the eye is drawn away from the majority light blue towards the minority, abnormal failures . . . These icons are pseudo-children with stylised blank bodies; they resemble automata, droids, or another science fiction invention.
> (Llewellyn & Mendick, 2011, p. 54)

This establishes difference as unacceptable. The implication of expected normalcy is reiterated through other New Labour titles such as *Keeping Up – Pupils who Fall Behind in Key Stage 2* (DCSF, 2009c) and *Getting There – Able Pupils who Lose Momentum in English and mathematics in Key Stage 2* (DCFS, 2007b). "Getting there" is quite problematic – it suggests both a finality and an essentialist view of children and their development. Overall, "this framework of expected levels and conversions, construct a 'normal' child, which purports to be, but is not, universal. Any moves away from normal connote danger/risk, and compel intervention to reconstitute the child within the normal" (Llewellyn & Mendick, 2011, p. 53).

In many of New Labour's text they remind us that the system has succeeded – this, of course, is the way that government narratives always already read – a government can only say it has made society better. For instance "the rigorous use of target-setting has led to high standards and consistent year-on-year increases in the proportion of pupils who reach or exceed national expectations" (DfEE, 2001, p. 10). And part way through their administration: "The education system in England is now widely recognised as a success. The first phase of reform launched in 1997 addressed the acute problems of the educational system that we inherited' (DfES, 2005, p. 13). However, we can contest any improvements; for instance there may indeed be 'real' improvements in grades, but what does this mean? Children are better educated? If so, in what way?

That is an argument worth considering particularly with regard to what has become to be expected from the mathematical child. I have already suggested that children are expected to progress at certain rates and that they are functional parts of the system. I now demonstrate this further by showing norms of educational discourse take on functional meanings. I do this by examining the discursive construction of both an emotive and a cognitive normative piece of language. What do educational discourses mean when they talk about confidence, and what do they mean when they talk about understanding? Both these are important aspects of education. There are perhaps more apparent terms I could have analysed – the majority of work concerning neoliberalism is written about assessment or 'closing the gap'. However, my intention is to use 'unproblematic' language to demonstrate how this functionality runs deep.

As explored earlier, skills became an important norm of New Labour's educational narratives, this shown in examples, such as

> [a] common belief shared by all these [successful] schools is that skills are learned for a purpose and not out of context . . . Skills are methodically built up, practiced and refined so that more challenging and complex work can be attempted.
>
> (DfES, 2007b, 21)

In the preceding, the implication is that mathematical skills are always for a purpose; they perform a function. In contrast, the term *understanding* is far less common; however, where it is found it arguably reads similarly to *skills* and takes on a functionality – being able to do. This is demonstrated in the following extract from the influential document the *Core Position Papers on Literacy and Numeracy* (DfES, 2006c):

> Children need to understand when and why the decimal point can disappear and can move about in the display. When £0.50 is entered, the number displayed is likely to be 0.5 as trailing zeros are not shown in decimal numbers.
>
> (DfES, 2006c, p. 59)

There is a knowing to the preceding extract – where the student is required to follow a procedure; a 'why' is alluded to but not followed through; it is very much about completion of the task. Another extract, "have a secure knowledge of number facts and a good understanding of the four operations" (DfES, 2006c, pp. 40, 57), is similarly ambiguous and favours facts in its discursive construction.

Hence, we have a position where understanding is found it is subsumed by the functional and performative found around it; the next extract makes this abundantly clear:

> These [outstanding] schools place a great emphasis on children understanding the key concepts attached to each subject. They do not, however, shy

74 *Unpacking educational policy*

away from teaching vital standard practices, for example, punctuation and grammar and mathematical algorithms. But the point here is that they make sure that children understand why these procedures are efficient and are fit for purpose.

(DfES, 2007b, p. 21)

That understanding here is constructed as "efficient and fit for purpose" is a very odd concept for something which in educational research is more abstract, or often seen as quite removed from knowledge. In educational research it is more the pinnacle of a hierarchy (e.g. in Bloom's taxonomy (1956) or the) or the good side of a dualism (e.g. in Skemp (1976)). which in turn means the mathematical child must be similarly functional. Instead, the understanding found in educational policy is more concerned with performing a task and the completion of that task, which very much fits neoliberal discourses of education and the neoliberal student.

For the functional discourse to work within neoliberalism, understanding must be constructed as uncomplicated and universal. In several extracts there is an implication that understanding will happen easily; for example,

This is shown in the following representative extract: "As children begin to understand the underlying ideas they develop ways of recording to support their thinking and calculation methods, use particular methods that apply to special cases, and learn to interpret and use the signs and symbols involved" (DfES, 2006c, p. 40). The production of mathematics here are quite functional ones which allude to a Platonic perspective on mathematics, one where mathematical reveal absolute truths (Ernest, 1991). There is definitive phrasing and deterministic ideas. My suggestion is that anyone reading this document and interpreting what it means for their school students to do mathematics, which assume a performative functionality, will assume that these children are the normative and anything else is defective.

Some may argue that the link between skills and understanding is quite obvious and one that may easily be conflated in documents, hence why I move to analyse another common work of education – a word that was very prominent under New Labour (Llewellyn, 2009); I start with a government advert that links understanding and confidence:

BERYL: Well you know looking back I know the exact time and place where I lost my confidence with maths. It was back in class 4C and I lost my ways with times-tables.
TEACHER: Seven eights are fifty six, eight eights are sixty four.
BERYL: I was too scared to put my hand up and say it's all goobledegook to me. But I've just taken this free adult maths course at my local college. They start you at the point where you get lost and build up your confidence from there. Now my fear of maths has just gone away. To get maths confident and get on call . . .

(Direct Gov, 2008)

In 2008, an advertisement appeared on UK Television; its aim was to encourage people to enrol on adult mathematics courses. The advertisement depicted a woman describing her 'difficult' experiences learning mathematics at school. She explained how taking the adult mathematics course helped improve her confidence. The woman is called Beryl – though this is not revealed in the advertisement but on the accompanying website. Earlier, I quoted it in full because it is typical of how confidence is produced within mathematics.

From the text, confidence is written as the key attribute/possession that gives power back to the individual in mathematics. In a neoliberal manner, Beryl finds a way out and regains control of the situation. This is possible, as the loss of confidence is not blamed on the student but on the mathematics and on other external factors such as 'teaching by rote'. The dialogue, mostly from Beryl's perspective, and the advertisement epitomise a neoliberal fantasy, in which confidence and an inner belief are keys to success.

The advert demonstrates how easy it is to be seduced by rhetoric that offers simple solutions for problems; in this case, confidence fixes problems with mathematics. Advertising, like government policy, constructs problems and proposes solutions to fix them. Hence, this is a stance that permeates education and this thesis. However, it illustrates how confidence can exclude some from mathematics by being part of the production of the mathematical child. As such, it demonstrates how Foucault's concepts of normalisation and governmentality circulate with contemporary discourses. In this instance, the person who is without confidence and who needs to be empowered is female and white and is constructed as 'working class' (shown in her visual representation and voice), and the person who dictates the regime is male, white and constructed as 'middle class'. This exemplifies essentialist notions that confidence is missing from women and girls, and as a consequence, mathematics belongs elsewhere.

The preceding advert connects confidence to the common-sense, good 'teaching for understanding'. Specifically, the advert implies that rote learning (the binary to understanding) and confidence are mutually exclusive for those, like Beryl, who are excluded from mathematics. I discuss in the next chapter how many in mathematics education researchers (such as Boaler, 1997b; Santos & Barmby, 2010) share this assumption. My concern is that this connection removes confidence of depth, complexity, and emotion, and instead, it becomes part of the "active cognitive subject" (Valero, 2002) which is the preferable mathematical child of mathematics education research and within this confidence becomes performative.

With regard to the written New Labour educational polices, *confidence* is a relatively common word; it has over 200 mentions whereas similar terms have far less: 13 for *self-esteem*, none for *self-concept* or *self-efficacy*, six mentions of *anxiety* or *anxious*. The choice of *confidence* is not innocent; other words such as anxiety do not belong within neoliberal discourse. *Confidence* is a far kinder word than *anxiety* which is suggests abnormality and is more often seen as a disorder (Spielberger, 1972). Confidence is far more neoliberal; it is something that everyone can aspire to; it is something that everyone can rationally imagine having; it is energising and enabling. Confidence is something everyone wants; anxiety is not. Confidence as liberator works within neoliberalism. It works on the premise that

76 *Unpacking educational policy*

anything is possible if we work hard and believe it to be true. It is a very appealing fantasy. However, how someone obtains confidence is more allusive, unless, of course, confidence has its own performative construction with, I argue, New Labour's does.

Mirroring Hardy's analysis (2007, 2009), I also found that in educational policy documents confidence is conflated with competence. This is particularly prevalent within *National Strategy* documents, which, as discussed, are the key manufacturers of knowledge concerning mathematics pedagogy. They clearly state that "practitioners must provide opportunities for practice to develop children's confidence and competence" (DfES, 2006b, p. 105); however, as I show in more detail in the following, these become one and the same.

The first example comes from Parliamentary Under-Secretary of State for Schools Andrew Adonis, in the introduction to the core document *Primary Framework for Literacy and Numeracy*, he states,

> It is in our primary schools and Foundation Stage settings that curiosity and enthusiasm for learning [are] first nurtured and our children develop the confidence to read, to write and to calculate. It is imperative that all our children develop these basic skills to sustain their learning and the confidence to access the curriculum as they move into secondary education.
> (Andrew Adonis in DfES, 2006b, introduction)

This extract represents almost one third of the text, and in it confidence is referenced twice. Thus, that a child should obtain confidence is an important aspect of education and learning mathematics. Moreover, confidence arguably becomes functional – it is about access and being able to do – it is very similar to policy documents construction of understanding. This conflation is found throughout the national Strategy documentation. For example,

> [t]he aim is that by the end of Key Stage 2, the great majority of children should be able to use an efficient written method for each operation with confidence and understanding.
> (DfES, 2006c, p. 41)

Again both confidence and understanding take on a functional performativity. The next few incidences are more explicit:

> As children become more confident users of the calculator they can be taught how to use the calculator's memory.
> (DfES, 2006c, p. 58)

> The challenge for teachers is determining when their children should move on to a refinement in the method and become confident and more efficient at written calculation.
> (DfES, 2006c, p. 41)

The aim is that children use mental methods when appropriate, but for calculations that they cannot do in their heads they use an efficient written method accurately and with confidence.

(DfES, 2006c, pp. 43, 45, 47, 50)

In the first quotation confidence is constructed as an obligatory feature of mathematical achievement and serves as a barrier to learning. In the other two extracts efficiency and accuracy have become indicators of mathematical success, and confidence becomes entwined with these performative traits. This is reiterated in *Making Good Progress*, where an aim for students is to "become more confident at 'reading' calculations and deciding on the most efficient method to use" (DCFS, 2008b, p. 5). In the preceding extracts confidence has taken on neoliberal discourses and has become functional and performative.

In the following extract, there is also a conflation of confidence with competence; however, confidence takes on more aspects of neoliberalism, such that it is tied to neoliberalism through the illusion of choice (Llewellyn, 2009):

Children should be equipped to decide when it is best to use a mental, written or calculator method based on the knowledge that they are in control of this choice as they are able to carry out all three methods with confidence.

(DfES, 2006c, p. 41)

Thus, confidence becomes performative and legitimises neoliberal discourses.

Neoliberal educational policy discourse of confidence removes emotions and/or doubt and instead discursively aligns with functionality and objectivity. Hence, confidence is constructed through its replacement of competence and through its links to the neoliberal subject. However, part of the neoliberal illusion of confidence is that it appears to be equitable and thus achievable by everyone. I argue this is not the case, as confidence is located more easily in some bodies than in others. For example, in the advertisement discussed previously confidence is missing from Beryl – a lower-class woman. This is emblematic of the wider discourses of confidence which are found more easily in some more powerful bodies than in others.

In educational policy confidence is naturalised within educational policy documents, such that only some can achieve, those who achieve highly. This 'naturalisation' is (re)produced through the *Making Good Progress* series of the *National Strategy* documents that describe "slow moving pupils" as "lack[ing] self confidence" and as "often girls" (DCSF, 2008b, p. 1) whilst underachieving pupils are "tentative and cautious when starting a new topic, particularly the girls" (DCFS, 2007b, p. 12). Thus, in a significant section of a major government education strategy, it is implied that you cannot be slow and confident in doing mathematics. Furthermore, that this is embodied by girls and women is reiterated throughout; for example able pupils who "lose momentum" are described as confident in English yet not in mathematics: "'these girls are really confident, but they are different when they are doing mathematics. They seem anxious about getting it right' (Year 6 teacher)" (DCFS, 2007b, p. 15).

In these educational policy documents the tendency is to place the problem with the girls. This 'victim blaming' has been much criticised, for instance in mathematics education by Walkerdine (1998a) and Boaler (1997b). Building on this, I argue that it is difficult for pupils (and girls especially) to break out of these cyclic defective categories, partly as it is difficult for pupils to appreciate their ability if it positions them as slow-moving and/or under-attaining and thus as outside of a normalised version of mathematical success (Llewellyn & Mendick, 2011). Therefore, speed and confidence are naturalised to the more able, and mathematics is done by those who can more easily perform these traits (Mendick, 2006). Moreover, confidence is naturalised within masculine identities (Bibby, 2002; Burton, 2004; Hardy, 2009). Hence, girls or women can too easily be constructed as under-confident and withdraw from mathematics, citing a lack of confidence as the reason, as they are caught up in discursive productions of femininity (Mendick, 2006; Walkerdine, 1990, 1998a). This leaves the majority of women in an impossible position; they are seen as weak for not having confidence, but it is also a position that they cannot comfortably inhabit because of their investment in femininity; conversely, 'real' men have to show confidence. Thus, confidence is discursively produced as an inner state (Llewellyn, 2009). This restricts the number of people who can be good at mathematics and perpetuates the myth of 'real' (born) mathematicians (Walkerdine, 1988).

Thus, overall I suggest that within New Labour confidence works as a barrier to success in mathematics; it is presented as equitable and achievable – a key part of neoliberalism – but instead is naturalised within those deemed to have higher ability. Moreover, the way that confidence is discursively constructed is that is performative. Confidence is a key part of New Labour's production of the mathematical child, as such it arguably more powerful than understanding – which is more often replaced by or constructed as skills. These discourses work to legitimise who can do mathematics, and in this case it is someone who can perform as the functional mathematical child.

There is one group who provide an exception to the rule – those who are deemed naturally able. Referring to the *Beryl advertisement* discussed earlier, the notion of 'ability' is remarkable by its absence; instead, the acquisition of confidence, through the correct teaching methods, is seen as the route to success in mathematics. In contrast to this, the highly 'able' mathematical 'genius' is a well-worn trope of popular culture. From the film *Good Will Hunting* (Van Sant, 1997), to the television show *The Big Bang Theory* (Crendowski, 2007–ongoing), the socially awkward inherently brilliant mathematician abounds (Mendick, 2006; Epstein, Mendick and Moreau, 2010). Thus, we are left with a quandary – is mathematics for these special few, or is it for everyone? Hence, mathematical 'ability' is a problematic construct, and whether it is constructed as 'natural' or 'developed', very many influence what is possible for the mathematical child, which is shown in educational policy discourse.

Within New Labour's mathematics educational policy documents, high-'ability' pupils are discursively constructed as 'naturally' gifted. This essentialising is cemented by the assertion that there are certain characteristics associated with 'able' pupils and, moreover, that there is a recommended pedagogy. For instance, this is shown in the DfEE (2000) document *Mathematical Challenges for Able Pupils in Key Stage 1 and 2* (DfEE, 2000). It states that mathematically 'able' pupils "grasp new material quickly; are prepared to approach problems from different directions and persist in finding solutions; generalise patterns and relationships; use mathematical symbols confidently; and develop concise logical arguments" (p. 4). This extract constructs a version of the 'able' mathematical child, as one who works fast, is confident, who understands and is a reasoned, 'natural' inquirer.

The document goes on to describe the appropriate pedagogy for working with able pupils. It talks of "extra challenges – including investigations using ICT – which they can do towards the end of a unit of work when other pupils are doing consolidation exercises" (DfEE, 2000, p. 5). Consequently, investigations and Information, Communication, Technology (ICT) are constructed as belonging to the 'able' whilst consolidation and practice exercises are positioned with those of lower 'ability'. The classroom is split between those who are functional and have to practise and those who are too special to need to. This supports, and draws on, familiar and exclusionary discourses of the gifted mathematician.

By 2006, if you were higher 'ability' in several subjects you were repackaged as "gifted and talented" (DfES, 2006a), stressing even more the specialness and the innate nature of these students' 'abilities'. Moreover, the documents made the distinction that it was 'ability', rather than attainment, that conferred the classification (DCSF, 2008a; DfES, 2006a). This perpetuates the production of a mathematical child with a fixed, 'natural' ability. By 2008, characteristics of the 'gifted and talented' pupil (who had been repackaged as a more neoliberal, managerial gifted and talented 'learner') include that they may

> be very articulate or verbally fluent for their age; learn quickly; show unusual and original responses to problem-solving activities; prefer verbal to written activities; be logical; be self-taught in his/her own interest areas; have an ability to work things out in his/her head very quickly; have a good memory that s/he can access easily.
>
> (DCFS, 2008a, p. 4)

As well as behavioural traits such as: "be easily bored by what they perceive as routine tasks; not necessarily appear to be well-behaved or well-liked by others" (DCFS, 2008a, p. 4). This appears to be a subset of traits of the high-'ability' mathematical child from 2000 already discussed. I argue that there is also an attachment to the 'able' mathematical child as frustrated and impetuous genius. It is also interesting to note what characteristics are absent that may be found in high-achieving people in society, for example creativity, team work, self-awareness, diligence, reliability, and organisation.

Moreover, the *gifted and talented* are encouraged to move at a faster rate than the norm. New Labour suggests that "it will be easier for young people to accelerate through the system – early achievement at Key Stage 3 or AS levels [a post 16 qualification] will be recognised in the achievement and attainment tables" (DfES, 2005, p. 57). Other government educational policy documents contain praise for schools that do this, thus validating this position (DfES, 2005). In addition, to support such schemes further, the government offered financial incentives (DCFS, 2007a). However, when progress/attainment is below expected levels, this production of a 'natural' mathematical child is normalised by New Labour. When pupils do not fit their projected trajectories they are labelled as defective. They are "able pupils who lose momentum" or "able pupils who make slow progress" (DCFS, 2007b) or 'able' pupils who make "less than expected progress" (DCFS, 2007b, p. 12). This keeps them as special but also draws on functional discourses of expected progress. Furthermore, it allows them to remain within the bounds of the 'natural' mathematical child.

In contrast the discursive production of low-'ability/-attaining' groups is very different. As mentioned earlier, it was similar at the beginning of the New Labour era when pupils were labelled as "very able or less able" (DfEE, 2000, p. 5). However, in later New Labour years, the language applied to and the discursive production of the "less able" pupils was repackaged to be more mobilising and more neoliberal. For instance, in educational policy documents lower 'ability' pupils are constructed as "under attaining" (DCFS, 2007a) or "underachieving" (DCFS, 2009b) or "slow moving" (DCFS, 2008b). The implication is that they have mobility and hence opportunity – their state is transient and hence can be improved. The language is maintained more generally by other New Labour educational policy documents that talk of "moving on in mathematics" or "narrowing the gap" (DCFS, 2009b). The inference is that lower 'ability' pupils are not fixed in their place, but they can move to a 'normal' state. This mobilising language provides a contrast to the 'gifted and talented' who are fixed as they always already have mobility through their status as 'naturally able' – they are a desirable kind of different. This message is reiterated by Williams (2008), in his independent review, who similarly uses "high ability" and "low attaining". This could encourage students and teachers to construct high achievement as internal and belonging to themselves and low achievement as external and somebody else's fault. This is problematic for many reasons, particularly as it sets up a division between groups of students in mathematics and labels some as 'real' mathematicians.

It is easy to see that there are good reasons to construct low-'ability' pupils as having moveable ability. However, when this is positioned against the static, natural, high 'ability', the message is incoherent and confusing. If we examine a trait, such as 'potential', that appears in much of New Labour documentation it is problematic. For instance, "all children and young people with outstanding academic ability or with particular sporting or artistic talent should be able to achieve their potential" (DfEE, 2001, p. 20). The statement, from New Labour's second education white paper, is written for "all children", and thus there is a nod to equity, which is common within New Labour's policies. However, the statement is found in a section for "gifted and talent children", and it specifically refers to those with "outstanding academic ability"; thus, this group is privileged as these are students have the greater potential. These pupils have inner qualities. This is problematic in relation to some of New Labour's promise of "narrowing the gap" (DCFS, 2009b) and the associated statements such as "[we must make] sure that all children benefit from rising standards and closing achievement gaps by bringing those who struggle up to the standards of those who achieve the most" (DfEE, 2001, p. 12).

This tension is accentuated by the sliding among ability, attainment, and progress. As I have shown, within educational policy, ability is ignored in low-'ability' groups, and progress/attainment can be overlooked when classifying high-'ability' groups; hence, it is easy to mix the terms. The mathematics education policy documents *Making Good Progress* (DCFS, 2008b) and *Keeping Up – Pupils who Fall Behind in Key Stage 2* (DCFS, 2009c) warn against this. They state that "in many schools the children who were making slow progress were placed in the lowest ability group and the planned teaching programme was unlikely to secure their progress to level 4 by the end of the key stage". However, this does contradict other statements from the documents, namely that speed is a marker of ability. Hence, the sliding is also done by New Labour educational policy documents; it is part of government discourses.

Thus, overall, I argue that when it comes to the more 'able' or 'gifted' pupils New Labour educational policy documents are caught up in essentialising notions of ability that construct it as innate (also argued by Gillborn & Youdell, 2001). However, I also argue that for the majority, ability is factiously written out of educational policy documents, so attainment can be constructed as fluid and possible for all. Thus, New Labour educational policy produces a discordant message that leads to division. Every student is required to perform as a functional mathematical child; however, there are 'gifted' students who are allowed that more flexibility; there is the top end and then the rest. This is a special kind of difference that is permitted and celebrated.

Thus, in spite of the child not being overtly described, the functional child of educational policy is very present within New Labour documentation and hence will probably have circulated to some extent within classrooms of that time. Much of this is what is appropriate within the confines of neoliberalism – what is interesting is perhaps how these discourses are accepted and rarely challenged. In addition, this functionality is rarely acknowledged alongside the image of New Labour as allowing from freedom and creativity. Instead, I suggest that operating as a key technology of power (Foucault, 1978/1998), New Labour's normative child was a functional one that laid the path for the subsequent Conservative-led governments.

Coalitions, conservatives, and the saviour of Shanghai

Since New Labour were voted out of office in 2010 the Conservative government have been in charge, either as part of a coalition government with the Liberal Democrats (2010–2015) or as the sole party of the government (2015–present day). Throughout this era the influence of the private sector on schools has accelerated; this has been on both a macro and micro level. For example England now has more than 3,000 academies, many of which are run by private companies. Becoming an academy not only removes schools from local authority control and influence but also removes the government from any responsibility; it is no longer liable for any school that is failing, as the accountability has shifted to the private company and to the self. At one time the government insisted all schools would become academies – though they quickly relented on this after public disapproval (Adams, 2016).

Within this (as under New Labour) leagues tables are still dominant and Ofsted still aggressively monitor the 'successes" of students and schools. A school is no longer closed for 'failing' its Ofsted judgement, but it can be forced to become an academy. Education is still a results-driven business.

Thus, at first glance, we can see that this is largely a continuation of New Labour's neoliberalism; however, one thing that is different is the apparent position of the government's role. Specifically, there is a movement away from New Labour's micromanaging of practices and the appearance of more power and freedom for schools and teachers. The Conservative-led government state that there will be "more and more schools run – and more and more decisions made – by teachers, not politicians" (Gove, 2014). In addition, when asked by a reader in *The Guardian* newspaper why they should vote Conservative the then education secretary Nicky Morgan first words were "We believe schools succeed when teachers are free to teach. That's why setting schools and teachers free has been central to our plan, and why we're going to do more" (Morgan, 2015b, *The Guardian*).

However, in the first instance this does not translate to freedom and power for school students; moreover, arguably, schools are monitored more and held more accountable than ever before. The Conservatives insist that they are more rigorous and that they have higher standards than previous governments (which is the normal discourse of derision applied to previous governments); they categorically state they will hold schools "to account for rigorous, fairly measured outcomes'"(DfE, 2016, 9). One instance of this is the changing of the Ofsted language of classification from *Satisfactory* to *Requires Improvement* – satisfactory is no longer acceptable, yet a transitionary phase that denotes the need for progress. Thus, there is the suggestion of freedom, yet there is more control through the measurement of outcomes, and the manner in which schools are held accountable; it is the realisation of neoliberal ideals, such that we govern ourselves but under the illusion of freedom (Rose, 1999a).

The Conservative government quickly settled into moulding their own educational governance by scrapping New Labour's priorities and practices, including *The National Strategies, Every Child Matters,* and *Teachers TV*. This meant the deletion of documentation – paper and websites – but also the removal of government-funded and -led training courses and advisors on every aspect of school life. Furthermore, this meant that the state pedagogy of teaching and learning was no longer to be found in the minutia of governmental discourse; arguably, there was space for other voices.

However, the Conservative government did not hold back in merely scrapping New Labour initiatives; it also introduced new curriculums to both the primary and the secondary sector – ruthlessly scrapping the former at the last minute. In 2015 (with the first results occurring in 2017) it also introduced a new classification system for its more 'rigorous' GCSEs (moving from grades A–F to a numbered system). Alongside this an Educational Baccalaureate (EBAcc) measurement and Progress 8 (DfE, 2017), were introduced; these are high-stakes assessments that draw from students' results in several subjects but where mathematics is given the highest priority (alongside English). This has led to a downgrading of arts and many humanities subjects, which were not prioritised under the system.

The privileging of mathematics and other STEM subjects is not covertly done; the former education secretary Nicky Morgan explicitly stated that "the subjects that keep young people's options open and unlock the door to all sorts of careers are the STEM subjects (science, technology, engineering and maths)" (Morgan, 2014). This statement is not unusual; it was not even deemed that controversial. As such, there has been a visible shift in what is outwardly preferenced under the Conservative government, and perhaps more so even than new Labour, mathematics is stated as one of their highest priorities. Its latest manifesto (The Conservative Party, 2017) states that every major city should have a mathematics specialist school, whilst the latest budget offers incentives for schools that maintain children studying mathematics post 16. Indeed, funding for mathematics has never been disadvantaged currently mathematics teachers are paid much more than other subjects whilst training and funding for various initiatives are in abundance. The importance and power of mathematics are a familiar discourse; it is the production of these truths that constitutes what is possible (Foucault, 2003b).

Increasing the stakes around mathematics is problematic for those who study it, as discussed, particularly that the image of mathematics as unobtainable is very part of the problem. But what did the Conservatives mean by studying mathematics – did they follow the functionality and skills of New Labour? Arguably, for the most part they did; however, the Conservative government, particularly under former education secretary Michael Gove, moved to prioritise a "knowledge-based curriculum" (Morgan,[4] 2015a). This 'proper' education was perhaps not dissimilar to Michael Gove's own grammar school education, one based on facts and 'proper' subjects.

In terms of the teaching and learning of mathematics, there was less overt prescription than New Labour, but strong messages were sent through the curriculum and what it prioritised. "In maths and science, the Expert Panel is focused on fundamental scientific knowledge and essential principles that are not subject to controversy and change every month or year" (Gove, 2011). This statement asks for stability and asserts that there are core principles of mathematics and science that are robust enough to step outside culture and trends. It is a critique of the many changes that were forced by New Labour, although it also heralds mathematics as incontestable and universal, as a solid foundation that should not deviate.

The new version of the curriculum contained more rote and procedure with standard examples of practice given as an exemplar. In addition, it was more rigorous than previous curriculums, or at least graded higher with some objectives moving to lower classifications. However, much of this is the recall of facts; for example children are required to know their times tables (up to 12) by age 9. Hence, mathematics becomes about knowledge production. Michael Gove's rhetoric demonstrates this clearly:

> As our society becomes more complex, so the level of mathematical knowledge every citizen requires has deepened. Critical personal finance decisions, from choosing a mortgage to thinking about pensions, depend on individuals being secure in the basics of numeracy. Understanding the decisions governments make; on debt, deficits and the design of taxes is impossible without a grounding in mathematics. Mastery of mathematics is key to success in the modern economy.
> (Gove, in an introduction to Vorderman, Budd, Dunne, Hart, and Porkess, 2011)

The first sentence is nonsense – society is no more complex for those doing mathematics today than it was thousands of years ago. More important, all the mathematics Gove mentions could be described as functional or utilitarian; in addition, arguably, many of those tasks could be done more easily by utilising technology. So it is hard to agree that the "mathematical knowledge every citizen required has deepened". The use of *understanding* is interesting and signifies that government and the progress of society are still the most important priorities – in spite of their allusions to the importance of schools and teachers. In contrast, their 2010 white paper titled "The Importance of Teaching" (DfE, 2010b) is an attempt to signal who is the most important person in the room – and it is not the school student. Thus, again there is an absence of children from the narrative. However, this direct positioning from Conservative ideology is more overt than New Labour's, which claimed to be 'child-centred', particularly in the second-half their tenure, but instead govern through the production of a homogenous functional child.

The Vorderman[5] et al. report (2011) was produced for the Conservatives when they were in opposition. Michael Gove provided the introduction whilst he was education secretary, hence signalling the acceptance of the report. Again in this report mathematics is tied to progress of the self and progress of the nation, the aims of the report being to assess

- where mathematics education currently stands in England,
- where it needs to be in order for us to compete internationally on an economic basis, and
- what is needed on an individual basis for students to be mathematically literate, and so able to fulfil their potential in future life (Vorderman et al., 2011).

This position is reiterated later on: "Unless major alterations in our mathematics education are made, and quickly, we are risking our future economic prosperity" (Vordeman et al., 2011). The report does not shy from being determined – it acknowledges that it is uncomfortable reading and that it is "frightening"; its message is that 'inadequate' mathematics teaching and learning "cannot be allowed to continue". Thus, again we see mathematics being tied to the self and tied to the nation and mathematics teaching and learning being constructed as not good enough.

Another interesting premise, and one that has bled into practise (and is thus discussed in Chapter 6) is the appreciation for mathematics teaching and learning in schools in Shanghai. Over the last decade Eastern countries have dominated national educational league tables (alongside Finland and Sweden), such as the TIMMS and PISA; this, alongside economic prosperity, has seen many Western educators seduced by Eastern promises. It should not be lost that this is an important reversal from Western colonisation and of the East borrowing progressive ideas and pedagogies from the West, which I discussed in the introduction.

As justification (through the PISA) Gove stated, "British 15-year-olds' mathematics skills are now more than two whole academic years behind 15-year-olds in Shanghai" (Gove in the introduction to the Vorderman et al., 2011); this gave rise to so-called mastery mathematics and the belief that "[m]astery of mathematics is key to success in the modern economy" (Vorderman et al., 2011). It is similar to statements made by politicians in the US who admonish their country's practice in relation to China. In an address to the Royal Society of mathematics and Science, Gove stated,

> And if we want mathematics to guide us into the future, it is easy to see in which direction history is currently moving: East . . . One of the lessons from the international evidence is that in East Asia there is [a] much greater focus on fundamental number concepts, fractions and the building blocks of algebra in primary school. They have minimum standards that they aim to get practically all children to reach so they have a firm foundation for secondary. It may be, therefore, that we will adopt the same approach and have much more emphasis on pre-algebra in primary and remove data handling and some other subjects from the primary curriculum. We should also bear in mind that in Shanghai, they have daily maths lessons and regular tests to make sure that all children are learning the basics.
>
> (Gove, 2011)

The message is one of content, of "firm foundations", of everyday lessons as routine, and of more assessment. Some of this is similar to New Labour – the daily lessons and testing – however, there is a shift in what is considered as progress. In the preceding, progress is not defined as the movement through small-scale levels; instead, there is more consideration that content should be embedded. The Vorderman report states, "It is sometimes suggested that restricting some pupils to a smaller curriculum would impair their chances of subsequent development. We think that argument needs to be challenged." (Vorderman et al., 2011, p. 5). It continues: "All young people should be entitled to understand mathematics at some level, and to the confidence boost that comes from it, rather than being forced to study topics that ensure failure for many of them". In relation to the discussion in the section on New Labour it is interesting to note that understanding and confidence still play a part; however, there is perhaps a different discursive construction of these terms. Confidence here comes from success in mathematics, which is very different from New Labour, where confidence was needed to do mathematics. Understanding is also perhaps not tied to being able to do. It should be noted these are not government words but a report supported by them.

The borrowing of ideas from the East applied to more than Shanghai and more than mathematics. In a thorough analysis of the West to East borrowing culture in England Forestier and Crossley (2015) explained the adoration by the Conservatives:

> The East Asian systems are described as 'restless improvers' and 'top performers' in policy discourse in England, including in the 2010 *Case for Change* (Department for Education, 2010a) accompanying the 2010 White Paper (Department for Education, 2010b) and in speeches and media articles (Gove, 2010a, 2010b, 2012a, 2012b), culminating in the revised National Curriculum published in July 2013 (Gove, 2013b). The UK Secretary of State for Education told the Parliamentary Select Committee on Education: 'I have been to Singapore and Hong Kong, and what is striking is that many of the lessons that apply there are lessons that we can apply here' (Gove, 2010a).
>
> (p. 667)

The vast amount of cited government texts demonstrate that the message from the Conservative government is clear – Eastern countries (or provinces), particularly Hong Kong and Shanghai, have a better curriculum and a better education system, and that is what England should aim for. Forestier and Crossley (2015) continue:

> The message is clear: if rigour is restored to the National Curriculum and public examinations, if principals have high levels of autonomy and if teachers can teach like those in Hong Kong and other high-performing jurisdictions, then England's children can achieve similar academic success, regardless of social background. Ultimately, this will contribute to future economic success (DfE, 2012; Gove, 2013b).
>
> (Forestier & Crossley, 2015, p. 668)

Although as they point out many Eastern countries do not attribute their success to the same aspects that Gove does. Gove revels in stating that he borrows randomly from around the world. Of course, for someone who advocates the importance of reading statistics it is odd that he has conflated correlation and cause and effect with the variables of his choosing. It is fairly obvious that to say why policies and practices work in education is far more complex than one initiative – it is, of course, complex – it is cultural, social, and political – all of which are missing from the earlier government discourses. "Many comparativists have warned of the dangers of simplistic borrowing and uncritical international transfer that are insensitive to local contexts and more likely to end in policy failure (Crossley & Watson, 2003; Steiner-Khamsi, 2010)" (Forestier & Crossley, 2015, p. 669).

The assumptions that this Conservative government uses are different from New Labour, but what both have in common is, in the first instance, simplicity – both construct education and doing mathematics as a straightforward procedure if you follow the rules. Second, they both construct mathematics as vital to the self and to the economy – this is an incontestable truth. A difference is that New Labour professed that everyone could succeed whilst the Conservatives are more content to keep a gap but think standards for all should rise. A second difference is that the Conservatives are clear in stating that they focus on the basics; New Labour assertions to the fundamental are hidden under the promise of inspiration. For both the onus is on the neoliberal self to achieve; there is no falling back on blaming government for any shortfall – this is more overt under the Conservative government.

Concluding remarks

This New Labour version of neoliberalism offered equity alongside standards and appeared to value both the Science and the Arts. However, this premise of equity is very much constructed on neoliberal tropes of opportunity, hard work, and self-determination (Llewellyn & Mendick, 2011). Furthermore, it was in the New Labour years that the performativity of the education system gained full steam and became normative; as Tony Blair foregrounded education within the political landscape and claimed he would drastically improve it, then measuring and regulating that performance became key. Thus, I contend that New Labour's equity is largely illusionary, and instead, its educational interventions are focused on constructing the correct way to be, and not on the diversity within and between students and teachers. Neoliberal discourses work to erode diversity and instead the stronger discursive construction of the functional educational Child is made – a normative child that is specifically constructed to fit a system, a child that has little space to deviate from this norm, a child that is founded without social and cultural context, a child that is a fiction.

In contrast the mathematical child of Conservative regime is more overtly focused on the fundamentals of mathematics, as the government borrows from the Far East. However, this Conservative child is only enabled by the functionalism of New Labour, where the standardisation of the measurement of the child was embedded in government metrics. For both governments operate through the illusion that people are free to govern themselves.

Throughout all this, mathematics has taken on an even more important relationship to the self and to society, and mathematics as a subject of privilege has become robustly embedded. What this means for doers of mathematics is explored in Chapter 6, but what this means to mathematics educational research is explored next.

Notes

1 Tony Blair was leader of the Labour Party (often termed New Labour) from 1994 to 2007 and British prime minister from 1997 to 2007.
2 'Crossing the threshold' for an English teacher concerns moving onto the upper pay scale – this requires a judgement that he or she has met satisfactory standards.
3 Ed Balls was secretary of state for children, schools and families from June 2007 to May 2010, and shadow secretary of state for education from May 2010 to October 2010.
4 Nicky Morgan was Secretary of State for Education from July 2014 to July 2016.
5 Carol Vorderman is a celebrity and media personality who co-hosted a game show where she solved problems with numbers.

5 Unpacking mathematics education research

A conversation in a corridor of a University:

"*You know I attended this meeting at xxxx school, and they didn't talk about – understanding. We have to get them to focus on teaching for understanding*"

Introduction

Education research is a dominant space in current Western educational discourse. The role of the expert academic, whilst often queried by politicians, governs teacher education programmes. Within this, educational establishments by their stature are often afforded the luxury of authority and neutrality. This chapter takes that as a starting point and examines the production of the mathematical child through an analysis of mathematics education research. To do this (and similar to the previous chapter), various norms and themes are unpacked that are commonly spoken about in mathematics education. In contrast to the functional child of educational policy, I show that a different type of mathematical child is privileged in dominant strands of mathematics education research. This I call the 'romantic' mathematical child.

The romantic child of mathematics education research

As discussed in Chapter 2 education research itself currently favours large-scale data sets and the 'what works movement'. The gold standard of educational research being RCTs, and the search for objective 'truths'. However, as discussed previously, education research itself should not be viewed as neutral (Patel, 2015) in spite of trends towards these 'objective' studies. Education research includes and excludes, enabling some questions to be examined and others to be foreclosed, some people to be worthy of study, and others not. Moreover, if the search is for the generalisable there is never space for acknowledging marginalised and minority voices. The common voice is not always one that includes everyone or seeks equity. For instance, I recently gained feedback on a funded PhD application with one of my undergraduate students; he wanted to explore participatory research with Trans Youth groups in order or improve their experience of compulsory education. The advice from more than one highly successful professor of education was to forget it – my student would not find enough participants to make the study valid. If this advice is followed, education research would only be conducted on large data sets that represent the dominant. As such, every minority voice, including trans people, people of colour, gay people, and the disabled would not be researched. Education research would only speak for the already privileged. That many view education as emancipation does not sit easily here.

As well as valuing some research and groups more than others, there are several other ways that educational research (re)produces hierarchies and privilege. Specifically, through governance and technologies or surveillance, such as citation, educational researchers are complicit in the production of certain truths. Who is cited and what is (re)produced are very much caught up in technologies of power. Some bodies are more easily cited than others, with women and people of colour falling down the line. For mathematics education I suggest these norms of citation take on a further act, specifically that there are certain things that are permissible to say in mathematics education research and certain things that are not warranted.

When I took the presentation of my results to a mathematics education research group at a UK university I was told my arguments were offensive. At first I was a little shook, there were people of much higher status and validity than me in the room casting their disapproval. However, on reflection, it is worth asking if is there a purpose in offending others or simply making them uncomfortable (which is more what I think I did). Is there a good reason to evoke those emotions? As many scholars and commentators have pointed out, for many white people they will have to be offended, or uncomfortable, if they ever want to acknowledge that white privilege and systemic racism exists. Perhaps offence is a place where transformation can happen.

The truths in mathematics education are seemingly more mundane: that mathematics is useful to society is one – that mathematics should be a key part of any school curriculum is a related other. But what if we did not perceive mathematics in this way; how would viewing mathematics as *not* integral to society change the way it was interpreted or accessed? Would it offer different possibilities for change in mathematics education? For many mathematics educators the usefulness and importance of mathematics are taken for granted – it is evoked directly or through indirect assertions. mathematics as powerful is a narrative that supports their work; thus, it may be difficult to comprehend any other position.

For educational research a truth is that research should seek to resolve situations and offer improvement. Thus, judgement and solutions are often demanded, and alternative views are in the minority (for an example from mathematics education see Pais, Stentoft, & Valero, 2010). My concern is that judgement tends to offer quick fixes to situations that are incredibly complex, and this becomes an accepted pattern of education. Moreover, there is always already an investment in the pursuit of a better way to do something. Mendick (2011), drawing on Dale (2001), points out the limitations of this:

> My own and others' readings of mathematics/education policy, practice and research indicate[ ] the persistence here of the anchoring narrative of

progress, as speaker after speaker 'straightforwardly invokes the premise of progress' [(W. Brown, 2001, p. 6)] ... As Dale points out, this is very different from researchers in sociology of religion or the family where the research agenda operates independently of their personal views on the social roles of religion or family. In contrast, in the sociology of education, education is treated less an object of study than as a resource.

(Mendick, 2011, pp. 50–51)

Rarely is education studied as an object or as part of the problem – it is a resource for achieving transformation – for realising progress. Brown and Clarke (2013), state that "there is a common assumption that research in mathematics education is about informing movement towards some improved conception of teaching" (p. 463); however, I suggest these notions of progress are much wider as, similar to educational policy, they also evoke progress of the individual and progress of the nation. As Mendick mentions, the invoking of progress runs through other educational discourses outside of research, although the problem with the academy is that it has the most authority.

The academy also has an assumption of neutrality. It is easier to imagine educational policy documents as being part of a wider political narrative; in contrast, educational research may most often be viewed as impartial and in pursuit of an objective truth. Following Foucault, universities are instead places to discipline and punish; they are places that control and shape a population. However, the questions that are asked and the studies that are researched are all part of a network of contingencies that make some things more researchable than others. I've already mentioned the problem of citation – that some bodies are easier to cite than others, that the normal citation of eminent voices (re)produces privilege. These voices are the ones that more easily obtain grants and funding. Moreover, I have already discussed the current trend for funding that privileges quantifiable research with large data sets and how this potentially excludes other ways of knowing as well as Othered groups of people. There is also the question of measurement – in that some things are easier to measure than others, affect being notoriously complex and attainment less so. It is clear that "research participates in constructing the boundaries of its own practice" (T. Brown & Clarke, 2013, p. 469).

All these complexities are found in mathematics education research. Arguably the premise of neutrality and objectify is even stronger with mathematics being embedded in an absolutist narrative. Moreover, there is great power in mathematics research itself that follows from its power in society. For mathematics education research, there are other specific truths that constrain possible discourses – one is the privileging of the active mathematical child:

> Most mathematics education research is based on the assumption of the centrality of learners in the processes of mathematical learning. This assumption views learners as active cognitive subjects at the 'centre' of the development of mathematical thinking in classrooms.

(Valero, 2002, pp. 542 – abstract)

This assumption draws from Rousseauian (1763/1884) romantic constructions of the past as well as developmental psychology that dominates education and mathematics education. It is a staged, "up the hill" progressive (Rorty, 1980) model of development that all children are expected to adhere to. It is a model of childhood built on the superiority of reason, rationality, and logic alongside the expectation of a 'natural' curiosity that leads to inevitable development:

> Modern theories of cognition have taken their central plank to be that reasoning is a centralised process, occurring on the basis of a naturalistic path of development, itself guaranteed by a structural model of thinking and of the world. This view taking some of its impetus from Descartes and from Kant has become an almost common sense wisdom.
> (Walkerdine, 1997, p. 57)

This child is always already a normalised developing child, one who is self-governing and freethinking, which fits the preference of autonomy within neoliberalism. As discussed this version of the mathematical child is not natural but is instead a production of discourses of developmental education that work to shape the child in a particular fashion (Burman, 1992, 2008a; Burman & Parker, 1993; Henriques et al., 1998; Walkerdine, 1997, 1998a). This investment runs deep in mathematics education research – researcher after researcher refers to the proper ways to do mathematics that centre on the 'active' learner' (Lundin, 2012), many of which fall under the guise of progressive or child-centred education. In spite of its allusions to inclusiveness, this progressive child is predominantly a cognitive being, and "cognitive activity is central to the whole educational enterprise" (Valero, 2002, p. 453) of mathematics education; as such, the social, cultural, and political are written out of discourses of the child. The child instead is someone predisposed to education and development – a being without a body and without a culture.

My concern with this particular 'romantic' discourse is that it masquerades under the pretence of freedom and liberation. An illustrative example is provided by the very influential work of Jo Boaler (1996, 1997a, 1997b, 1997c, 1997d, 1998a, 1998b, 1998c, 2002). Her popularist work is positioned as "legitimate classroom practice" (de Freitas, 2013, p. 7).

Boaler's influential study compared mathematics departments – one that taught mathematics in a progressive/reform manner and one that followed a more 'traditional' pedagogical approach; she termed these "open and closed" approaches to mathematics education (in the US version of the research they are termed as reform and traditional). In the open classroom the child is instructed to work 'freely' on mathematical activities, within specific social groups. As such, this child must be naturally curious and have a predisposition for mathematical inquiry. Boaler argued here, and in later similar studies (Boaler, 2009, 2016), that this was 'real' mathematics, thus implicating a 'real' mathematical child and anything and anyone else is automatically deemed inferior. This argument remains a constant throughout Boaler's work: "real mathematics . . .

the whole subject that involves problem solving, creating ideas, and representations, exploring puzzles, discussing methods and many different ways of working" (Boaler, 2009, p. 2). Indeed, she returned to the participants of the study to demonstrate that the 'real' mathematics of the 'open' classroom, had enabled the pupils as 'real' citizens, with highly skilled or professional jobs (Boaler, 2009) in comparison to the 'deficit' model of pupils from the 'closed' mathematics classroom.

Specifically, Boaler used Lave and Wenger's (1991) "situated cognition" and "communities of practice" to suggest that "notions of knowing should be replaced with notions of doing" (Boaler, 1997b, p. 92). This allows her to argue that pupils taught in an open manner can transfer mathematical techniques to other situations. In simple terms, situated cognition relies on the principle that learning is relational to the context whilst communities of practice refer to a group of people with a shared interest whose development relies on learning from each other (Boaler, 1997b; Lave & Wenger, 1991), although Lave and Boaler can both be critiqued similarly such that they do not "really theorise how subjects are produced – practices" (Walkerdine, 1997, p. 59). What is ignored is the role of the pedagogy and the teacher in facilitating the child's behaviour. Everyone – including the apparently free – is a product of discourse, and under neoliberalism, governmentality is ubiquitous; thus, the freedom that we believe we have is instead a form of governance (N. Rose, 1999a). People are governed, not practices, through the production of normalised subjects (Foucault, 1977, 1978/1998; N. Rose, 1999a). In Boaler's classroom students are still produced in a specific way, they are still products of their environment. In this case, the mathematical child feeds liberal educators' dreams of the autonomous teacher and student – arguably this may well succeed because it is a very attractive fantasy on which education is based (Walkerdine, 1990). Furthermore, it is this liberal child that is used a model for the global version of acceptable childhood (Wells, 2015)

Boaler further romanticises the mathematical classroom and further essentialises children's identities by talking of girls "quest for understanding". She argues that girls remove themselves from the mathematics classroom when rote learning is dominant:

> Throughout my 3-year case study, students, in conversations noted during lessons and in interviews, expressed concern for their lack of understanding of the rules they were learning. This was particularly acute for the girls, not because they understood less than the boys, but because they appeared to be less willing to relinquish their desire for understanding and play the 'school mathematics game' . . .
>
> J: He'll write it on the board and you end up thinking, well how comes this and this?, how did you get that answer? why did you do that?, but . . .
> M: You don't really know because he's gone through it on the board so fast and . . .

> J: Because he understands it he thinks we all do and we don' t. (Jane and Mary, year 11, set 1)

> Here the students contrast 'learning' and 'understanding', with the need to 'get things done', set against the demands of a fixed pace of coverage of topics.
> (Boaler, 1997c, pp. 292–293)

There are also other ways of reading this extract, for instance that the students are concerned with being able to do (explored in the next chapter) or that the pace of the classroom is not suitable. Furthermore, the 'girls' may be giving Boaler an answer she was searching for, or this may be a group identity; Lacan's interpretation of desire is "about the quest for a secure identity" (Walshaw, 2004, p. 130). Regardless, in Boaler's interpretation girls are homogenised; they are said to 'desire' something (a highly gendered word). This essentialism is also evident in her book *Elephant in the Classroom* (Boaler, 2009) and her more recent *Daily Telegraph* article (Boaler, 2014), where even the commenters attest to this concern. As one of them points out, if you change the comparison to race, you can see how dangerous the essentialising argument becomes. Oddly, Boaler states that the "science of the brain shows that anyone can do well in maths, and there is no such thing as a 'maths person'" (Boaler, 2014, para. 8) yet reiterates the argument that girls prefer learning in certain ways. This is an incongruent message – that we are born a certain way, but we are not; everyone can do mathematics, but certain mathematics excludes some people.

It is clear that comparative approaches to research can over-simplify situations; they are designed to be divisive and to position one as good and the other as lacking, which creates a false and unnecessary division. A feud is created between mythical opposed positions, education being full of these "discourses of dichotomy" (Alexander, 2010, p. 21). In this situation, one way of doing mathematics is correct, and one version of the child is valued. Writing in 2008, in a critique of the report of the *Foundations for Success: The Final Report of the National mathematics Advisory Panel (NMAP)* (2008) in the US, Boaler (2008) admonishes others for such a division:

> In framing its review, the task group posed this question: "How effective is teacher-directed instruction in mathematics in comparison to student-centered approaches?" (Gersten et al., 2008, p. 12). This question . . . sets up a dangerous dichotomy between two forms of teaching that bear little relation to the reality of mathematics classrooms in the United States. Indeed the question is reminiscent of the sort of dichotomous thinking that characterized the "math wars".
> (p. 588)

An academic is entitled to develop his or her position, especially reflecting on how Boaler has been harshly criticised in the US for her progressive teaching stance. Moreover, part of her argument is that the NMAP's interpretation of student-centred teaching is too extreme. She continues, stating that "fortunately, mathematics education has moved beyond such dichotomized thinking to a broader appreciation of the varied and complex roles in which effective teachers of mathematics need to engage" (Boaler, 2008, p. 588). In particular, Boaler argues that research in mathematics education has moved on from being concerned with learning to what the teacher does – more in line with the 'what works' movement. However, writing in 2016, Boaler is overwhelmingly suggesting that there is a specific and right way to do mathematics, and this leads to 'real' attainment (Boaler, 2016). Thus, there is always already a correct kind of mathematical child.

Linking to the already-discussed preference for the active child of mathematics education, for many educational researchers the quest for understating is their main objective. They are supported in this position by a range of theorists, including the hierarchies of Bloom's taxonomy (1956), where knowledge is the lowest rung on the ladder and dialectics models; such Skemp (1976), who perpetuates the divisions by his divisive instrumental and relational understanding; and the Piagetian stages. Thus, there is a hierarchy of pedagogy where understanding is at the top and something that must be front and present within any mathematics classroom (Hossain, Mendick, & Adler, 2013). There are many aside from Boaler in the mathematics education that avow to this position – that the active pupil results in a 'real' mathematician. Many researchers "centred their analyses on individuals shaping their practice in response to the perceived reform agenda" (Remillard & Kaye, 2002; Van Zoest & Bohl, 2002)" (T. Brown & Clarke, 2013, p. 464). In addition, Battista, who has written extensively about the 'correct' kind of understanding, states that "a teacher cannot explain to her students the principles underlying the multiplication algorithm if she does not explicitly understand them herself" (D. L. Ball, 1988, p. 36). Moreover, many pre-service teacher textbooks clearly promote the principle, having titles such as *Primary mathematics: Teaching for Understanding* (Barmby, Harries, Higgins, & Suggate, 2009) and *Understanding mathematics for Young Children* (Haylock & Cockburn, 2008). Hardy (2009) similarly notes that another popular textbook states that many pre-service teachers " 'have the wrong kind of understanding of their subject' (Suggate, Davis, & Goulding, 2006, preface)" (p. 387). As such, a position is constructed of a right kind of mathematics and, by implication, a right kind of mathematical child. Like Walkerdine, I ask, "[W]hy is there such remorseless and unrelenting pressure to 'prove' that real understanding causes real attainment" (Walkerdine, 1998a, p. 39)?

Confidence (which was unpacked in the previous chapter) functions similarly in mathematics education research literature to privilege 'progressive' pedagogies. This position is (re)produced and perpetuated by many in mathematics education research. For instance Santos and Barmby (2010) in discussing a progressive classroom state that

> pupils manifested improved attitudes towards mathematics inside and outside the classroom, such as positive attitude while working, pride in their work, had fun and built confidence in their own abilities to tackle the tasks.
> (p. 203)

In the preceding extract, mathematics is constructed as something that should be positive and fun, and confidence is produced as a natural product of this. What is absent are spaces for doubt, confusion, negativity, or emotion.

Another example is provided by Liljedahl (2005, 2011/2006). He states that as a result of changing pedagogy, "the majority of the participants [pre-service teachers] demonstrate significant changes in their beliefs and attitudes about mathematics, as well as their beliefs and attitudes about their own ability to do mathematics" (2005, p. 232). He quotes a pre-service teacher Melanie:

> Of all the problems that we worked on my favourite was definitely the pentominoe problem. We worked so hard on it, and it took forever to get the final answer. But I never felt like giving up, I always had confidence that we would get through it. Every time we got stuck we would just keep at it and suddenly one of us would make a discovery and we would be off to the races again. That's how it was the whole time – get stuck, work hard, make a discovery – over and over again. It was great. I actually began to look forward to our group sessions working on the problem. I have never felt this way about mathematics before – NEVER! I now feel like this is ok, I'm ok, I'll BE ok. I can do mathematics, and I definitely want my students to feel this way when I teach mathematics.
>
> (2005, p. 232, 2011/2006, p. 168)

Whilst I agree with Hannula (2006) that "these examples show that both relatively stable emotional traits as well as rapidly changing emotional states have an important role in mathematical thinking and learning" (p. 211), I am concerned that it has to come from a romantic vision of problem-solving and that this is causally connected to developing 'understanding'. There is no reason that 'never giving up' cannot be connected to other ways of doing mathematics. The concern is that the teacher in question (Melanie) becomes concerned with a correct version of mathematics and of the mathematical child. There are many more examples that corroborate this romantic view; for instance Duffin and Simpson (2002), whose work is subtitled "The Tension Between the Cognitive and the Affective", state that confidence (alongside comfort) is "the internal characteristics of understanding" (p. 90). The concern with this is that the affective side merely becomes a by-product of cognition. Within this, confidence becomes a 'natural' and required part of child 'development' and of the mathematical child. When confidence is more easily available to some than others particularly for those who already have privilege.

Establishing a correlating, causal relationship between confidence and gender is well documented (Hannula, Maijala, & Pehkonen, 2004), with Fennemma and Sherman (1977), in a very well-cited research article, being one of the earlier and more influential works to validate the assertion that confidence is found less with girls and women. Indeed, the negativity of this relation is enhanced via its relation to attainment; specifically, some studies indicate that the relationship between self-confidence and achievement is intrinsically part of gender (e.g.

Hannula et al., 2004). Thus, in spite of counterarguments (e.g. found in Burton, 2004; Walkerdine, 1998a) and in spite of many researchers arguing that confidence and gender norms are facilitated by the teacher, the classroom, and deeper sociological relations, this powerful story is reproduced within mathematics education research in ways that posit these relations and these genders as real. This is shown in the following example, where discourses are inscribed into common-sense practice. In this extract, the authors measure attitude and confidence via scales. They view confidence as being different at various points during the problem-solving process:

> *After* having worked on one of the problems (problem 4) boys also showed more confidence than girls. . . . The results at this level confirm that boys and girls tune in differently when processing mathematical problems. For boys a relevant aspect of the mathematical learning environment is the challenge and competition it elicits. Their constructive attribution beliefs call for favourable scenarios which generate confidence rather than doubt. Girls may more than boys believe that doing math is applying a set of rules. When they are not sure that they know 'the' necessary rule they may want to protect their ego by lowering their affects and expectations.
> (Boekaerts, Seegers, & Vermeer, 1995, p. 259)

Thus, whilst they acknowledge that confidence is not one-dimensional, their simplistic classification of boys and girls negates this work and fixes it to an essentialised performance. Moreover, the authors invalidate girls' ways of experiencing mathematics; I would argue that doubt need not be seen as inferior to confidence; it is only that it is positioned as such. In addition, they discredit the expectations they have of 'girls'' 'ways of doing mathematics', by positioning rule following as inferior, which is the same point that Walkerdine (1989) made in the 1980s.

Confidence was also mentioned in Boaler's (1997b) work, where it was again judged to be absent from girls. As discussed there, what is missing from this is an acknowledgement of how girls are products of the practices that make it more difficult for them to be viewed as confident or that

> we also have a set of expectations about the way we expect people of different sexes to behave. A man who freely expresses his emotions or freely discusses emotional issues is considered remarkable or out of the ordinary. A woman who behaves in a very confident way is considered extra-ordinary.
> (Jones & Smart, 1995, p. 161)

As discussed, Boaler suggested it was 'traditional' teaching methods that supported this, but I would contest this.

There are many other examples within mathematics education research that specifically link confidence and competence (or anxiety and attainment; e.g. Coben, 2003; Dorman, Adams, & Ferguson, 2003; Jones & Smart, 1995; Karimi & Venkatesan, 2009; Kyraciou, 2005; Kyraciou & Goulding, 2004; Ma,

1999; Tobias, 1985). Within these works, statements of correlation and of cause and effect are often evoked as common-sense wisdom. This is particularly evident in work that draws on the 'normal' psychological subject. Here, you find statements that present as the truth; for example "the correlation between mathematics anxiety and academic performance is negatively significant" (Karimi & Venkatesan, 2009, p. 33) or "self-efficacy is a strong predictor of related academic outcomes" (Pajares, 1996, p. 5). Much of this work ignores or misunderstands the wider structural relations that set out what is possible for people studying mathematics, and of course, this work essentialises the mathematical child.

It is the connection to 'ability' that is particularly concerning as it can position the mathematical child as natural and confidence as restricted to pupils who fit. One such example is provided by Kyraciou:

> The link between confidence and competence is an important one, because attainment is always normative – some pupils must inevitably do less well than others, and it is this sense of doing less well than one's peers that can all too easily lead to disaffection and anxiety in mathematics, and create a vicious circle of low self-confidence and underachievement.
>
> (2005, p. 168)

He is suggesting that since a spectrum of achievement is unavoidable, the correlating spectrum of levels of confidence is similarly so. Even if this does occur, my issue is with its acceptance as 'inevitable'. Moreover, the statement ignores any structural elements that facilitate it. In particular, it accepts the link between low achievement/ability and low confidence as 'real' and as causal (similar to the last chapter). As such, the mathematical child is bound by the connection between confidence and competence, and more often than not, this is fixed. This reduces the development of confidence and leads it primarily to be concerned with the development of cognition, leaving complexity and emotion as secondary concerns. As such, the mathematical child becomes a developed cognitive one who displays models of confidence as discussed previously. This does not take into account that, "assessed ability is socially constructed . . . rather than an attribute of the person" (Erickson, 1986, p. 125).

Burton argues that if we accept this correlation then "persistently, a link is made with 'confidence' in ways that can affect a pupil's self-image and consequent choices" (Burton, 2004, p. 357). In "confidence is [constructed as] everything" she highlights the problems associated with labelling pupils; in particular, she questions the idea that confidence stems from individuals, which is a common position in mathematics education research (Jones & Smart, 1995). This is similar to Chetcuti and Griffiths (2002), who examine self-esteem in relation to social justice. They contend that this commonly held view of the individualistic notion of self-esteem (and, I would argue, confidence) ignores the wider conceptions of power relations that lead to the marginalisation of some pupils. The "situation that many people feel powerless in the presence of mathematical ideas has been systematically reinforced by our culture, which sees mathematics as accessible to a talented few" (Willis, 1990, p. 206), I agree with Willis that the "power resides not in the mathematics but in the myth of mathematics – in the meritocratic prestige of mathematics as an intellectual discipline" (Willis, 1990, p. 205). Additionally, I suggest that confidence acts similarly, that the power of confidence is, in its fictitious status, the power to create the normal and ideal mathematical child. The salient point is that those "talented few" are often dominant groups, such as the middle-class male (Walkerdine, 1998a).

A further way that mathematics education research constructs the romantic child is though specialness. For many in mathematics education research, the special mathematician is not part of its acknowledged discourses; however, it is indirectly constructed by the way that their acknowledged discourses operate. The 'natural' problem-solver is part of this deeply embedded hierarchy that constructs the mathematical child as special. It is always already part of mathematics education research, which I show in the following.

The first illustration is from the mathematician Polya, who applied heuristics to problem-solving. In an influential, and well-referenced text, within mathematics education research (with more than 6,000 citations on Google Scholar), Polya (1945/2014) talks of both the 'natural' problem-solver and the use of common sense. He also talks of the expedition of these:

> All the questions and suggestions of our list are natural, simple, obvious, just plain common sense; but they state plain common sense in general terms. They suggest a certain conduct which comes naturally to any person who is seriously concerned with his [*sic*] problem and has some common sense . . . If the teacher wishes to develop in his students the mental operations which correspond to the questions and suggestions of our list, he puts these questions and suggestions to the students as often as he can do so naturally.
>
> (pp. 3–5)

Thus, here there is an appreciation of the 'natural' reasoned 'man', through "natural, simple, obvious, just plain common sense". The tone of the language is factual and the use of "common sense" constructs the doing of mathematics and the mathematical child as inherent and innate. However, what Polya refers to as 'natural', or common sense, is, of course, dependent on cultural and sociopolitical context; it constructs the 'common sense' of the time. In spite of this 'inborn' 'ability' to see and do mathematics, there is also an acknowledgement of the facilitation of this, as the teacher governs the classroom. Hence, it is clear that the teacher is complicit in this production of commonality and 'natural' reason. The work of Polya and others in developmental psychology is very influential in mathematics education research; hence, the story constructed is of 'natural' reason.

Similar messages are found in the more recent work in mathematics education research that draws upon developmental psychology. One typical example is offered in the following:

> Problem solving, a way to reach a goal that is not immediately attainable, is a hallmark of mathematical activity and an important means of developing mathematical knowledge. Problem solving is natural to young children

because the world is new to them, and they exhibit curiosity, intelligence, and flexibility as they face new situations.

(Tarim, 2009, p. 325)

Here, Tarim, like Polya, posits a natural mathematical problem-solver; hence, (re)producing natural and inherent mathematical ability as 'real'. Similar to others in mathematics education research, she also expects pupils' mathematical ability to develop from experience, perhaps inevitably as Piaget or Rousseau did. Within this, the child is constructed as acultural and asocial, as a vessel who is already 'natural' and who continues to 'develop' in a 'natural' (predetermined) way. However, the 'natural' problem-solver, whilst appearing universal in Polya's statement, authenticates the mathematical genius that everyone does not conform to.

As I have discussed dominant branches of mathematics education research are invested in problem-solving; they are invested in progressive education and demonstrating that this is the only way to learn mathematics. However, there are a few counterexamples to the connection between problem-solving and mathematical achievement; one is provided by Schiefele and Csikszentmihalyi (1995). They note that "the majority of studies confirm that cognitive student characteristics explain a large part of the observed variance in [mathematical] achievement" (p. 163). The authors examine correlations between mathematical ability and motivation and conclude that

> [q]uality of experience in mathematics class was mainly related to interest in mathematics and, to a lesser extent, to achievement motivation. Inconsistent with our hypothesis, ability was not at all correlated with experience. Even feelings of self-esteem, concentration, or skill seemed to be unaffected by ability. Achievement, however, was most strongly related to level of mathematical ability.
>
> (p. 176)

This contradicts some of my previous points specifically that they are confident and that they should experience mathematics in an 'active' way. However, by measuring mathematical ability and achievement as distinct, they maintain the idea that aspects of mathematical ability are 'natural'. This sliding between ability and achievement/attainment is a problematic discourse.

Discussions of ability are not found all over mathematics education research, especially in more recent publications; instead, often mathematical ability is noticeable by its absence. Boaler (2009) called it "the elephant in the classroom", something of which we dare not speak but which is always there.

Nunes and Bryant's (1997) edited collection *Learning and Teaching mathematics: An International Perspective* demonstrates the predicament with which academics are faced – trying to argue that 'ability' is inherent whilst maintaining that everyone can do mathematics. Nunes and Bryant explicitly use Piaget's definition of intelligence, stating that "intelligence (but note, one form of intelligence only!) and mathematical reasoning are the same because both are ways of solving problems in an adaptive, not arbitrary, and coherent fashion" (p. xiii). In addition, they are concerned with being able to think and reason, more than being able to do or perform functionally. As such, they link success in mathematics to reasoning, to intelligence, and to ability, very much in line with Piaget. However, they contest the argument I have just made: that this produces mathematics 'ability'/understanding as innate. They do this by drawing on the idea of stages of development (also similar to Piaget):

> If mathematical understanding were innate, one would not expect children to have to go through a series of earlier stages in which their understanding of some mathematical idea is not just incomplete but rather takes a different form before they achieve a full understanding of the idea in the question.
> (Nunes & Bryant, 1997, p. 45)

Though as I argued earlier, someone who can 'develop naturally' is an always already 'able' child, though this is often through covert surveillance. This way of being is heavily entrenched in discourses of inherent 'ability'.

Thus, Nunes and Bryant are not circulating the discourses of an innate mathematical 'ability' explicitly; however, there is a nod to the natural. Nunes and Bryant go broader than cognition and draw on social and cultural context. Moreover, they are circulating the discourse of mathematical reasoning, as the pinnacle of a hierarchy of stages of development, and the meaning of intelligence. It is a correct way to be 'able'.

Whilst these explicit discourses of 'natural mathematical ability' are not everywhere, mathematics education research does contain many other nuanced suggestions of the natural, the inevitable, and the intuitive. Some of these works have great influence; for example Schoenfeld (1992), who provides an overview and critique of trends in mathematics education, emphasises his own preference for orienting teaching towards "mathematical thinking". For this he draws on communities of practice and states that "the person who thinks mathematically has a particular way of seeing the world, of representing it, of analysing it" (Schoenfeld, 1992, p. 363). Hence, in spite of Schoenfeld's broad conclusions, he advocates a particular way of doing mathematics and, within this, the mathematical child becomes special. Schoenfeld does not intentionally advocate a naturalised mathematical child; however, his positioning invokes one.

Somewhat similarly, in a report on a review of mathematics education research, Watson states that "it is well known that very young children develop intuitive ideas that form the foundations of later formal mathematics" (A. Watson, 2010, p. 1). Again, Watson is not stating that some people are good at mathematics and others are not; however, she acknowledges that some of mathematics is intuitive and hence natural. In a sister paper/report, when discussing her preferred "bottom-up" approach to mathematics pedagogy, she states that

> a complementary 'bottom up' view includes consideration of the development of students' natural ability to discern patterns and generalise them, and

their growing competence in understanding and using symbols; however this would not take us very far in considering all the aspects of school algebra.

(A. Watson, 2009, p. 8)

Watson is not stating that she uses "students' natural ability" or that it is important; however, by its inclusion, there is an implicit acknowledgement of its being. It is possible that 'natural ability' surreptitiously saturates documents, and hence discourses of mathematics education research.

The most explicit positioning of a 'natural' 'ability' in mathematics education research comes from two places: projects that blur the boundaries between practice and research (some of which is explored in the next chapter) and researchers that write about 'gifted' students/learners. For the former, mathematics ability is routinely ascribed as natural, and this 'ability' dictates what mathematics the pupils should do. Indeed, "stereotyped goals [by ability] can be found even in a document of such generous intentions as the Cockcroft (1982) report" (Ruthven, 1987, p. 250). A typical more recent example is found on the NRICH (Enriching mathematics) website (NRICH, n.d.) based at Cambridge University, which is generally held in high regard by both practitioners and researchers:

> Ability is usually described as a relative concept; we talk about the most able, least able, exceptionally able, and so on. If mathematical ability is similar to other physical differences between individuals then we might expect it to approximate to a normal distribution, with few individuals being at the extreme ends of the spectrum . . . A hard-working student prepared well for an assessment can succeed without being highly able. Conversely not all highly able mathematicians show their abilities in class, or do well in statutory assessments.
>
> (McClure, n.d. para.1, 10, 11)

In the brief article, McClure, the NRICH project director, suggests that ability is inherent but not always related to attainment. She draws on those that suggest various presentations of natural ability in mathematics: Krutetskii (1976), Bloom (1956), and Straker (1983), from more than 30 years ago. Krutetskii's description of mathematical ability is similar to that of a problem solver (Orton, 2004). This is reiterated in this statement from McClure's article:

> The message here then is that in order to discover or confirm that a student is highly able, we need to offer opportunities for that student to grasp the structure of a problem, generalise, develop chains of reasoning.
>
> (McClure, n.d. para. 8)

Hence, as before, the 'natural ability' that is prescribed is a certain type of mathematical ability. It is active reasoning that is always already sought by mathematics education research.

Research articles that specify the 'gifted, natural learner' encompass broader fields and disciplines than mathematics education research – though they permeate its boundaries. Indeed, there are many journals that are specifically constructed around 'gifted'/'able' pupils. These include *Gifted Child Quarterly*, the *Gifted Child Newsletter*, the *Journal for the Education of the Gifted*, and *Gifted Education International*. Whilst none of these is specific to mathematics, many of the articles are exclusively about mathematics, with titles such as "Gender Differences in Gifted and Average-Ability Students Comparing Girls' and Boys' Achievement, Self-Concept, Interest, and Motivation in mathematics" (Preckel, Goetz, Pekrun, & Kleine, 2008). Within this, and other such articles and journals, natural ability is produced as 'real', with the choice of 'gifted' conjuring notions of innate qualities. In the article mentioned earlier, this essentialising is taken further by the analysis of gender. The discourses stemming from the articles are similar to those already discussed, specifically that gifted pupils require opportunities to be active and be creative problem-solvers. However, some clarify this around the suggestion of inclusive practice. One such example is from the journal *Gifted Child Quarterly*, where Mann (2006) not only stresses that creativity is for all but also suggests that it is most important for the gifted. He states that "teaching mathematics without providing for creativity denies all students, especially gifted and talented students, the opportunity to . . . fully develop his or her talents" (p. 236). As discussed previously, this both affirms a natural 'ability' and the discourse that creativity/ problem-solving/understanding is only or mainly relevant to the more mathematically 'able'.

The positioning of mathematical ability as innate, and 'real' mathematics as achieved through problem-solving, is concerning. First, even if you are successful at mathematics (via academic grades) you are only viewed as a 'real' mathematician if you have achieved this through 'natural' 'ability' and understanding, not through 'hard work' (Walkerdine, 1998a). Thus, some pupils are more easily labelled as 'naturally able' and hence good at mathematics, which is inequitable.

The production of 'natural mathematical ability' as 'real' is probably not the intention of mathematics education research; instead, mathematics education research positions itself and progressive pedagogies as the route to equity in mathematics (e.g. Boaler, 1997b; Boylan & Povey, 2012). In addition, they fiercely advocate all 'ability' grouping as another route to this, although setting by 'ability' is endemic in mathematics classrooms (both primary and secondary).

Some researchers, such as Zevenbergen (2003), are aware of the psychological and hierarchical constructions of learning mathematics that facilitate this production of mathematical ability and could enable grouping by 'ability':

> In the current educational climate, there is a dominance of psychological discourses; views of social justice that focus on liberal, individualistic perspectives; and a view of mathematics being a hierarchical ontology. Within a field such as this, there is considerable influence for constructing a habitus that

would legitimate practices associated with grouping students according to need and ability.

(pp. 4, 5)

However, Zevenbergen stops short of specifically criticising or analysing mathematics education research's role in this production

The evidence-based trends of neoliberalism

More recent trends in mathematics education research, particularly those associated with direct governance, and 'impact', could be seen as a threat to the 'romantic' child of mathematics education; however, I contend that a correct developmental path for the Child was a precursor to the overt surveillance and targets we currently see in education in many parts of the world.

The child that is able to move through predetermined stages as Piaget or other similar developmental paths is not dissimilar to the child of targets found within educational policy and neoliberalism, even though they are presented very differently – one through a functional performance and one through performance disguised as freedom.

What is perhaps most interesting is the neoliberal performativity that has come through mathematics education from the use of people such as Dweck (2008) and her growth mind-sets. This suggests that 'all can do mathematics' if you have the right attitude and if you attempt mathematics with the correct approach, which is supported by Boaler (2016).

At first glance, this sits in contrast to my critique of the mathematical child who was situated in innate ability. However, what a neoliberal 'it's down to you' position can achieve is that systems and structures are ignored – that confidence is more easily found in some bodies than others, that opportunity is presented more easily for some than others are ignored. For mathematics that means there are many people who are excluded from mathematics – as they are not the right kind of mathematical child. Thus, again, a certain cognitive mathematics Child is maintained.

Mathematics education research has been leisurely in privileging RCTs. In terms of large-scale studies, mathematics education was said to be slow to respond to the call for evidence through large data sets, although many RCTs use mathematical attainment (often alongside literacy) as a measure and an indicator of success. Thus, illustrating the power of mathematics as a measure, as a subject and as a key part of society. Although as before, I suggest this measure is not particularly useful – it is an image of mathematics as a marker of intelligence. It perhaps helps that mathematical content is relatively easy to measure.

Concluding remarks

Thus overall, and in spite of recent shifts in the direction of educational research, I would still contend that mathematics research education is invested in certain positions and that many of these directly or indirectly ascribe a specific mathematical child. mathematics has to be constructed as important within research; without this position, the value of doing research into mathematics education is contested. In addition, the amount of money given to mathematics education may be questioned. However, this means that mathematics education researchers are already starting from a position of privilege, a certain lens to view what they do as vital.

This privileging already attributes something special to those who do mathematics; however, I suggest this is proliferated by the way that dominant discourses of mathematics education construct 'real' ways of doing mathematics. Even if it is not explicitly written, the underlying discourse is that there is a 'natural' way to do mathematics and this can lead to the idea of the 'natural' mathematician. The taken-for-granted privileging of problem-solving, of developing understanding, and of underlying confidence all add to the normalised construction of a romantic mathematical child, where many of these traits are said to be found inherently. The preference for the 'active learner' of mathematics education has been an integral part of mathematics education research from its inception to the present day, with very few in mathematics education acknowledging their own role in its production.

6 Spaces of enactment

A statement from a pre-service teacher:

"I always immediately think that I should have done something different with those children and I just worry that I don't know what to do".

Introduction

Discourses of the mathematical child operate differently across the domains discussed in the previous two chapters, however how these discourses relate to practice is another question. This chapter discusses teachers (practising or pre-service teachers) in relation to how these practitioners make sense of these discourses. For instance do they merge and work to make the teacher a criticality informed practitioner, or do they cause confusion about what is best practice? Pre-service teachers, being at the beginning of their careers and arguably most open to advice, are particularly susceptible. They have little background knowledge to make sense of the multitude of discourses to which they are exposed, some of which are in conflict or competition (Walshaw, 2007). Calderhead (1988), for one, has suggested that the value of student-'teachers'/learners'' personal experiences is quite high in shaping their own conception of teaching and learning. Whilst Brown, Jones, and Bibby (2004) note that if pre-service teachers had negative experiences of mathematics they were "determined to deliver the subject in terms other than their own experience" (p. 174).

In seeking the teachers' perspectives, I am concerned not only with what is said within mathematics education but also with what is allowed to be heard and what is produced in the performance of the classroom. Thus, both the macro level of systems and the micro level of practice are studied. Specifically, I take into account that there is a difference between the intentions of policy and the practice by groups and individuals (S. J. Ball, 2006).

This chapter is in two parts. The first discusses a group of pre-service teachers in a University in England. The second discusses teachers (and pre-service teachers) interacting online.

These different spaces for research very much demonstrate how teaching has moved from something that was contained by the classroom and school to a profession where discourses permeate across local and global environment by the use of social media. Blogs and social media such as Twitter and Pinterest have reshaped the way that schoolteachers view their practice. The virtual space has broken physical and discursive barriers to allow the transfer of information regardless of space, place, or position of power.

Pre-service teachers of New Labour

This section uses a case study of a group of six pre-service teachers who studied from a primary education undergraduate degree situated in the North of England. These students were interviewed and observed teaching over the full period of their studies, from 2006 to 2009. They were selected initially from a larger cohort to show a range of normative constructions.

The predominant use of interviews is similar to other poststructural case studies which are based on participants' identities. For example this is the case for Ball, Maguire, and Macrae's (2000) four-year longitudinal study of post-16 students, for Brown and McNamara's (2011) study of teacher identity in relation to educational policy, and for Mendick's (2006) study of post 16 student's mathematical identities.

The use of a case such as this is not to look for causal factors or underlying characteristics but, instead, to suggest interpretations and nuances based on coming to know the data. Moreover, the central purpose is to offer rich description of the case discussed (Hamilton & Corbett-Whittier, 2013; Merriam, 2009; Stake, 1978, 1995), acknowledging that poststructuralism seeks to expose and explore the messiness and inconsistencies between accounts (Tierney, 2000). Specifically, for the interviews, I am concerned with how the pre-service teachers take up some discourses and resist others as they construct the world around them. "In a significant sense, then we live by stories – both in the telling and the realizing of the self" (K. J. Gergen, 2001, p. 248); thus, "narratives do not reflect so much as they create the sense of 'what is true'" (K. J. Gergen, 2001, p. 249). Hence, this section explores how people present themselves during interviews and conversations as they are constructing versions of themselves that they want to be seen as the truth. My approach towards the participants was to develop an ethics of care around the participants (Christians, 2000). This included involving them in the research process, using ethical interview techniques, and minimising disruption to the participants' schedules. They are also presented here through pseudonyms.

The construction of the mathematical child as a functional automaton: the 'shoulds'

Throughout the interviews, all the pre-service teachers discursively produce progress as a key concept in the mathematics classroom. Specifically, there seems to be a push for linear progress for all, such that everyone achieves at the same rate, regardless of other internal or external factors. This very much fits the functional production of progress within New Labour educational policy. This construction is shown in Nicola's interviews, where the completion of the work is produced as the goal, as in the following extract. (The school students choose their own names for their 'ability' group, suggesting a knowing and subversive subject positioning – a constrained agency)

NICOLA: The other day I had four kids that did the Comets work [lower group] and the Spoons work [higher group] in the same amount of time the Spoons did their own work. And the rest of the Comets did their work. And it was like they should really be working with Spoons.

The extract demonstrates how the mathematics classroom can be constructed around normalcy and comparison, of what pupils "should really be" doing. Pupils are assumed to move at predetermined rates, and this is the construction favoured by the teacher. In addition, it demonstrates how the pupils' position can be fixed within this, in accordance with markers of ability/attainment that suit 'normal' trajectories. These constructions are very similar to the ones given by Nicola and Sophie, in the following extract, which is indicative of the wider data and taken from a group discussion:

ANNA: What do you think of having targets?
NICOLA: I think there's too many of them. Because you are changing, like sometimes you're changing topic like do one week on it and then you're on to the next thing and by the end of the second week they've forgotten what you did the first week because you haven't got the time to go back over.
SOPHIE: I think you do need some targets set but there's so much to do in the year, some kids you can go and do it one week, they'll be perfect at it, go and do a couple of weeks of other work and then you come back and they'll have completely forgotten it. So you can't win . . . because you were trying to meet all the targets and all the strands, you had to skimp on certain weeks and certain bits and pieces.

Again, there is an expectation of what should happen in the mathematics classroom – what is "perfect" and demonstrating this within the lesson. There is an expectation of normalcy and pupils behaving as machines to maintain their progress from lesson to lesson. The mathematical child is constructed as objects or "target groups" that "need to be pushed that little bit further".

There are several debates that follow from the preceding: first, for forward movement to be maintained, forgetting things, or making mistakes, becomes problematic – an illegitimate mathematical discourse. Second, as targets surveil the classroom, and the push for progress becomes the push to move at a fast pace and cover the objectives of the mathematics curriculum, progress can be measured by, or conflated with, speed and/or quantity and coverage. Both of these suggest particular connotations for mathematics pedagogy, for the mathematics teacher and, of course, for the mathematical child. The teacher (and the system) could be read as exerting an external force on the mathematical child, as he or she is processed through the production line at a predetermined speed, regardless of who they are. They are machines that have to keep up with this production line.

This is particularly evident where pupils do not fit normal trajectories. There is an attempt to reconstitute defective groups within the normal, within what we should do, as demonstrated in the following indicative extracts, which are from separate interviews:

NICOLA: [T]he lower ability are pushed and they will be helped to the point where they will catch up with the other kids.
LOUISE: [I]f I say I'm working with a target group I need to work with that group 'cos I need to push them on.

However, as shown in all the preceding extracts, the push for progress is not as straightforward as discourses constructed in educational policy. Accordingly, the pre-service teachers express difficulties taking the construction fully onboard. For instance, the extract from Nicola and Sophie demonstrates that tensions are evident between the pressure to obtain targets and the perceived needs of their students. Both pre-service teachers seem be uneasy about moving through fictional targets at a regulated speed and they express some desire to work more flexibly. Within this, they criticise the system (the number of objectives in the curriculum); however, it also becomes acceptable for them to criticise their students when they fall short of these expectations. The pupils take the brunt of the blame and are positioned as defective. As such, the child, rather than the system, is broken. These sentiments are shown throughout the earlier interviews and in Kate's interviews. The following extract is indicative of her other statements:

KATE: [T]hey're second to bottom set so um, so I had to make sure I targeted my lesson at that, but they tended to get it one minute and it was over their head the next . . . Wednesday I think it was, they'd not got estimation even though we'd done it two weeks ago, they could not get it, so we had to spend all of today doing estimation and they finally got it but if I asked them again on Monday they wouldn't be able to do it.

The label (and perceived level) of the 'ability' group (or set) seems to dictate the teacher's assumptions about the targets and levels; thus, it dictates the curriculum and pedagogy. Moreover, there is an expectation of linear temporality, and any child who cannot meet these criteria is deemed defective. 'Blame' is 'easily' placed with the abnormal pupils, and they become malfunctioning functional automata. However, there is another option for those who do not fit the functional, linear system of progress. Instead of blaming the pupil, you can, of course, blame yourself – the teacher, which is discussed, through Jane, in the next section.

The frustration of the mathematical child as functional automaton: the constitution of blame around the self

Jane is also caught up in expectations of what pupils 'should' do; she also assumes progress means speed. For example,

> JANE: See I've got to keep moving on for the higher ones and the ones that get it because there's no point keep doing that because they're just going to get bored, but what do I do with those ones who don't get it? Do I just move, you know, it's difficult weighing it up because this was supposed to be a consolidation lesson for those children who still didn't get it.

The confusion that stems is that her pupils must move forward, but they must all progress at the same rate – which is impossible. The linear functionality of educational policy does not mirror the messy realities of the classroom. Pupils who "still didn't get it" are thus problematic – as the comparison to the normal child is enforced.

Thus, for Kate, Nicola, Sophie, and Jane there is tension concerning the functional expectations of educational policy in relation to their fuzzy classroom experiences. Jane also feels the need to consolidate the work and possibly to make mathematics comfortable. She does not want children to struggle. Although rather than solely blame the pupils, Jane takes the responsibility onto herself. This is shown throughout her interviews; one example is used as an illustration in the following:

> JANE: [B]ut he still can't work it out in the way that we were working it out and that worries me because I don't know where to go with him now . . . He just still doesn't understand . . . Not that they should all understand. I don't think it's anything, I never think it's anything to do with them. I always immediately think that I should have done something different with those children and I just worry that I don't know what else to do because I've had them sat on the carpet yesterday doing it. They could do it yesterday but when they go to the tables something happens and they just can't do it and I'm not sure why.

Jane seems to be aware that she should be ensuring that her pupils make progress, as straightforwardly and homogeneously as suggested in New Labour educational policy documents and/or possibly as intrinsic to the natural development of the 'romantic' inquiring mathematical child of mathematics education research.

However, in reality the school pupils are neither functional automata nor romantic natural inquirers. Jane states, "When they go to the tables something happens"; their messy behaviour is not something that is written into normative educational discourses. Hence, the space that is available is one of deviance: that something must be wrong with the pupils or with Jane. In Jane's case she seems to take the majority of responsibility for the 'lack of progress' onto herself and positions herself as abnormal and as an unsuccessful teacher. There is tension around 'impossible' discourses of progress and of the mathematical child.

Jane's story

We can further explore the tensions around impossible discourses by examining the term *understanding* discussed in the previous two chapters. As Jane suggests earlier, she is frustrated when a student does not understand – when the message from educational research is that this is the most important aspect of studying mathematics. Furthermore, she is frustrated with her own learning and is able to use the university lectures diminishing rote learning to validate her problems with mathematics. She states, "I really enjoyed the lectures about rote learning because it made sense to me that that's the way I'd learned."

JANE: I just used to think well surely if I had an embedded understanding it must have come back somehow and then I realised that in some areas I didn't have an embedded understanding, I just rote learned stuff and even though I did understand that, this is what I've realised in the past few months that even though I did a lot better in year 10 and 11, I think it was still all rote learning . . . I don't think there was any understanding towards it, because you know I still don't understand things, and sometimes I wonder how I got a B, because in the things I got a B in I don't understand how to do

Thus, this university-perpetuated story of rote learning equals bad and understanding equals good supports Jane in redistributing blame from herself to the situation; as Boaler's (1997b) research suggests, Jane may have a "quest for understanding", and this lack of opportunity prevents her being successful at mathematics. Jane has never had the opportunity to be the mathematical child.

However, if we unpack the term *understanding* further we can see that Jane's version of understanding fits with educational policy and understanding as being able to do:

JANE: I always remember at school thinking every time we did anything in maths 'why are we doing this? I don't get it, why are we doing this? Why do we have to do it this way? I don't understand.' And it was never explained so when I was doing my maths teaching I always made a point of saying 'we're doing it this way because it's easier'.

In the preceding extract it is clear that being able to understand is conflated with being able to do – understanding takes on a functionality of performance. Moreover, it is about doing the task in an efficient way, which very much follows advice

112 Spaces of enactment

from neoliberal educational policy. There are other memories that assert the position of understanding being framed around access and functionality. She states,

> JANE: You never got taught anything, you just worked through a workbook and the workbook was supposed to explain how to do things but I quite often never understood what the workbook meant because there was not very often any example.

So when Jane states that "[e]veryone else was understanding it and I wasn't", it is more likely that she is frustrated at not being able to do the task – and she perceives that everyone else can. The romantic discourses of educational research and the functional discourse of educational policy are not aligned, which creates tension for Jane and someone is to blame. Perhaps she is caught between the discourses of romanticism and functionality, between mathematics education research and educational policy.

During part of the interview, in my rather ineffective way, I offered Jane a path to understanding:

> JANE: Yeah, and you have to put a three down and a one up so you add another one to the tens column, they said 'why' and I was, just like, 'well just so you know where it's going' and they were like, 'why, why do you put it there? Why can't you just put it somewhere else?' 'Well that's just the way we do it'.
> ANNA: Where else did she want to put it?
> JANE: Underneath.
> ANNA: Oh, right, ok. In the same column though because it's the column that's the important bit.
> JANE: Yeah, I know that but it was still like, well, you know.
> ANNA: It was ((inaudible)) question really.
> JANE: ((laughter)) I know, you're a maths person ((laughter)). It was a question that just completely threw me because I never thought that.
> ANNA: Some people do put it underneath.
> JANE: Do they?

Jane rejected my attempt to explain mathematics or to think deeper herself about the way mathematics works. There are many things happening in the above extract, the most important probably being I am indirectly identifying myself as a maths person someone who 'understands' mathematics – consequently I am Othering myself from Jane. Thus, there is an alternative reading to Boaler's 'quest for understanding' in that not having understanding can be a safe space, a place that offers security. Not understanding could be a method of self-protection from the inevitable failure that romantic discourses afford: subject positions being both constraining and enabling (Foucault, 1980a, 1989i) and resistance being more than just compliance.

Jane knows what she is *supposed* to think – mathematics educational research has told her this; she knows what she and her students are *supposed* to achieve – educational policy has told her this. When these supposed ideas do not match her experience, it becomes a very difficult position. Jane falls back on positioning the mathematical child as something special and unachievable to all.

This special mathematical child must also act confidently, confidence and mathematics being actions that cannot (within dominant discourses) function separately. Jane's reading of confidence similarly adds to the barriers around mathematics. She states,

JANE: I think knowledge can only take you so far and if you haven't got the confidence then you haven't got the ability to absorb the knowledge really because you've got this presumption that you can't do it . . . The average achievers because they weren't very confident in maths were quite happy to sit back and let the higher achiever do all the work and everything

In the preceding text achievement becomes a fixed state (which I will return to later on in this chapter). In addition, confidence is similarly constructed (like understanding) as a gatekeeper to accessing mathematics. This appearance of being 'able to do' being a precursor for actually being able to do. As before, confidence is an easier barrier to imagine overcoming for the 'average' doer of mathematics. Though for confidence to become measurable it can easily become essentialised as an innate quality in mathematics education research, and the pre-service teachers' emotional discourses suggest that they essentialise it further. In Jane's case, it becomes a reason to keep her as a non-mathematical person. She states,

JANE: I'm not very confident teaching maths, I'm not very confident at maths . . . If I'm not confident I can't pretend to be confident

She reiterates this by making the mathematical person confident:

JANE: [B]ut you know like when I was saying how that girl tried to like knock my confidence at the same time, because she was very good at maths.

Consequently, it restricts mathematics to certain groups, as Jane states in an earlier interview there are "those who can, do it [Mathematics] and those who can't". These binary oppositions position people/groups into mutually exclusive boxes giving some pupils access to mathematics and keeping others without (Mendick, 2006), as confidence and mathematics are positioned as an inner state (Hardy, 2009). Again, we are positioning the mathematical child as special – as 'all knowing' and not doubting. There is something almost inhuman about this production.

Jane's is a particularly strong story which demonstrates the tension between the various discourses of 'understanding', 'confidence', and the concern with being 'able-to-do'. She constructs a story of the real mathematician that is out of reach to her and many others; she keeps it out permanently out of reach by the various fixed traits she constructs. She states, "[T]hat's what I think I need, more confidence", which may very well be the most acceptable discourse for Jane to give.

In the following, I explore differences and similarities between Jane's and other pre-service teachers Sophie and Nicola. Particularly, both stories highlight how understanding is reserved for the most able, which limits mathematics to certain pupils and excludes others. This is a more common story.

Sophie's story: understanding and the most able

Sophie's discursive positioning is similar to Jane's in that she also produces understanding as important to the mathematical child and as something that was absent from her own education. The following extract is typical of Sophie's interviews:

SOPHIE: That is all I remember from year 6 was those multiplication grids. I hated them . . . Then at the end of GCSE's it was the case again, the same thing just recalling facts over and over again. Still not understanding but learning the multiplications or learning the actual formula and things like that without understanding them.

She states that she believes that rote learning is wrong: "I didn't like that way of teaching at all, just teaching by rote". In addition, she pronounces that you should "try and get the understanding, that's what you need to have initially, you've to have understanding there before you can develop it all". Thus, Sophie may seek understanding, or indeed, this could be the acceptable discourses that are available to Sophie, as they are the ones permitted by mathematics education research and hence by her university.

Thus, similar to Jane, she presents as frustrated with the rote learning she has experienced in mathematics. In addition, and like Jane, she seems to have difficulties dealing with situations where 'understanding' could arise. For instance, when it comes to her teaching Sophie seems to be utilising these rote methods and replicating her own experience:

SOPHIE: The class chanting works good. The first time they did that really quite well. They used to be so slow and they'd die down between the 7 times 4 and the 9 times 4 but they have improved quite a bit with taking tables home and things like that.

Academic conceptions of understanding are missing from the preceding exchange; instead, the emphasis is on practice, speed, and being able to do/recall. Thus, like Jane, there is a disconnect between a desired outcome and the realisation of that outcome. Or perhaps, like Jane, understanding is similarly concerned with functionality and being able to do. This is clearer in the next extract; it is not dissimilar to my exchange with Jane (discussed previously). Specifically, when faced with developing her mathematics, Sophie expresses fear for the process (or the connections) or for what some (Barmby et al., 2009; Skemp, 1976) might term *understanding*. She expects mathematics to come to her naturally, which is a familiar and constricting story (Mendick, 2006):

SOPHIE: That's my worst one! I hate the tables. 7s and 8s. 9s, I know the trick with your hand so that's not a problem. 5s and 10s and 3s are fine. 4s are fine. It's just 7s and 8s.
ANNA: Would you be happier, would you just like to know them and be able to recall them or work them out?
SOPHIE: I would love to be able to know them by rote and just be able to say '7 8s are . . . whatever it is' and know it, off hand, but I just can't. I haven't got that in my head. Whereas some people are more- they can visualize numbers so easily and I just can't do that. I need to sit down and go through them all one by one and get to the answer.
ANNA: Right, so you know your 4s?
SOPHIE: Yeah.
ANNA: You could double your 4s to get your 8s.
SOPHIE: I can't do that because that's doing too much of a process so I could probably try that. I just think it's going to complicate it more.
ANNA: I do it.
SOPHIE: I'll give it a try but . . .
ANNA: Some people wouldn't know them all but would calculate to get each individual one.
SOPHIE: Yeah.
ANNA: Or if you know 8 8s is 64, use that to get back to 7.
SOPHIE: Mmm. But it's all working out your long methods isn't it?
ANNA: Yeah.
SOPHIE: I'm not good at that sort of thing of working out how to do things and making it complicated. I'd rather it just came to me naturally. But I'm never going to be that one! (laughter) Unfortunately.

As with my conversation with Jane, this exchange may be a rejection of me as a teacher or as a mathematical person, with Sophie feeling positioned as the Other. It is perhaps a comfortable position for Sophie to choose; however, it is not a position that is allowed in neoliberal educational policy or in mathematics education research, where everyone is constructed as being able to achieve.

Sophie takes the position that 'real' mathematics comes naturally to a lucky few; which contrasts to the extract where she asks her pupils to practice timestables. This also complicates the relationship to understanding, suggesting that those without it see it as a natural gift. Thus, it does follow the hierarchical view of mathematics, where the 'real' mathematical child is naturally able. As such, this positions those who achieve results by hard work as not (authentically) mathematical (Walkerdine, 1998a), which excludes many from the subject.

Nicola's story: the person who identifies as mathematical

Nicola's story has similarities and differences to the two described earlier. In the first instance, Nicola is different in that she self-identifies with mathematics. In

116 *Spaces of enactment*

addition, perhaps she is more aware of the position from some of mathematics education research that mathematical progress is concerned with connectivity (e.g. Barmby et al., 2009). This is shown in the following extract:

NICOLA: I had two kids in my class last year; they didn't have the basic understanding.
ANNA: So what do you think they missed out on that stopped them getting access to the Year 5 Maths or the Year 4, whichever it was?
NICOLA: The basic concept of a number really . . . because they can tell you the numbers from 1 to 100 in order quite easily . . . But understanding, giving them multiplication tables and things it was all learnt by rote, there was no concept of the fact that five times four is five lots of four.

Although here, and similar to most mathematics education research, Nicola positions understanding against rote learning, perpetuating reductive binaries. However, rather than viewing understanding as part of a stage of development, in practice she seems to construct the mathematical child as a fixed category, and hence, this position is only available to some:

ANNA: Could you see yourself ever teaching by these sort of rote ways that you don't particularly like?
NICOLA: To be honest I think it's beneficial for certain kids. You're always going to have the odd kid in your class that just can't cope with like abstract ways of learning and needs to learn by rote.

Thus, where for 'low achievers', 'failure' would be seen as an opportunity for correction in neoliberal educational policy texts, here the students' 'abnormality' is constructed as static. The concern is that these lower achievers (rote learners) are positioned as non-mathematical children and are no longer asked to understand (Bibby, 2001). This message runs throughout Nicola's interviews and is shown in the following extract. Here, she reiterates these divisions by restricting using and applying, the strand of the curriculum which many (including Boaler, 1997b; J. Rose, 2009; Williams, 2008) associate with 'understanding', to the most able.

NICOLA: My Highers can do fractions, equivalent fractions everything. The Lowers don't even understand basic fractions. The Highers are very good with their times-tables. Or one boy, you can ask him anything in his zero to twelve times-tables, he's like that ((clicking of fingers)), you get it back. He understands it perfectly. It's like using and applying is, I find more important for them [the Highers].

Her assumption that true mathematics comes inherently or instinctively seems to validate the perspective that teaching for understanding should be directed to the naturally able mathematical child. This is perhaps validated with reference to herself. For instance, discussing her sister she states that "she was good at maths, she wasn't naturally as good as I always [was]". Thus, like Sophie she views the mathematical child as innately and naturally mathematical.

However, in the preceding extract, the version of understanding is more aligned to the recall of knowledge and speed, which is very different from Boaler's romantic child and different from her previous statements. An alternative reading is that these are more performed and noticeable traits of cognitive ability, or from a poststructural perspective they could be viewed as social markers presented as understanding. This is just one case, though her interview also exemplifies Walkerdine's (1990) point that boys are more easily afforded the luxury of the appearance of understanding even when it is not apparent in their attainment. What is clear is that the version of understanding described above is not primarily concerned with connections or with Boaler's romantic curious child, in spite of previous concerns that it should be.

Similar to Jane, Nicola also constructs confidence as belonging to the naturally able:

NICOLA: One of the biggest problems is their [low attaining pupils] confidence. That plays more of a part than anything.

A concern is that this causal assumption is too easily made, and the importance of confidence can supersede competence resulting in exclusion based on behaviour. Thus, we are stuck in a catch-22 position where confidence is a precursor for competence, yet you cannot be confident if you do not have competence. Thus, confidence is restricted to the already 'able', and as elsewhere there is homogenising around an 'ability' group. The restricting of confidence is broader than towards the mathematically 'able'; instead, it is towards pupils who can do confidence as performance. For example, Leah also assigns confidence more easily to boys – "I would say that probably in maths, boys are more confident on this table" – which is a common stereotypical generalisation (Walkerdine, 1998a). Leah is not saying that all boys are more confident than girls, but she is making assumptions based on an abstract rather than a concrete notion, one that is not equitably measurable. An example from Nicola is shown in the following excerpt:

NICOLA: I knew she'd be hesitant about it because she's one of those people who doesn't have the confidence. She can do it . . . She's a really clever girl. She can do anything you put in front of her; she just hasn't got the confidence to believe in herself.

Here Nicola talks of a female pupil that has competence ("she can do it") but denies her confidence ("she just hasn't got" it). This suggests it is more complicated than simply conflating competence and competence. As here, despite being academically successful at mathematics, the female pupil is constructed as lacking something and as not belonging to the group of 'real mathematicians' (Walkerdine, 1988). Attainment must be based on performances of 'understanding' and 'confidence' to fit the idealised mathematical child.

A neoliberal "can-do" approach to mathematics

Confidence is slightly different to understanding as it fits much more easily into neoliberal discourse of self-improvement, which at times Nicola buys into: "when the shutters come down it's about convincing them they can do it". Consequently, the pupils are asked to adopt a "can do" attitude, where emotion is constructed as the driver of cognition, as shown by some of the other pre-service teachers:

LEAH: They've given up on it because they just don't have the confidence to say I can do it or they just don't want to do it because they don't feel like they can.

KATE: It is self-esteem, a bit more confidence with their work. They can do it but they don't believe that they can do it I think.

The pre-service teachers talk of needing to instil into students the attitude that "they can do it", which is very similar to Burton's (2004) observations of students' conceptions of confidence as a 'can-do' approach to studying mathematics. This is also shown where Louise constructs her own approach to mathematics:

LOUISE: I've got the maximum, I stormed it! Stormed the GCSE and got a B 'cos I did the intermediate paper, erm, but I wish I'd gone in for the higher one because I felt, felt it was a bit tedious to be honest . . . I just picked it up really, really, quickly.

This is not an uncommon statement for Louise. She acts as 'confident' in relation to mathematics and constructs this as integral to her performance as someone who is naturally good at mathematics. She constructs confidence as from within and belonging to her – which is the case of some of the pre-service teachers.

However, she also makes the complex connection between mathematics and confidence clear:

LOUISE: So maybe if she can do it with shape she'll start building up her confidence and maybe that'll help her confidence in numbers too, so . . . I think it's [confidence] huge. That's why I like to give a lot of praise.

The mathematics is almost 'magically' responsible for an inner state, similarly to the advertisement discussed in the introduction to the Chapter 4. As Nicola puts it, "maths is able to give you a confidence boost or to do the complete opposite". Thus, doing mathematics and being confident are 'intrinsically' connected. This construction permeates much of the pre-service teachers' talk, which results in particular classroom behaviours, for example Louise's use of praise or Jane's assumptions about why groups of pupils behave the way they do. Again, and similar to educational policy, there is a sliding between confidence and competence.

These constructions are notably different to academic conceptions where building confidence comes alongside competence and through specific teaching methodologies. Similarly, but more explicitly in educational policy, confidence is viewed as an end result and a by-product of successful doers of mathematics. This contrasts with a student's competence or cognition, which in the classroom is often viewed as fixed and as an inner state and so as less easily influenced.

From this, I suggest that pre-service teachers can experience tension between the expectations of the functional mathematical child and being able to do and the romantic attraction of the naturally curious mathematical child from mathematics education research. However, they do not find many of these children in their classroom practice or within themselves. Thus, each pre-service teacher takes on the discourse of understanding as all important to varying degrees; however, within that, how they interpret understanding is not straightforward. It is particularly complex in a neoliberal climate where pupils are subjects to be measured and are required to demonstrate progress. As such, it may be that understanding and/or the mathematical child must take on aspects of performativity. However, this performance of understanding is not equally available to everyone. Very similarly, confidence is not equally available to everyone

Thus, confidence as enabler is quite problematic; it is a chimera that allows neoliberal discourses to circulate, yet they never can be realised, as confidence is more easily found in some bodies than others. For the group of pre-service teachers, they are in a catch-22; confidence is a prerequisite for competence, yet you cannot have confidence if you do not have competence; confidence is restricted to the already (assigned as) able. The concern here is that the pre-service teachers' essentialise students more so than educational policy documents, particularly on groupings and assigned ability.

This can be dangerous from the point of excluding and including only certain people into mathematics. In this case, 'real' mathematics is reserved for the already (assigned) able (Walkerdine, 1998a) and is possibly monitored through measurable, social markers such as speed. Within this the mathematical child is mostly constructed as naturally able, in spite of the awareness of neoliberal counter-discourses that everyone can achieve

The already-assigned able mathematical child

There are several extracts where the pre-service teachers seem to follow the neoliberal position of New Labour educational policy, that everyone can do mathematics. For instance, in Year 1 of her studies Jane states:

JANE: I don't think it takes a type of person I think it takes a type of education. I think it's the way you're taught it that makes you decide whether you're good or bad at maths.

Jane constructs being good at mathematics as dependent on how students are taught. This relates to earlier discussions where Jane recounted not enjoying how she was taught mathematics as 'not being able to 'understand' (do)' and how this resulted in her 'lacking confidence'. Jane is perhaps unique in this small group of pre-service teachers and demonstrates the most outwardly negative reading of mathematics lessons. She could be read as a functional mathematical child, whose success in mathematics is dependent on external factors, such as good teaching.

In contrast, Louise and Nicola construct being able to do mathematics in a more neoliberal fashion, as concerned with choice, independence, and the empowerment of self:

LOUISE: Everybody's certainly got the ability to be good at maths but it's whether they choose to or whether they choose not to. And I think a lot of it again, learning from this course [university], it stems from your early years and what your attitude towards teaching, towards maths is then. Like, most of my teachers had it pretty negative, but I was lucky enough to be able to put myself out of that.

Similar to Jane, Louise asserts that everyone can do mathematics, but different from Jane, Louise takes responsibility for being good at mathematics onto herself (rather than the teacher). In the following excerpt, she expands on this by drawing on neoliberal fantasies of the always already 'able' mathematical child as someone who understands, is confident (already discussed), and is an independent problem-solver, aligning to the romantic discourses of mathematics education research.

LOUISE: No, I've always enjoyed maths, always enjoyed maths, I think it was just the actual day of my exam because I'd been predicted a much higher grade, and I did the higher paper, and I, I know, roughly, I can't remember the exact, the exact exam but I know around the time of my GCSEs 'cos I was ill but I couldn't stay off, and to be honest I didn't revise that much, I got, I knacked it up for myself, so, that's why I ended up with a poor grade but I've always enjoyed maths . . . for some reason I seem to have a brilliant understanding of it and it wasn't from my teachers, where did I get it from? . . . I'm probably one of the few who really enjoy maths.

This positioning is very typical of Louise's interviews and is consistent throughout the three years of the degree programme; there is a strong desire to be seen as good at maths (Mendick, 2006). Her discussion signifies the dilemma that educators are faced with when discussing ability; she states that everyone can achieve and tries to remove ability by discussing her choice (in a neoliberal fashion). However, she is drawn into essentialising qualities of the 'naturally able' mathematical child.

Nicola similarly constructs herself as the always-already 'able' mathematical child, the romantic inquirer of mathematics education research and 'gifted and talented' policy documents. She states that her success in mathematics was not related to the teaching she experienced but was due to herself:

ANNA: Do you think, would you say you're particularly good at maths, or . . .
NICOLA: I've always been good at maths, but getting past GCSE I think I've, just not 'cos the effort,

ANNA: Okay, so you didn't choose it [A-level mathematics]?
NICOLA: Well I did, but I did it for a month, and got bored of it and gave it up at A-Level.

Both Nicola and Louise are keen to take responsibility for their own progress. They also had the strongest positioning of themselves as the naturally 'able' mathematical child – the romantic natural inquirer. This is consistent throughout their interviews.

By Year 3 of the course, Nicola relates this to her students and widens the mathematics, rather than moving students on to the next objective. This seems to be restricted to those she ascribes as more 'able'. Hence, the task becomes one of herding the students on to similar trajectories rather than pushing for objective-specified progress.

NICOLA: So instead of pushing them on to another objective I try and give them a more challenging way of doing it, like with multiplication, while I'm doing basic multiplication, like for what is two times two days, I give them a grid that's got like five numbers in it.

This there are tensions around the various productions of progress, and we can ask if progress is about the completion of content-based objectives of educational policy or is it about "meaningful learning" (Battista, 1999), more akin to mathematics education research. Leah similarly expands the mathematics for those designated as more able.

LEAH: I feel frustrated because I wish I had more time to spend and I feel like pressurised because of the way you're expected to teach so much . . . I think as long as you focus on one thing and you bring it up to the level of that, the high ability children by expanding on it, it's okay that they do that or even just throwing in other elements and things I've done over the year.

Here, Leah produces a specific group of students as different to functional machines, this very much follows the mathematical child of mathematics education research. However, for Leah (and for Nicola) this 'real' mathematics is reserved for the already more able. This replicates the binary division that can be found in certain mathematics is only suitable for the natural gifted (traces of which are found in both policy and research) – thus reifying the natural mathematical child. This creates the myth of the 'real' mathematician and keeps mathematics out of reach to many, as Jane illustrates.

JANE: Because, if like, the higher achievers find a different way of doing it then that's fine, but just for the lower achievers to know that, you know, that first thing it should circle the lowest number, and then they need to find out how low it is, and those were the key bits I wanted them to realise . . . But I think it's important for them to understand what they're doing, and why they're doing it, you know, to know that they are finding the smallest number.

Thus, Jane she restricts thinking and choice to the "higher achievers." Within this the mathematical child is a naturally inquisitive child who is capable of performing understanding. This is possible only for those who, unlike her, are deemed naturally able: someone who is outwardly successful at mathematics (with a grade B) yet it is still not good enough. Although as before, the understanding that is attached to the 'normal' 'non-mathematical' students is about functionality and being able to do.

Jane is aware of the romantic ideal; she is also aware of her own discursive contradictions that restrict this version of mathematics:

JANE: I think the main thing is to let children explore maths, to not, you know not let it just be abstract, let it be concrete by them exploring it and looking at examples and things and to know that it's not just me that struggles with maths, everybody does to a certain extent and I think the biggest thing I've learnt is that you have to work through it yourself and explore it yourself, you know, just because you don't get the answer right the first time doesn't matter I think. But I think there will always be that ingrained thing with me that it's either right or wrong.

Jane is perhaps aware that the romantic version of mathematics belongs to a privileged, select group of people: those who are naturally curious and exist only through their cognition – this is the 'real' mathematical child.

As already shown, the pre-service teachers' essentialise students more so than educational policy documents. They form judgements based on groupings and perceived 'ability'. Moreover, they often see students as defined by ability over other characteristics; it was the most dominant theme of their interviews. However, they also have functional expectations in that they know there are certain levels that pupils should achieve. This results in confusion and frustration. As such, when ability is enacted in the classroom it is not used to mobilise pupils as the fantasy of educational policy suggests; instead, ability demobilises, particularly for the lower groups, the ones who are most in need of movement.

The attachment of a fixed ability to students of mathematics is a discourse that seems to permeate both pre-service teacher talk and popular culture and society. It is difficult to find a story where someone once was weak at mathematics and got better. Instead, stories of the mathematical genius from a young age persist – such as the Anne-Marie Imafidon who gained a GCSE in mathematics at 11 and a master's degree from Oxford in mathematics at 19. This story in undoubtedly wonderful for Imafidon and women in STEM, but it is not usual, and it does nothing to break down the privileging of mathematics as something unique and done by only a talented few.

I have got better at writing by practising and by reading many diverse works. I can see this by looking at items I wrote 10 years again and comparing them to now. Potentially mathematics struggles to follow discourses such as these, as it is experienced as objective after objective after objective; you succeed in one aspect, and then another vast mountain comes along. In that respect you can see why mathematics education researchers look for a more 'open' or project-based approach to mathematics; they have the hope that this is equitable to all. However, the way it is realised in practice is that it does the opposite – it excludes. Just as there are those that do functional mathematics more easily there are those that will approach 'investigative mathematics more easily, in this way studying mathematics is always already divisive. Whilst it is held up as such as a marker of intelligence, such a marker of success at school, and such an important part of society, there is a struggle to find ways around this.

Social media and the 2.0 generation

Since the above research was conducted in England, and after the New Labour years, there has been a move away from Continued Professional Development (CPD) through centralised government, and potentially overt government rule. As discussed in Chapter 4, *The National Strategy* – New Labour's flagship strategy – was abandoned early under the next government' s rule, alongside elements such as *Every Child Matters*. Moreover, the educational narrative that stems from the current Conservative government is that power has been dispersed to the people on the ground. The official rhetoric is that the Conservative government categorically promotes "more and more schools run – and more and more decisions made – by teachers, not politicians" (Gove, 2014, para.11). As such, there has been a visible movement away from the micromanaging of practices seen under New Labour. However, what does remain is the monitoring of the 'success' of school students, teachers, schools, and local authorities, as this "norm becomes the criterion for evaluating individuals" (Foucault, 1989g, 197) and schools. Specifically, the government is clear that it will hold schools "to account for rigorous, fairly measured outcomes" (DfE, 2016, p. 9). Thus, the official message is that teachers and schools are 'free' to do what they want, but if they 'fail', they will be disciplined and punished and shaped in the government's mould. As such, it is the idea of freedom that is presented, but instead, society is weighted under increasing regulation and systems of control. The illusion of self-governance is key to the success of neoliberalism (Rose, 1999a).

In spite of this covert surveillance, the dominant spaces of educational pedagogical discourse have arguably moved beyond 'traditional' policy and research to a more fluid arena infiltrated by teacher 'expertise'. Whilst the judgments of schools are similar to the New Labour era, the spaces for discussions have altered drastically over the last seven years. In the first instance, the increasing privatisation of the sector has led private companies to conduct training and CPD for schools, some of which are run by practising or former teachers. In addition the general trend towards teacher-led CPD, with teachmeets – which are informal places to share 'best' practice – and more 'in-house' training, suggests that teachers voices are finding more of a place within mainstream pedagogical discourses; these teachers have agency yet are subjected to many forms of governance.

I suggest this movement has been enabled not only by a shift in governance but also by the change in the manner that teachers can interact. Particularly, the rise of social media (including Twitter, Pintrest, blogs, and vlogs) has given a space that plays with traditional hegemonic power boundaries, as well as with time, space, and place. Schoolteachers no longer have to limit their discussion to their classroom; they are no longer contained by their department or their school.

Web 2.0 technologies have drastically altered how we interact with people on both a local and a global level. Technologies, in general, disrupt our interpretations of space and time, but for recent users of the internet this has multiplied with the shift towards audience participation. No longer is the web a place to story or obtain information; it is now a place to share ideas and engage in active conversation. Thus, providing there is access to the Internet, a schoolteacher in a remote South American village can communicate with an educator in a remote part of Norway. An educator's resources that are shared on the Internet could theoretically be used by anyone around the world who has accessed the educator's site. The point is the classroom is no longer the container, and no longer is the teacher limited to receiving information from experts. The internet has "became a place where you participated; a dynamic space that was shaped (both intentionally and inadvertently) by your own actions and contributions" (Seargeant and Tagg, 2014, p. 2); it is a place to be an active contributor.

In addition, the Internet not only disrupts place; it also challenges traditional societal power relationships. It is possible that the online digital world can be read as a Foucauldian heterotopia – (an)other space. Heterotopias are sites that are outside of normal rules and boundaries of society, where "the displacement of time is matched by the disruption of space" (Johnson, 2006). Foucault argues that places such as cemeteries, asylums, and prisons fall under this description; these are spaces that sit outside the norms of modern society, where time takes on a different meaning, where space is constrained around a specific location. The internet similarly plays with both time and space. The localised time of your setting may not translate to the people you communicate with, or the activity you engage with. Moreover, time can be persevered and replayed. Tweets or posts on social media forums can be stored and reposted years later or set to post in advance. The space is similarly non-normative. The digital space does not exist in the physical world; instead, it is created by the user and those that interact with it. Users can present as whomever they choose; they can play with their own representation of identity. "Cyberspace is often anarchic, playful, and even carnivalesque" (Danet, Cyberpl@y 2001, p. 8). This is a 'staged' self that can be carefully created and edited and may have very little to do with a 'day-to-day' lived experience. Thus, the digital space is one that blurs boundaries between fiction and reality, a further part of heterotopias (Foucault, 1998). Further than this, the heterotopia allows for the breaking of power boundaries. There are not the same rules: The pre-service teacher can have more followers on Twitter than the headteacher; the chance to present is largely open to anyone who can find a voice. "Blogs, Twitter, and social media networks on the World Wide Web have opened up the conversation and levelled the playing field of the ordinary people to explore themselves without the usual gatekeepers" (Cross, 2011, p. 1). The methods of surveillance are not as regulated as the classroom or the school.

"The expectation becomes that this content is less regulated, more fluid, and more diverse, and that the dividing line between private or personal communication and publishing or broadcasting can be increasingly blurred" (Seargeant and Tagg, 2014, p. 4). The private and professional blend as the teacher becomes a noted online expert, as discussed recently by *The Secret Teacher*[1] in *The Guardian*.

Examining examples of these experts and the discussions they have allows us to query these power relations. It is possible that a space/place like Twitter, where there are "visible displays of one's networks of followers or friends" (Seargeant & Tagg, 2014, p. 9) and thus overt markers of celebrity/expertise, merely creates its own hierarchies and normative positionings. For example if we examine the best-selling books on education, many of those are written by very successful tweeters on Twitter – commonly (and possibly disparagingly) referred to as the twitterati;. Ross McGill is one of those – who has postponed himself as the "most influential blog on education In the UK" (McGill, 2016), with more than 140,000 followers – @teachertoolkit. McGill is producing himself as a neoliberal brand. The same is true for Tom Bennett, another prominent tweeter who has used his success for new opportunities. A former teacher he is now the founder of ResearchEd and an educational behaviour tsar for the current Conservative government. ResearchEd is advertised as "the online home for anyone interested in educational research, what it means, and how it can – or can't – make a difference in the classroom" (ResearchED, 2016); thus, it is said to perform a bridge between research and the classroom; educational research has long been criticised for its lack of application to the classroom. ResearchEd has been very successful, hosting conferences in various parts of the (Western) world. Its website, titled 'workingoutwhatworks', and the logo designed around a microscope signal its alignment to 'serious' 'scientific' inquiry, following trends in educational research. It is clear that to be taken seriously educational research is not a fuzzy social science but is an objective incontestable place of absolute truth.

For practitioners of mathematics there are similarly superstars that are held in high regard, and there is certainly a blurring of boundaries between research and practice. There is also a rise in general pedagogies that focus on practical advice; however, the binary 'Math Wars' are still evident, which is shown in the following illustrative discussion from Twitter – which took place in June 2014. I have kept them anonymous out of respect of their confidentiality, in spite of this discussion being in the public domain. I have also presented it as one conversation, when, in reality, Twitter works through reactions to individual posts.

PERSON B: You're missing an interesting tension in the new NC [National Curriculum], which is worth the 350,000 discussing. How are 'fluency & 'enquiry' related? @PersonC
PERSON A: @PersonB @PersonC Fluency is the foundation you need for enquiry?
PERSON B: Now this is the discussion we should be having @PersonA . . . or is it fluency developed more effectively as part of enquiry? @PersonC
PERSON A: @PersonB @PersonC No, that's just cognitive overload. Enquiry is the pinnacle of maths, not the foundation.

PERSON C: @PersonA @PersonB Is this really a discussion we need? Maths has been taught for a long time . . . we already know how to do it
PERSON E: @PersonA @PersonB @PersonC enquiry & fluency are [*sic*] surely be a cycle. New maths wasn't created by practicing what was already known.
PERSON C: @PersonE @PersonA @PersonB Oh God XXXX now you have got me involved in this nonsense! I'm biting my lip
PERSON A: @PersonC @PersonE @PersonA *sits back and opens the popcorn*
PERSON B: Disappointing, @PersonA! Thought you were open to debate. @PersonC
PERSON A: @PersonB @PersonC OH [sic] I am, just worth making the joke
PERSON B: I think that argument underestimates the skill of teachers who can balance cognitive demand with inquiry & exploration. @PersonA @PersonC
PERSON D: @PersonB @PersonA @PersonC I'd say it's a dissuasion you [sic] trying to manufacture out of your own self interest.
PERSON B: @PersonD @PersonA @PersonC Possibly, but obviously the authors of the NC thought fluency & enquiry are compatible; others disagree.
PERSON A: @PersonB @PersonD @PersonC Of course they're compatible you can't do enquiry without fluency (which is the reward of enquiry)
PERSON B: @PersonC @PersonD @PersonA Perhaps that's where we depart, because it works the other way round as well: fluency is the reward of enquiry?
PERSON A: @PersonB @PersonD @Person No. Fluency can be established without enquiry.

There are many aspects of this discussion that are worth examination. First, the teaching and learning of mathematics are still seen as within these binaries. The attempt by @PersonE to discuss a cyclical relationship is ignored; second, the admonition from either side that the other side is dangerous to teachers and students; third, these tweeters are experts in receipt of incontestable truths. For all these points, it is easy to see how someone may be seduced by a clear binary solution. In addition, that @PersonB states that "maths has been taught for a long time . . . we already know how to do it" is both arrogant and naïve. As stated, the teaching and learning of mathematics are often positioned as not good enough; moreover, many children find learning mathematics very difficult. The concern with Twitter is that whilst it offers space for anyone to become an expert, part of anyone's success is around 'entertaining' tweets and personality (see tweets 7–9 earlier). Moreover, the cult of celebrity is apparent, where you need to be in the on-trend crowd saying the on-trend things; as *The Guardian*'s Secret Teacher states, "[i]t felt like one big club I wasn't allowed to be a member of" (Secret Teacher, 2016).

Thus, there is a shifting of power through Twitter, however arguably new power regimes are created, through self-styled experts that work on the power of celebrity. For example, a recent call for action from 'educational reformers' (Vaughan, 2016) consisted of several prominent users of Twitter, alongside founders of academy chains and frees schools. As such, it is possible to suggest that these educational 'reformers' are deliberately positioning themselves away from the 'experts' of the academy. Thus, Twitter may mirror the privatisation of education that stems from current neoliberalism societies.

It is fair to say that Twitter and social media do offer more access to professional development. Teacher- and education-related hashtags[2] are often trending, as teachers actively discuss their ideas and practice. As such, it is clear that there is an appetite to debate educational expertise and not just to impart knowledge, and Twitter offers an exciting discursive space to do this. Teachers are no longer predominantly influenced by the academy or by educational policy; however, the old narratives of mathematics and the binary 'maths wars' of 'inquiry' versus 'traditional' mathematics or inquiry as the pinnacle or as the foundation of mathematics are still found. In this sense, as there are preferred versions of mathematics; there is always a preferred homogenous mathematical child, who often bears little relation to many children who experience the mathematics classroom.

Concluding remarks

Overall, there are many competing discourses that go into what it means to be a teacher. There is also a gap between what someone may say is the rhetoric and the action. Language is complex and should be viewed as such; it is not universal, innocent, or transparent. Thus, when teacher or teacher-educators discuss best practice, it would be advisable if they gave more consideration to the power that certain language brings. Certain ways of teaching are seen as legitimate classroom practice (by some), and there are very real targets that are expected from policy and accountability. What actually happens in the classroom is much messier, much more fluid. Children are not homogenous, they are not simply cognitive, and they do experience the world as such. This can leave teachers and students in very difficult positions when they do not experience the world as dominant discourses tell them they should and when they do not make the right kind of progress.

As they play with space and time, Twitter and social media bring new opportunities and new ways of gaining knowledge. However, with the short tweets and sound bites and the need to appear as expert, there is a tendency that people are looking for over-simplistic solutions. This is understandable in education, but one-size-fits-all has never really worked. Moreover, it can exclude and set many up to fail.

Notes

1 The Secret Teacher is a regular blog/article in *The Guardian* newspaper, which is written by different anonymous contributors – who are assumed to be teachers.
2 A hashtag is a type of metadata used to theme information on social media.

7 Messy bodies
What next?

An academic conclusion

I began this book by contesting the lens through which mathematics education, in general, and mathematics education research, specifically, produces itself, arguing that we are bound by the parameters that produce us and that as such, we can only see, say, and hear certain positions. As Foucault states, people, institutions, and societies

> govern (themselves and others) by the production of truth (I repeat once again that by production of truth I mean not the production of true utterances but the establishment of domains in which the practice of true and false can be made at once ordered and pertinent).
>
> (2003c, p. 252)

Once we accept these positions as real, we are always already bounded by them, as methods of maintaining this production. Hence, we may be propagating practices that exclude many from mathematics. That is the crux of this book, as I unpack norms of the mathematical child and the work these do in relation to who is included and excluded from mathematics: that mathematics is deeply embedded in progress of the self and the state, that the 'good' of mathematics is all many are permitted to see.

Specifically, I argue that in educational policy, the mathematical child is produced as a functional automaton and within the dominant strands of mathematics education research, as a 'natural' romantic inquirer. Moreover, I contend that these constructions were most often hidden from view and thus are taken for granted as the truth. As such, they were always already parts of the documentation, and the mathematical child is always already predetermined and constituted around this version of the normal. Furthermore, this leads to inclusions and exclusions from the mathematics classroom.

Both of these productions of the mathematical child, from mathematics education research and New Labour educational policy, are based on the normal cognitive child, but this takes different forms within these different domains. Specifically, and as stated, the construction of the mathematical child of mathematics education research is a 'romantic' natural inquirer, someone who is keen to achieve and thrives on problem-solving and discovery. This position draws from a Rousseauian perspective where the child is a state of nature (Rousseau, 1755/2007) and/or from developmental psychology, which is constructed around the natural child and the concept of maturation (James et al., 1998). However, as Walkerdine (1998b) clearly demonstrates, the child of developmental psychology was defined by the process that produces them. Both Rousseau and developmental psychology assume that the child is natural and free to make decisions. Hence, the position of mathematics education research both produces progress as a hierarchy of reason and rationality, as well as romanticising a "golden age" of the past. The mathematical child of New Labour educational policy is similar in that it is concerned with the cognitive child but different in that its basis is not in nature or hierarchical development but instead is in the child as a functional automaton. This mathematical child is a product of a programmed production line who completes objectives through the demonstration of outputs in a mechanistic fashion. Hence, what is missing from both these productions is the mathematical child as social or cultural, as different or messy. Furthermore, what is absent is the mathematical child as different on different days and as connected to the wider world. Instead, we see how both mathematics education research and educational policy construct and thus produce a version of the normal mathematical child that is an impossible fiction.

Throughout, I demonstrated that these were impossible fictions that pre-service teacher struggled to find in their mathematics classrooms. Instead, I argued that both teacher and their pupils are complex doers of mathematics, caught up in cognitive, social, cultural, and emotional positions. Moreover, they are not universal or uniform categories and do not behave as such. The mathematics classroom, the student-teacher, and the pupils were all messy. Teaching is a process which is caught up with the teacher's identities, similarly doing mathematics is caught up with the child's identities. As such, what is mathematically possible for any pupil is a complex hybrid of these.

One of the most overriding aspects of the mathematics classroom that strongly influenced the construction of the mathematical child within the student-teachers' classrooms was the construct of mathematical ability, specifically, for everyone to have mobility and opportunity; the mathematical child is constructed as special and as more (naturally) 'able'; this gives them mobility and the right to greater 'progress'. These children perform 'real' mathematics through demonstrating 'understanding' and 'confidence'. Furthermore, this position is enhanced through mathematics education research's commitment to the romantic natural inquirer and to progressive pedagogies, despite a widespread critique of ability within the field. In contrast, the concept of 'natural' ability for the less able in educational policy is disregarded. Instead, anyone below the norm is repositioned as "under-attaining", and as functional automata they are expected to move seamlessly through targets and levels. However, in practice this does not happen because of the wider discourses which construct many as outside the bounds of the mathematical child.

130 *Messy bodies*

Teachers do (and will) struggle with tensions between competing discourses, especially when such value is attached to them. Moreover, they will find it particularly difficult when discourses do not acknowledge each other. What is perhaps most concerning, and what is drawn out of this book, is the inherent assumptions that are constructed about the mathematical child and the reification of the normal. These are not to be disregarded, "this fiction of what a normal person is like has important effects, according to Foucault, in courtroom, prisons, and various other institutions such as universities" (Pickett, 1996, p. 453). In this case, there are assumptions about what progress pupils should be making and how they should do and demonstrate this. Furthermore, this determines who has value.

I would like to suggest some implications, or rather considerations, for teachers, education policy makers, and educational researchers. In the first instance, I suggest we should question what else we do when we place certain behaviours, such as progress, understanding, and confidence upon pedestals. Moreover, we should interrupt these dominant discourses of mathematics education. For example, we can disrupt what we mean by progress by contesting the need to demonstrate it as linear and as unproblematic. Instead, we must query what we mean by progress and examine its cultural relevance. We do not need to privilege understanding but instead see it as part of a complex process of learning that includes gaining knowledge. Instead of confidence, we could at times encourage doubt and questioning. We could foster acceptance around worry and suggest that struggling with mathematics can be conducive to learning it. In addition, we could stop producing children's understanding and confidence as highly valued characteristics and instead question how we identify them in children as a way of disrupting their naturalisation within some bodies and not others. Also, we could allow emotional responses to mathematics, ones that can at first appear negative. Hence, we must acknowledge that children doing mathematics are not simply cognitive beings but are complex and made up of emotions and social and cultural subjectivities. Finally, we should all consider what work we do when we promote something as necessary or good, particularly that mathematics is incontestable as a vital part of society.

It is important that these final points are considered not only by mathematics teachers but also by mathematics education researchers, who too often construct themselves as removed from the discourses that circulate and create positions or 'problems' within mathematics. Hence, I challenge some of the norms upon which mathematics education is based. Particularly, I suggest that the mathematics education research community 'should' look for alternative ways around essentialising and/or normalising the mathematical child. More than this, they 'should' examine themselves in relation to what they do and what they promote. They could ask what their work would look like if it did not start with the promotion of mathematics education,

Of course, I too am not removed from this. However, in this book I have deliberately attempted to disengage from trends in mathematics education and its dominant discourses. Throughout I have used Foucault to do this and to be aware of the parameters that produce us. As Foucault states it is,

> [d]iscourse – the discourse that names, that describes, that designates, that analyzes, that recounts, that metaphorizes, etc. – constitutes the field of the object and at the same time creates power effects that make it possible for subjugation to take place.
>
> (1989f, p. 157)

For policy makers, it is fairly obvious that they need to adopt a less simplistic one-size-fits-all approach to many things. However, two sizes are just as damaging creating more divisions. For all the mathematics educational community I am suggesting more complexity and nuance and more messy, fuzzy areas and less box fitting and less best fit. I acknowledge this is difficult in an era which privileges an over-simplistic 'what works' version of educational research, policy, and practice. Beyond this I do not wish to offer 'better' alternatives; as Foucault states,

> [t]he work of an intellectual is not to mold the political will of others; it is, through the analyses that he [*sic*] does in his own field, to re-examine evidence and assumptions, to shake up habitual ways of working and thinking, to dissipate conventional familiarities, to re-evaluate rules and institutions and starting from this re-problematization (where he occupies his specific profession as an intellectual) to participate in the formation of a political will (where he has his role as citizen to play).
>
> (1989b, pp. 462–463)

Mathematics and Education both appeal to a progressive future of emancipation and for the good of society. Thus, I suggest it is these hidden forms of control that masquerade as liberation that warrant further consideration.

An alternative personal conclusion

I have often been told I need to be more confident. I am not sure why or why people make that judgement. In all honesty I would rather they judge me on my competence rather than on the *appearance* of whether I know what I am talking about. I like to doubt – I think there is something honest and intellectual about holding an opinion as a possibility rather than as an incontestable fact.

How do they judge that I am not confident in what I say anyway? Is it that I offer my ideas as one possible solution or that I do not present myself in the manner that people expect? Why should I? As a small-in-stature, young-looking, comprehensive school–educated gay woman I am not sure I am offered the appearance of confidence; as an older heterosexual man, maybe I would be (although I am aware of the privilege that the white colour of my skin and my cisgender identity both afford me). For me, there is security in uncertainty; there is freedom in doubt.

In my first university job I expected to find this freedom, and instead, I found that there was a particular message to adhere to – there was an expected, departmental-favoured way of talking about the teaching and learning of Mathematics – that mathematics should undoubtedly be taught in pursuit of this vague term called *understanding* – I was sad that this was expected. I felt very much straitjacketed and could not find the freedom within. It was not what I thought an academic position entailed.

When I was 8 years old, my school report said I thought mathematically; once the was written, I thought that was who I was. And science and mathematics were more important than the arts anyway. Clever people studied science and mathematics; these subjects led to real jobs that made a difference. So I was told . . .

An alternative succinct conclusion

ONE: The Child is seen as the hope of the nation rather than just the relationship to itself;

TWO: The mathematical child is an amplified version of this with societies investment in rationality and reason;

THREE: Mathematics is seen as integral to society is a myth that the majority cannot think outside;

FOUR: Mathematics teaching and learning are constructed as not good enough;

FIVE: Governments and educational research are all deeply invested in these myths and the power of mathematics;

SIX: Governments and educational research construct doing mathematics as a cognitive activity;

SEVEN: Mathematics is a socially and culturally constructed activity;

EIGHT: Governments and educational research enact very specific ways of doing mathematics that do not speak to each and bear little relation to teacher and student experience;

NINE: Governments and educational research construct their own homogenous versions of the mathematical child;

TEN: The standardised child of neoliberalism was enabled by the Western developmental psychological child;

ELEVEN: These fictitious constructions and myths keep mathematical out of reach to many;

TWELVE: The authority of these institutions makes them difficult to contest;

THIRTEEN: It is almost impossible for the majority to question an investment in any of this – you cannot bite the hand that feeds you.

References

Acker, S. (Ed.). (1989). *Teachers, gender and careers*. London: Falmer Press.
Acker, S. (1999). *The realities of teachers' work: Never a dull moment*. London: Cassell.
Adams, R. (2016). Government drops plans to make all schools in England academies. *The Guardian*. Retrieved May 2017, from www.theguardian.com/education/2016/may/06/government-backs-down-over-plan-to-make-all-schools-academies
Adams, R., & Weale, S. (2017). New Ofsted Chief: 'I want everyone to see us as a force for improvement'. *The Guardian*. Retrieved May 2017, from https://www.theguardian.com/education/2017/jan/09/ofsted-chief-inspector-schools-amanda-spielman
Ahmed, S. (2013). *Making feminist points*. Retrieved from https://feministkilljoys.com/2013/09/11/making-feminist-points/
Alexander, R. J. (1994). *Innocence and experience: Reconstructing primary education*. Stoke-on-Trent: Trentham.
Alexander, R. J. (2004). Still no pedagogy? Principle, pragmatism and compliance in primary education. *Cambridge Journal of Education, 34*(1), 7–34.
Alexander, R. J. (Ed.). (2010). *Children, their world, their education: Final report and recommendations of the Cambridge primary review*. Abingdon: Routledge.
Allen, A. (2014). *Benign violence: Education in and beyond the age of reason*. Basingstoke: Palgrave Macmillan.
Apple, M. W. (2003). *The state and the politics of knowledge*. New York: Routledge Falmer.
Archard, R. (1993). *Children: Rights and childhood*. London: Routledge.
Arestis, P., & Sawyer, M. (2005). Neoliberalism and the third way. In A. Saad-Filho & D. Johnson (Eds.), *Neoliberalism: A critical reader*. London; Ann Arbor, MI: Pluto Press.
Ariès, P. (1962/1996). *Centuries of childhood*. London: Pimlico.
Ball, D. L. (1988). *Research on teaching mathematics: Making subject knowledge part of the equation*. East Lang, MI: Office of Educational Research and Improvement.
Ball, S. J. (1993a). Education markets, choice and social class: The market as a class strategy in the UK and the USA. *British Journal of Sociology of Education, 14*(1), 3–19.
Ball, S. J. (1993b). Education policy, power relations and teachers' work. *British Journal of Educational Studies, 41*(2), 106–121.
Ball, S. J. (1994). *Education reform: A critical and post-structural approach*. Buckingham; Philadelphia: Open University Press.

References

Ball, S. J. (2003). The teacher's soul and the terrors of performativity. *Journal of Education Policy, 18*(2), 215–228.

Ball, S. J. (2006). *Education policy and social class: The selected works of Stephen J. Ball.* Abingdon, Oxon: Routledge.

Ball, S. J. (2008). *The education debate.* Bristol: The Policy Press.

Ball, S. J., Kenny, A., & Gardiner, D. (1990). Literacy, politics and the teaching of English. In I. Goodson & P. Medway (Eds.), *Bringing English to order.* London: Falmer.

Ball, S. J., Maguire, M., & Macrae, S. (2000). *Choice, pathways and transitions post-16: New youth, new economies in the global city.* London; New York: RoutledgeFalmer.

Barmby, P., Harries, T., Higgins, S., & Suggate, J. (2009). The array representation and primary children's understanding and reasoning in multiplication. *Educational Studies in mathematics, 70*(3), 217–241.

Battista, M. T. (1999). Fifth graders' enumeration of cubes in 3D arrays: Conceptual progress in an inquiry-based classroom. *Journal for Research in mathematics Education, 30*(4), 417–448.

Battiste, M. T. (2013) *Decolonizing education: Nourishing the learning spirit.* Saskatoon, Canada: Purich Publishing

Best, S., & Kellner, D. (1991). *Postmodern theory: Critical interrogations.* Basingstoke: Communications and Culture.

Bibby, T. (2001). *Primary school teachers' personal and professional relationships with mathematics.* London: King's College, University of London.

Bibby, T. (2002). Shame: An emotional response to doing mathematics as an adult and a teacher. *British Educational Research Journal, 28*(5), 705–721.

Blair, T. (1996). *Leader's speech: Blackpool 1996.* Blackpool: The Labour Party

Bloom, B. (Ed.). (1956). *Taxonomy of educational objectives: Handbook 1, cognitive domain/by a committee of college and university examiners.* London: Longmans.

Boaler, J. (1996). Learning to lose in the mathematics classroom: A critique of traditional schooling practices. *Qualitative Studies in Education, 9*(1), 17–34.

Boaler, J. (1997a). Equity, empowerment and different ways of knowing. mathematics *Education Research Journal, 9*(3), 325–342.

Boaler, J. (1997b). *Experiencing school mathematics: Teaching styles, sex and setting.* Buckingham: Open University Press.

Boaler, J. (1997c). Reclaiming school mathematics: The girls fight back. *Gender and Education, 9*(3), 285–305.

Boaler, J. (1997d). When even the winners are losers: Evaluating the experience of "top set" students. *Journal of Curriculum Studies, 29*(2), 165–182.

Boaler, J. (1998a). Alternative approaches to teaching, learning and assessing mathematics *Evaluation and Program Planning, 21*(2), 129–141.

Boaler, J. (1998b). Mathematical equity: Under achieving boys or sacrificial girls? *Journal of Inclusive Education, 2*(2), 119–134.

Boaler, J. (1998c). Open and closed mathematics approaches: Student experiences and understandings *Journal for Research in mathematics Education, 29*(1), 41–62.

Boaler, J. (2002). *Experiencing school mathematics: Traditional and reform approaches to teaching and their impact on student learning.* Mahwah, NJ: Lawrence Erlbaum Associates.

Boaler, J. (2008, December). When politics took the place of inquiry: A response to the National mathematics Advisory Panel's review of instructional practices. *Educational Researcher*, 588–594.

Boaler, J. (2009). *The elephant in the classroom: Helping children learn and love maths.* London: Souvenir Press.

Boaler, J. (2014). Britain's maths policy simply doesn't add up. *Daily Telegraph.* Retrieved from www.telegraph.co.uk/education/educationnews/11031288/Britains-maths-policy-simply-doesnt-add-up.html

Boaler, J. (2016). *Mathematical mindsets: Unleashing students' potential through creative math, inspiring messages and innovative teaching.* San Francisco, CA: Jossey-Bass.

Boekaerts, M., Seegers, G., & Vermeer, H. (1995). Solving math problems: Where and why does the solution process go astray? *Educational Studies in mathematics,* 28(3), 241–262.

Boero, P. (2008). *Autonomy and identity of mathematics education: Why and how to use external theories.* Paper presented at the 11th International Congress on mathematics Education, Rome.

Boylan, M., & Povey, H. (2012). Ability thinking. In D. Leslie & H. Mendick (Eds.), *Debates in mathematics education* (pp. 7–16). Abingdon, Oxon; New York: Routledge.

Britzman, D. (2000). "The question of belief": Writing poststructural ethnography. In E. A. St Pierre & W. Pillow (Eds.), *Working the ruins: Feminist poststructural theory in methods in education.* New York: Routledge.

Brown, M., Askew, M., Millet, A., & Rhodes, V. (2003). The key role of educational research in the development and evaluation of the National Numeracy Strategy. *British Educational Research Journal,* 29(5), 655–672.

Brown, T., & Clarke, D. (2013). Institutional context for research in mathematics education. In M. A. Clements, A. J. Bishop, C. Keitel, J. Kilpatrick, & F. K. S. Leung (Eds.), *Third international handbook of mathematics education* (pp. 459–484). New York; London: Springer.

Brown, T., Jones, L., & Bibby, T. (2004). Identifying with mathematics in Initial Teacher Training. In M. Walshaw (Ed.), mathematics *education within the postmodern* (pp. 161–180). Greenwich: Information Age Publishing.

Brown, T., & McNamara, O. (2011). *Becoming a mathematics teacher.* Dordrecht; Heidelberg; London; New York: Springer.

Brown, W. (2001). *Politics out of history.* Princeton, NJ; Oxford: Princeton University Press.

Buckingham, D. (2000). *After the death of childhood: Growing up in the age of electronic media.* Malden, MA: Polity Press.

Buckingham, D. (2011). *The material child: Growing up in consumer culture.* Cambridge; Malden, MA: Polity.

Buckingham, D., & Scanlon, M. (2003). *Education, entertainment and learning in the home.* Buckingham; Philadelphia: Open University Press.

Burman, E. (1992). Development psychology and the postmodern child. In J. Doherty, E. Graham, & M. Malek (Eds.), *Postmodernism and the social sciences.* New York: St Martin's Press.

Burman, E. (2008a). *Deconstructing developmental psychology.* London: Routledge.

Burman, E. (2008b). *Developments: Child, image, nation.* Hove, Sussex; New York: Routledge.

Burman, E., & Parker, I. (1993). *Discourse analytic research.* London; New York: Routledge.

Burton, L. (2004). "Confidence is everything" – Perspectives of teachers and students on learning mathematics. *Journal of mathematics Teacher Education,* 7(4), 357–381.

Calderhead, J. (1988). *Teachers' professional learning*. London: Falmer Press.
Caputo, J. D. (Ed.). (1997). *Deconstruction in a nutshell: A conversation with Jacques Derrida*. New York: Fordham University Press.
Carabine, J. (2001). Unmarried motherhood 1830–1990: Genealogical analysis. In M. Wetherell, S. Taylor, & S. Yates (Eds.), *Discourse as data: A guide for analysis* (pp. 267–310). London: Sage in association with The Open University.
Central Advisory Council for Education. (1967a). *Children and their primary schools: A report of the Central Advisory Council for Education (England). Vol.1, the report.* London: HMSO.
Central Advisory Council for Education. (1967b). *Children and their primary schools: A report of the Central Advisory Council for Education (England). Vol.2, Research and surveys*. London: HMSO.
Chetcuti, D., & Griffiths, M. (2002). The implications for student self-esteem of ordinary differences in schools: The cases of Malta and England. *British Educational Research Journal, 28*(4), 529–549.
Christians, C. (2000). Ethics and politics in qualitative research. In N. K. Denzin & Y. S. Lincoln (Eds.), *Handbook of qualitative research* (pp. 133–155). Thousand Oaks; London; New Delhi: Sage.
Clarke, B., Clarke, D. M., Emanuelsson, G., Johansson, B., Lambdin, D. V., Lester, F., . . . Walby, K. (Eds.). (2004). *International perspectives on learning and teaching mathematics*. Goteburg: National Center for mathematics Education, Goteburg University.
Coben, D. (Ed.). (2003). *Adult numeracy: Review of research and related literature*. London: National Research and Development Centre for Adult Literacy and Numeracy.
Cockcroft, W. H. (1982). mathematics *counts: Report of the committee of inquiry into the teaching of mathematics in schools under the chairmanship of Dr W H Cockcroft*. London: HMSO
Coffey, A., & Delamont, S. (2000). *Feminism and the classroom teacher: Research, praxis, and pedagogy*. London: Falmer Press.
Conservative and Unionist Party. (2017). *Forward, together: Our plan for a stronger Britain and a prosperous future*. London: The Conservative Party.
Cook, D. T., & Kaiser, S. B. (2004). Betwixt and be Tween: Age ambiguity and the sexualization of the female consuming subject. *Journal of Consumer Culture, 4*(2), 203–227.
Crendowski, M. (Writer) (2007–ongoing). *The big bang theory*. Burbank, CA: Warner Bros.
Cross, M. (2011). *Bloggerati, twitterati: How blogs and Twitter are transforming popular culture*. Santa Barbara, CA: Greenwood Publishing Group.
Crossley, M., & K. Watson. (2003). *Comparative and international research in education – globalisation, context and difference*. Abingdon: Routledge.
Curtis, B. (2006). *Is the primary National strategy transforming or ossifying English primary schools*. Paper presented at the Nordic Educational Research Association Conference. University of Orebo, Sweden.
Dale, R. (2001). Shaping the sociology of education over half-a-century. In J. Demaine (Ed.), *Sociology of education today* (pp. 5–29). Basingstoke: Palgrave Macmillan.
Danet, B. (2001). *Cyberpl@y. Communicating online*.Oxford; New York: Berg.

Darling, J. (1994). *Child-centred education and its critics.* London: Paul Chapman Publishing.

Davies, B. (2003). *Frogs and snails and feminist tales: Preschool children and gender.* Cresskill, NJ: Hampton Press.

Davison, D. M., Mitchell, J. E., & Montana, B. (2008). How is mathematics education philosophy reflected in the math wars. *The Montana mathematics Enthusiast,* 5(1), 143–154.

DCFS. (2007a). *The children's plan: Building brighter futures.* London: DCFS.

DCFS. (2007b). *Getting there: Able pupils who lose momentum in English and mathematics in key stage 2.* London: DCFS.

DCFS. (2008a). *Identifying gifted and talented learners – getting started.* London: DCFS.

DCFS. (2008b). *Making good progress in key stage 2 mathematics.* London: DCFS.

DCFS. (2009a). *21st century schools: Your schools, your children, our future.* London: DCFS.

DCFS. (2009b). *Moving on in mathematics: Narrowing the gap.* London: DCFS.

DCSF. (2009c). *Keeping up – pupils who fall behind in key stage 2.* London: DCFS.

de Freitas, E. (2013). What were you thinking? A Deleuzian/Guattarian analysis of communication in the mathematics classroom. *Educational Philosophy and Theory,* 45(3), 287–300.

Derrida, J. (1994). *The Villnova roundtable: A conversation with Jacques Derrida.* Villanova, PA: Villanova University.

Derrida, J. (1998). *Resistances of psychoanalysis* Stanford, CA: Stanford University Press.

Dewey, J. (1902/1956). *The child and the curriculum; and the school and society.* Chicago; London: University of Chicago Press.

Dewey, J. (1916). *Democracy and education: An introduction to the philosophy of education.* New York: Palgrave Macmillan.

DfE. (2010a). *The case for change.* Crown Copyright. Retrieved April 29, 2013, from www.education.gov.uk/publications/eOrderingDownload/DFE-00564-2010.pdf

DfE. (2010b). *The importance of teaching: The white paper 2010.* London: HMSO.

DfE. (2012). *New primary curriculum to bring higher standards in English, maths and science.* Crown Copyright. Retrieved June 11, 2013, from www.education.gov.uk/inthenews/inthenews/a00210127/newnatcurric

DfE. (2013). *School leaving age.* Retrieved September 5, 2013, from www.gov.uk/know-when-you-can-leave-school

DfE. (2014). *Raising the participation age.* Retrieved September 2014, from www.gov.uk/government/policies/increasing-opportunities-for-young-people-and-helping-them-to-achieve-their-potential/supporting-pages/raising-the-participation-age

DfE. (2016). *Educational excellence everywhere: The schools white paper.* London: DfE.

DfE. (2017). *Progress 8 and attainment 8: Guide for maintained secondary schools, academies and free schools.* London: Crown.

DfEE. (1997). *Excellence in schools.* Annesley: DfES.

DfEE. (1999). *National numeracy strategy framework for teaching mathematics.* Annesley: DfES.

DfEE. (2000). *Mathematical challenges for able pupils in key stages 1 and 2*. Annesley: DfES.
DfEE. (2001). *Schools: Achieving success*. Annesley: DfES.
DfES. (2003a). *Every child matters*. Annesley: DfES.
DfES. (2003b). *Aiming high: Raising the achievement of minority ethnic pupils*. Annesley: DfES.
DfES. (2004). *Increasing pupils' rate of progress in mathematics*. Annesley: DfES.
DfES. (2005). *Higher standards, better schools for all*. Norwich: HMSO.
DfES. (2006a). *Identifying gifted and talented pupils: Getting started*. Norwich: DfES.
DfES. (2006b). *Primary framework for literacy and mathematics*. Norwich: DfES.
DfES. (2006c). *Primary framework for literacy and mathematics: Core position papers underpinning the renewal of guidance for teaching literacy and mathematics*. Norwich: DfES.
DfES. (2007). *Making great progress – schools with outstanding rates of progression in key stage 2*. Norwich: DfES.
Dilnot, C., & Boliver, V. (2017). Admission to medicine and law at Russell Group universities: The impact of A-level subject choice. In P. J. Burke, A. Hayton, & J. Stevenson (Eds.), *Widening participation in higher education: Towards a reflexive approach to research and evaluation*. London: Trentham Books.
Direct Gov. (2008). *Beryl: Get confident and get on TV advertisement*. Retrieved May 1, 2008, from http://geton.direct.gov.uk/tv-advert.html
Donald, J. (1985). Beacons of the future: Schooling, subjection and subjectification. In V. Beechey & J. Donald (Eds.), *Subjectivity and social relations* (pp. 214–249). Milton Keyes: Open University Press.
Donaldson, M. (1978). *Children's minds*. London: Fontana/Collins.
Dorman, J. P., Adams, J. E., & Ferguson, J. (2003). A cross-national investigation of students' perceptions of mathematics classroom environments and academic efficacy in secondary schools. *International Journal of mathematics Teaching and Learning, 15*, 123–176.
Driscoll, M. P. (1994). *Psychology of learning for instruction*. Boston: Allyn and Bacon.
du Gay, P. (1996). *Consumption and identity at work*. London: Sage.
du Gay, P., Hall, S., Janes, L., Mackay, H., & Negus, K. (1997). *Doing cultural studies: The story of the Sony Walkman*. London; Thousand Oaks; New Delhi: Sage.
Duffin, J., & Simpson, A. (2002). Understanding their thinking: The tension between the cognitive and the affective. In D. Coben, J. O'Donoghue, & G. E. FitzSimons (Eds.), *Perspectives on adults learning mathematics* (pp. 83–99). New York: Kluwer Academic Publishers
Dweck, C. (2008). *Mindset: The new psychology of success*. New York: Ballatine Books.
Edelman, L. (2004). *No future: Queer theory and the death drive*. Durham; London: Duke University Press.
Elkind, D. (2007/1981). *The hurried child: Growing up too fast too soon* (25th anniversary ed.). Cambridge, MA: Da Capo Press.
Epstein, D. (1995). In our (new) right minds: The hidden curriculum and the academy. In L. Morley & V. Walsh (Eds.), *Feminist academics: Creative agents for change* (pp. 56–72). London: Taylor and Francis.
Epstein, D., Mendick, H., & Moreau, M.-P. (2010). Imagining the mathematician: Young people talking about popular representations of maths. *Discourse: Studies in the Cultural Politics of Education, 31*(1), 45–60.

Erickson, F. (1986). Qualitative methods in research on teaching. In M. C. Wittrock (Ed.), *The handbook of research on teaching* (pp. 119–161). New York: Palgrave Macmillan.

Ernest, P. (1991). *The philosophy of mathematics education*. London: Falmer Press.

Fennema, E., & Sherman, J. (1977). Sex-related differences in mathematics achievement, spatial visualization, and affective factors. *American Educational Research Journal, 14*, 51–71.

Fevre, R. W., & Bancroft, A. (2010). *Dead white men and other important people: Sociology's big ideas*. London: Palgrave Macmillan.

Flax, J. (1987). Postmodernism and gender relations in feminist theory. *Signs, 12*(4), 621–643.

Forestier, K., & Crossley, M. (2015). International education policy transfer – borrowing both ways: The Hong Kong and England experience. *Compare: A Journal of Comparative and International Education, 45*(5), 664–685.

Fosnot, C. T. (2013). *Constructivism: Theory, perspectives, and practice*. New York: Teachers College Press.

Foucault, M. (1970/2002). *The order of things*. Abingdon, Oxon: Routledge.

Foucault, M. (1972/2002). *The archaeology of knowledge*. London: Routledge.

Foucault, M. (1975). Interview with Roger-Pol Droit. *Le Monde*.

Foucault, M. (1977/1991). *Discipline and punishment: The birth of the prison*. London: Penguin.

Foucault, M. (1978/1998). *The history of sexuality (volume one): The will to knowledge*. London: Routledge.

Foucault, M. (1980a). *Power/knowledge: Selected interviews and other writings 1972–1977*. New York: Pantheon.

Foucault, M. (1980b). Prison talk. In C. Gordon (Ed.), *Power/knowledge: Selected interviews and other writings 1972–1977* (pp. 37–54). New York: Pantheon.

Foucault, M. (1980c). Truth and power. In C. Gordon (Ed.), *Power/knowledge: Selected interviews and other writings 1972–1977* (pp. 109–133). New York: Pantheon.

Foucault, M. (1980d). Two lectures. In C. Gordon (Ed.), *Power/knowledge: Selected interviews and other writings 1972–1977* (pp. 79–108). New York: Pantheon.

Foucault, M. (1984). Space, knowledge and power. In P. Rabinow (Ed.), *The Foucault reader* (pp. 239–256). London: Penguin.

Foucault, M. (1988). "The minimalist self", interview with Stephen Riggins. In L. Kritzman (Ed.), *Michael Foucault: Politics, philosophy, culture: Interviews and other writings, 1977–1984* (pp. 1–19). London: Routledge.

Foucault, M. (1989a). An aesthetics of existence. In S. Lotringer (Ed.), *Foucault live: Collected interviews, 1961–1984* (pp. 450–454). New York: Semiotext(e).

Foucault, M. (1989b). Concern for truth. In S. Lotringer (Ed.), *Foucault live: Collected interviews, 1961–1984* (pp. 455–464). New York: Semiotext(e).

Foucault, M. (1989c). The eye of power. In S. Lotringer (Ed.), *Foucault live: Collected interviews, 1961–1984* (pp. 226–240). New York: Semiotext(e).

Foucault, M. (1989d). The order of things. In S. Lotringer (Ed.), *Foucault live: Collected interviews, 1961–1984* (pp. 13–18). New York: Semiosext(e).

Foucault, M. (1989e). Power affects the body. In S. Lotringer (Ed.), *Foucault live: Collected interviews, 1961–1984* (pp. 207–213). New York: Semiotext(e).

Foucault, M. (1989f). Schizo-culture: Infantile sexuality. In S. Lotringer (Ed.), *Foucault live: Collected interviews, 1961–1984* (pp. 154–167). New York: Semiotext[e].

Foucault, M. (1989g). The social extension of the norm. In S. Lotringer (Ed.), *Foucault live: Collected interviews, 1961–1984* (pp. 196–199). New York: Semiotext(e).

Foucault, M. (1989h). Talk show. In S. Lotringer (Ed.), *Foucault live: Collected interviews, 1961–1984* (pp. 133–145). New York: Semiotext(e).

Foucault, M. (Ed.). (1989i). *Foucault live: Collected interviews, 1961–1984.* New York: Semitext(e).

Foucault, M. (1998). Different spaces. In J. Faubion (Ed.), *Aesthetics: The essential works* (Vol. 2, pp. 175–185). London: Allen Lane.

Foucault, M. (2003a). The ethic of the concern of the self as a practice of freedom. In P. Rabinow & N. Rose (Eds.), *The essential Foucault: Selections from essential works of Foucault, 1954–1984* (pp. 25–42). New York; London: The New Press.

Foucault, M. (2003b). Governmentality. In P. Rabinow & N. Rose (Eds.), *The essential Foucault: Selections from essential works of Foucault, 1954–1984* (pp. 229–245). New York; London: The New Press.

Foucault, M. (2003c). Questions of method. In P. Rabinow & N. Rose (Eds.), *The essential Foucault: Selections from essential works of Foucault, 1954–1984* (pp. 246–258). New York: The New Press.

Foucault, M. (2003d). The subject and power. In P. Rabinow & N. Rose (Eds.), *The essential Foucault: Selections from essential works of Foucault, 1954–1984* (pp. 126–144). New York; London: The New Press.

Foucault, M. (2003e). Technologies of the self. In P. Rabinow & N. Rose (Eds.), *The essential Foucault: Selections from essential works of Foucault, 1954–1984* (pp. 145–169). New York; London: The New Press.

Foucault, M. (2003f). What is enlightenment? In P. Rabinow & N. Rose (Eds.), *The essential Foucault: Selections from essential works of Foucault, 1954–1984* (pp. 43–57). New York; London: The New Press.

Foucault, M. (2003g). Nietzsche, genealogy, history. In P. Rabinow & N. Rose (Eds.), *The essential Foucault: Selections from essential works of Foucault, 1954–1984* (pp. 351–369). New York: The New Press.

Gergen, K. J. (2001). Self-narration in social life. In M. Wetherell, S. Taylor, & S. Yates (Eds.), *Discourse, theory and practice: A reader* (pp. 247–260). London: Sage.

Gersten, R., Ferrini-Mundy, J., Benbow, C., Clements, D. H., Loveless, T., Williams, V., . . . Banfield, M. (2008). *Chapter 6: Report of the task group on instructional practices.* Washington, DC: U.S. Department of Education. Retrieved October 26, 2008, www.ed.gov/about/bdscomm/list/mathpanel/report/instructional-practices.pdf

Gillborn, D., & Youdell, D. (2001). The new IQism: Intelligence, "ability" and the rationing of education. In J. Demaine (Ed.), *Sociology of education today* (pp. 65–99). Basingstoke: Palgrave Macmillan.

Gillies, D. (2008). Quality and equality: The mask of discursive conflation in education policy texts. *Journal of Education Policy, 23*(6), 685–699.

Gittens, D. (1998). *The child in question.* London: Palgrave Macmillan.

Gittens, D. (2009). The historical construction of childhood. In M. J. Kehily (Ed.) *An introduction to childhood studies* (pp. 35–49). Maidenhead: McGraw-Hill Education; Open University Press.

Gorard, S. (2013). *Research design: Creating robust approaches for the social sciences.* London: Sage.

Gorard, S. (2014). A proposal for judging the trustworthiness of research findings. *Radical Statistics, 110,* 47–59.

Gorard, S. (2015). Rethinking "quantitative" methods and the development of new researchers. *Review of Education, 3,* 72–96. doi:10.1002/rev3.3041

Gove, M. (2010a, December 14). *Oral evidence on the schools white paper.* Retrieved May 2017, from www.parliament.co.uk

Gove, M. (2010b, December 28). Michael Gove: My revolution for culture in classroom – why we must raise education standards so children can compete with rest of the world. *Daily Telegraph.* Retrieved July 10, 2013, www. telegraph.co.uk/education/8227535/Michael-Gove-my-revolution-for-culture-in- classroom.html

Gove, M. (2011) *Michael Gove speaks to the Royal Society on maths and science.* DfE. Retrieved May 2017, from www.gov.uk/government/speeches/michael-gove-speaks-to-the-royal-society-on-maths-and-science

Gove, M. (2012a). *Speech: Michael Gove to the education world forum.* DfE. Retrieved December 2017, www.gov.uk/government/speeches/michael-gove-to-the-education-world-forum

Gove, M. (2012b). *Letter to Tim Oates.* Retrieved June 12, 2012, http://media.educa tion.gov.uk/assets/files/pdf/l/secretary%20of%20state%20letter%20to%20 tim%20oates%20regarding%20the%20national%20curriculum%20review%2011%20june %202012.pdf

Gove, M. (2013a). I refuse to surrender to Marxist teachers hell-bent on destroying our schools: Education secretary berates "The New Enemies of Promise" for opposing his plans. *Daily Mail,* March 23. Retrieved March 25, 2013, www.dailymail.co.uk/debate/article-2298146/I-refuse-surrender-Marxist- teachers-hell-bent-destroying-schools-Education-Secretary-berates-new-enemies- promise-opposing-plans.html

Gove, M. (2013b). *Written statement to Parliament: "Education Secretary Michael Gove Sets out Plans for the New National Curriculum".* Retrieved July 10, 2013, www.gov.uk/government/speeches/education-reform-schools

Gove, M. (2014). *Michael Gove speaks about the future of education reform.* DfE. Retrieved May 2017, from www.gov.uk/government/speeches/michael-gove-speaks-about-the-future-of-education-reform

Grek, S., Lawna, M., Lingard, B., & Varjoc, J. (2009). North by northwest: Quality assurance and evaluation processes in European education. *Journal of Education Policy, 24*(2), 121–133.

Griffin, G. (1997). Teaching as a gendered experience. *Journal of Teacher Education, 48,* 7–18.

Grimshaw, T. (2007). Problematizing the construct of "the Chinese learner": Insights from ethnographic research. *Educational Studies, 33*(3), 299–311.

The Guardian. (2016). Secret teacher: I refuse to be a Kardashian with a PGCE. Retrieved October 2016, from www.theguardian.com/teacher-network/2016/jan/30/secret-teacher-refuse-kardashian-with-a-pgce-social-media-toxic

Guthrie, E. R. (1933). Association as a function of time interval. *Psychological Review, 40*(4), 355–367.

Hadow, W. H., & Great Britain, Board of Education, Consultative Committee on the Primary School. (1931). *Report of the Consultative committee on the primary school.* London: HMSO.

Hamilton, L., & Corbett-Whittier, C. (2013). *Using case study in education research.* London; Thousand Oaks, CA; New Delhi; Singapore: Sage.

Handal, B. (2003). Philosophies and pedagogies of mathematics. *Philosophy of mathematics Education Journal, 17.* Retrieved May 2012, from www.people.ex.ac.uk/PErnest/pome17/handal.htm

Hannula, M. S. (2006). Affect in mathematical thinking and learning. In J. Massz & W. Scholoeglmann (Eds.), *New mathematics education research and practice* (pp. 209–232). Rotterdam: Sense Publishing.

Hannula, M. S., Maijala, H., & Pehkonen, E. (2004). *Development of understanding and self-confidence in mathematics: Grades 5–8*. Paper presented at the Proceedings of the 28th conference of the International Group for the Psychology of mathematics Education, Bergan, Norway.

Hardy, T. (2007). Participation and performance: Keys to confident learning in mathematics. *Research in mathematics Education, 9*, 21–32.

Hardy, T. (2009). What does a discourse orientated examination have to offer teacher development? The problem with primary mathematics teachers. In L. Black, H. Mendick, & Y. Solomon (Eds.), *Mathematical relationships in education: Identities and participation* (pp. 185–197). New York: Routledge.

Harvey, D. (2005). *A brief history of neoliberalism*. Oxford: Oxford University Press.

Haylock, D., & Cockburn, A. D. (2008). *Understanding mathematics for young children: A guide for foundation stage and lower primary teachers*. London; Thousand Oaks, CA; New Delhi; Singapore: Sage.

Hendrick, H. (1997). Constructions and reconstructions of British childhood: An interpretative survey, 1800. In A. James & A. Prout (Eds.), *Constructing and reconstructing childhood: Contemporary issues in the sociological study of childhood* (pp. 34–62). London; Philadelphia: Falmer Press.

Henriques, J., Hollway, W., Urwin, C., Venn, C., & Walkerdine, V. (Eds.). (1998). *Changing the subject*. London; New York: Routledge.

H. M. Government. (2009). *New opportunities: Fair chances for the future*. London: HMSO.

Hobsbawm, E. (1994). *Age of extremes: The short twentieth century 1914–1991*. London: Abacus.

Holton, D., Anderson, J., Thomas, B., & Fletcher, D. (1999). Mathematical problem solving in support of the curriculum? *International Journal of Mathematical Education in Science and Technology, 30*(3), 351–371.

Hossain, S., Mendick, H., & Adler, J. (2013). Troubling "understanding mathematics in-depth": Its role in the identity work of student-teachers in England. *Educational Studies in mathematics*, 35–48.

Hultqvist, K., & Dahlberg, G. (Eds.). (2001). *Governing the child in the new millennium*. London: RoutledgeFalmer.

Hursh, D. W. (2007). Marketing education: The rise of standardized testing, accountability, competition, and markets in public education In E. W. Ross & R. Gibson (Eds.), *Neoliberalism and education reform*. Cresskill, NJ: Hampton Press.

James, A., Jenks, C., & Prout, A. (1998). *Theorizing childhood*. Cambridge, UK: Polity.

James, A., & Prout, A. (1997). *Constructing and reconstructing childhood*. London; Philadelphia: Falmer Press.

Jenks, C. (2005). *Childhood* (2nd ed.). Abingdon, Oxon: Routledge.

Johnson, P. (2006). Unravelling Foucault's "different spaces". *History of the Human Sciences, 19*(4), 75–90.

Jones, L., & Smart, T. (1995). Confidence and mathematics: A gender issue? *Gender and Education, 7*(2), 157–166.

Karimi, A., & Venkatesan, S. (2009). mathematics anxiety, mathematics performance and academic hardiness in high school students. *International Journal of Educational Sciences, 1*(1), 33–37.

Kenway, J. (1990). Education and the right's discursive politics: Private versus state schooling. In S. J. Ball (Ed.), *Foucault and education: Disciplines and knowledge* (pp. 167–206). London; New York: Routledge.

Kenway, J., & Bullen, J. (2001). *Consuming children: Education-entertainment-advertising*. Buckingham, MK: Open University Press.

Kline, S. (1995). *Out of the garden: Toys, TV, and children's culture in the age of marketing*. London: Verso.

Krutetskii, V. A. (1976). *The psychology of mathematics abilities in schoolchildren* (J. Teller, Trans., & J. Kilpatrick, Eds.). Chicago: University of Chicago Press.

Kyraciou, C. (2005). The impact of daily mathematics lessons in England on pupil confidence and competence in early mathematics: A systematic review. *British Journal of Educational Studies, 53*(2), 168–186.

Kyraciou, C., & Goulding, M. (2004). *A systematic review of the impact of daily mathematics lessons in enhancing pupils' confidence and competence in early mathematics*. London: EPPI-Centre, Institute of Education.

Labour Party. (1997). *New labour: Because Britain deserves better (The Labour Party manifesto)*. London: The Labour Party.

Lather, P. (1991). *Getting smart: Feminist research and pedagogy with/in the postmodern*. New York: Routledge.

Lave, J., & Wenger, E. (1991). *Situated learning: Legitimate peripheral participation*. New York: Cambridge University Press.

Lerman, S. (1983). Problem-solving or knowledge-centred: The influence of philosophy on mathematics teaching. *International Journal of Mathematical Education in Science and Technology, 14*(1), 59–66.

Lerman, S. (1990). Alternative perspectives of the nature of mathematics and their influence on the teaching of mathematics. *British Educational Research Journal, 16*(1), 53–61.

Lerman, S. (1994). Articulating theories of mathematics learning. In P. Ernest (Ed.), *Constructing mathematical knowledge: Epistemology and mathematics education* (pp. 41–49). London: Falmer Press.

Liljedahl, P. (2005). *Sustained engagement: Preservice teachers' experience with a chain of discovery*. Paper presented at the Proceedings of the Fourth Congress of the European Society for Research in mathematics Education. Sant Feliu de GuÃxols, Spain.

Liljedahl, P. (2011/2006). Learning elementary number theory through a chain of discovery: Preservice teachers' encounter with pentominoes. In R. Zazkis & S. R. Campbell (Eds.), *Number theory in mathematics education: Perspectives and prospects* (pp. 141–172). New York; Abingdon, Oxon: Routledge.

Llewellyn, A. (2009). "Gender games": A post-structural exploration of the prospective teacher, mathematics and identity. *Journal of mathematics Teacher Education, 12*(6), 411–426.

Llewellyn, A., & Mendick, H. (2011). Does every child count? Quality, equity and mathematics with/in neoliberalism. In B. Atweh, M. Graven, W. Secada, & P. Valero (Eds.), *Mapping equity and quality in mathematics education* (pp. 49–62). Dordrecht; New York: Springer.

Lloyd, G. (1993). *The man of reason: "Male" and "female" in western philosophy*. London: Routledge.

Locke, J. (1693/1932/1989). *Some thoughts concerning mathematics education*. Oxford: Clarendon.

Luke, C. (1989). *Pedagogy, printing and protestantism: The discourse on childhood*. New York: SUNY Press.

Lundin, S. (2012). Hating school, loving mathematics: On the ideological function of critique and reform in mathematics education. *Educational Studies in mathematics, 80*(1–2), 73–85.

Ma, X. (1999). A meta-analysis of the relationship between anxiety toward mathematics and achievement in mathematics. *Journal for Research in mathematics Education, 30*(5), 520–540.

MacLure, M. (2003). *Discourse in educational and social research.* Buckingham: Open University Press.

MacLure, M. (2010). The offence of theory. *Journal of Education Policy, 25*(2), 277–286.

Mann, E. L. (2006). Creativity: The essence of mathematics. *Journal for the Education of the Gifted, 30*(2), 236–260.

McClure, L. (n.d.). *Supporting the exceptionally mathematically able children: Who are they?* Retrieved July, 2014, from http://nrich.maths.org/7740

McGill, R. (2016). *Te@cher Toolkit: The most influential blog on education in the UK.* Retrieved October 2016, from www.teachertoolkit.me

McNeal, J. U. (2007). *On becoming a consumer: The development of consumer behavior patterns in childhood.* London: Routledge.

Mendick, H. (2006). *Masculinities and mathematics.* Maidenhead: Open University Press.

Mendick, H. (2011). *Is progress good for mathematics/education?* Paper presented at the British Society for Research into Learning mathematics, London.

Merriam, S. B. (2009). *Qualitative research: A guide to design and implementation.* San Francisco, CA: Jossey-Bass.

Moi, T. (1988). Feminism, postmodernism, and style: Recent feminist criticism in the United States. *Cultural Critique, 9,* 3–22.

Monk, D. (2009). Childhood and the law. In M. J. Kehily (Ed.), *An introduction to childhood studies* (pp. 177–197). Maidenhead: McGraw-Hill Education; Open University Press.

Morgan, N. (2014). *Nicky Morgan speaks at the launch of You Life campaign.* Retrieved March 2017, www.gov.uk/government/speeches/nicky-morgan-speaks-at-launch-of-your-life-campaign

Morgan, N. (2015a). *Nicky Morgan: Why knowledge matters.* DfE. Retrieved March 2017, www.gov.uk/government/speeches/nicky-morgan-why-knowledge-matters

Morgan, N. (2015b). Conservative education policies: You asked the questions. *The Guardian.* Retrieved March 2017, from www.theguardian.com/education/2015/apr/21/conservative-education-policies-schools-nicky-morgan

Morris, M. (1988). *The pirate's fiancee: Feminism, reading, postmodernism.* London: Verso.

National mathematics Advisory Panel. (2008). *Foundations for success: The final report of the National mathematics Advisory Panel.* Washington, DC: U.S. Department of Education.

Newman, J. (2001). *Modernising governance: New labour, policy and society.* London: Sage Publications.

Nias, J. (1999). Primary teaching as a culture of care. In J. Prosser (Ed.), *School culture* (pp. 66–81). London: Paul Chapman.

NRICH. (n.d.). *NRICH: Enriching mathematics.* Retrieved from http://nrich.maths.org/frontpage

Nunes, T., & Bryant, P. (1997). *Learning and teaching mathematics: An international perspective*. Hove, Sussex: Psychology Press.

Oancea, A., & Pring, R. (2008). The importance of being thorough: On systematic accumulations of "What Works" in education research. *Journal of Philosophy of Education, 42*, 15–39.

Ofsted. (2008). mathematics: *Understanding the score*. London: Ofsted.

Orton, A. (2004). *Learning mathematics: Issues, theory and classroom practice*. New York: Bloomsbury Publishing.

Orton, A., & Frobisher, L. (2005). *Insights into teaching mathematics* (2nd ed.). London: Continuum.

Ozga, J. (2009). Governing education through data in England: From regulation to self-evaluation. *Journal of Education Policy, 24*(2), 149–162.

Pais, A. (2013). *Conversation 2: Theory to analyze the macro dimension of classroom interactions* Paper presented at the mathematics, Education and Contemporary Theory 2. Manchester: Manchester Metropolitan University

Pais, A., Stentoft, D., & Valero, P. (2010). *From questions of how to questions of why in mathematics education research*. Paper presented at the Sixth International mathematics Education and Society Conference, Berlin, Germany.

Pais, A., & Valero, P. (2011). Beyond disavowing the politics of equity and quality in mathematics education. In B. Atweh, M. Graven, W. Secada, & P. Valero (Eds.), *Mapping equity and quality in mathematics education* (pp. 35–48). Dordrecht; Heidelberg; London; New York: Springer.

Pajares, F. (1996). Self-efficacy beliefs in academic settings. *Review of Educational Research, 66*(4), 543–578.

Patel, L. (2015). *Decolonizing educational research: From ownership to answerability*. New York: Routledge.

Patton, P., & Meaghan, M. (1979). *Michel Foucault: Power, truth, strategy*. Sydney: Feral Publications.

Phillips, D. C. (Ed.). (2000). *Constructivism in education: Opinions and second opinions on controversial issues. Ninety-Ninth yearbook of the National Society for the Study of Education*. Chicago, IL: University of Chicago Press.

Piaget, J. (1933). Social evolution and the new education. *Education Tomorrow, 4*, 3–25.

Piaget, J. (1957). The child and modern physics. *Scientific American, 197*, 46–51.

Piaget, J. (1980). Twelfth conversation. In J.-P. Bringuier (Ed.), *Conversations with Jean Piaget* (pp. 128–132). Chicago: University of Chicago Press.

Piaget, J., & Garcia, R. (1989). *Psychogenesis and the history of science*. New York: Columbia University Press.

Piaget, J., & Inhelder, B. (1969/2000). *The psychology of the child*. New York: Basic Books.

Pickett, B. L. (1996). Foucault and the politics of resistance. *Polity, 28*(4), 445–466.

Plato. (375BC/2003). *The republic* (D. Lee, Ed.) London: Penguin.

Plato. (380BC/2009). *Protagoras*. Rockville, MA: Serenity Publishers.

Plowden, B. (1967). *Children and their primary schools*. London: HMSO.

Polya, G. (1945/2014). *How to solve it: A new aspect of mathematical method*. New York: Princeton University Press.

Popkewitz, T. (1988). Educational reform: Rhetoric, ritual and social interest. *Educational Theory, 38*(1), 77–93.

Popkewitz, T., & Brennan, M. (1997). Restructuring of social and political theory in education: Foucault and a social epistemology of school practices. *Educational Theory, 47*(3), 287–313.

Postman, N. (1982/1994). *The disappearance of childhood.* New York: Vintage Books Ed.

Preckel, F., Goetz, T., Pekrun, R., & Kleine, M. (2008). Gender differences in gifted and average-ability students comparing girls' and boys' achievement, self-concept, interest, and motivation in mathematics. *Gifted Child Quarterly, 52*(2), 146–159.

Pring, R. (1989). Subject-centred versus child-centred education – a false dualism. *Journal of Applied Philosophy, 6*(2), 181–194.

Raymond, A. M. (1997). Inconsistency between a beginning elementary school teacher's mathematics beliefs and teaching practice. *Journal for Research in mathematics Education,* 550–576.

Remillard, J. T., & Kaye, P. (2002). Supporting teachers' professional learning by navigating openings in the curriculum. *Journal of mathematics Teacher Education, 5*(1), 7–3.

ResearchEd. (2016). *About.* Retrieved September 2016, from www.workingoutwhatworks.com/en-GB/About

Robertson, P. (1976). Home as a nest: Middle class childhood in nineteenth century Europe. In L. DeMause (Ed.), *The history of childhood* (pp. 407–431). London: Souvenir.

Romberg, T. A. (1997). The influence of programs from other countries on the school mathematics reform curricula in the United States. *American Journal of Education, 106*(1), 127–147.

Rorty, R. (1980). *Philosophy and the mirror of nature.* Oxford: Blackwell.

Rose, J. (2009). *Independent review of the primary curriculum: Final report.* London: DfES.

Rose, M. (2000). Looking back: 1985. mathematics *in School, 29*(3), 31.

Rose, N. (1991). Governing by numbers: Figuring out society. *Accounting Organisation and Society, 15*(7), 673–692.

Rose, N. (1999a). *Governing the soul* (2nd ed.). London: Free Association Books.

Rose, N. (1999b). *Powers of freedom: Reframing political thought.* Cambridge: Cambridge University Press.

Rousseau, J. (1755/2007). *Discourse on the origins of inequality* (G. D. H. Cole, Trans.). Minneapolis: Filquarian Publishing.

Rousseau, J. (1763/1884). *Emile, or, concerning education: Extracts, containing the principle elements of pedagogy found in the first three books/by Jean-Jacques Rousseau; with an introduction and notes by Jules Steeg.* London: D.C. Heath & Company.

Rousseau, J. (1763/2007). *Emile or on education.* Sioux Falls, SD: NuVision Publishing.

Ruthven, K. (1987). Ability stereotyping in mathematics. *Educational Studies in mathematics, 18*(3), 243–253.

Saad-Filho, A., & Johnston, D. (Eds.). (2005). *Neoliberalism: A critical reader.* London; Ann Arbor, MI: Pluto Press.

Santos, S., & Barmby, P. (2010). Enrichment and engagement in mathematics. In Joubert, M. and Andrews, P. (Eds.) Proceedings of the British Congress for mathematics Education April 2010, University of Manchester.

References 147

Sarup, M. (1993). *An introductory guide to post-structuralism and postmodernism* (2nd ed.). Georgia: University of Georgia Press.

Schiefele, U., & Csikszentmihalyi, M. (1995). Motivation and ability as factors in mathematics experience and achievement. *Journal for Research in mathematics Education, 26*(2), 163–181.

Schoenfeld, A. H. (1992). Learning to think mathematically: Problem solving, metacognition, and sense making in mathematics. In D. A. Grouws (Ed.), *Handbook of research on mathematics teaching and learning* (pp. 334–370). New York: Palgrave Macmillan.

Schoenfeld, A. H. (2002). Making mathematics work for all children: Issues of standards, testing, and equity. *Educational Researcher, 31*(1), 13–25.

Seargeant, P., & Tagg, C. (2014) *The language of social media: Identity and community on the internet* (pp. 1–20). Basingstoke; New York: Palgrave Macmillan.

Simon, M. A. (1995). Reconstructing mathematics pedagogy from a constructivist perspective. *Journal for Research in mathematics Education, 26*(2), 114–145.

Sjoberg, S. (2007). Constructivism and learning. In E. Baker, B. McGaw, & P. Peterson (Eds.), *International encyclopaedia of education* (3rd ed., Vol. 10, pp. 1–11). Oxford: Elsevier.

Skemp, R. (1976). Relational understanding and instrumental understanding mathematics *Teaching, 77*, 20–26.

Skinner, B. F. (1938). *The behavior of organisms: An experimental analysis.* Englewood Cliffs, NJ: Prentice-Hall.

Skinner, B. F. (1974). *About behaviorism.* New York: Knopf.

Smith, A. (2004). *Making mathematics count: The report of Professor Adrian Smith's inquiry into post-14 mathematics education.* London: The Stationary Office

Smith, L. (2001). Jean Piaget, 1986–1980. In J. Palmer (Ed.), *Fifty modern thinkers on education* (pp. 37–44). Abingdon, Oxon; New York: Routledge.

Soriede, G. E. (2007). *Narrative construction of teacher identity.* Bergen: University of Bergen.

Spielberger, C. D. (1972). Conceptual and methodological issues in anxiety research. In C. D. Spielberger (Ed.), *Anxiety: Current trends in theory and research* (pp. 481–493). New York: Academic Press.

Stake, R. (1978). The case study method in social inquiry. *Educational Researcher, 7*(2), 5–8.

Stake, R. (1995). *The art of case study research.* Thousand Oaks, CA; London; New Delhi: Sage.

Straker, A. (1983). *Mathematics for gifted pupils.* London: Longmans.

Steiner-Khamsi, G. (2010). The politics and economics of comparison. *Comparative Education Review, 54*(3), 323–342.

Suggate, J., Davis, A., & Goulding, M. (2006). *Mathematical knowledge for primary teachers.* London: David Fulton.

Sugrue, C. (1998). *Complexities of teaching: Child-centred perspectives.* London: Falmer.

Tarim, K. (2009). The effects of cooperative learning on preschoolers' mathematics problem-solving ability. *Educational Studies in mathematics, 72*(3), 325–340.

Taylor, S. (2001). Locating and conducting discourse analytic research. In M. Wetherell, S. Taylor, & S. Yates (Eds.), *Discourse as data: A guide for analysis.* Milton Keyes: Sage in association with the Open University.

Thomas, G. (2007). *Education and theory: Strangers in paradigms*. Maidenhead: Oxford University Press.
Thomas, G. (2016). After the gold rush: Questioning the "gold standard" and reappraising the status of experiment and randomized controlled trials in education *Harvard Educational Review*, *86*(3), 390–411.
Threadgold, T. (2000). Poststructuralism and discourse analysis. In A. Lee & C. Poynton (Eds.), *Culture and text: Discourse and methodology in social research and cultural studies*. Lanham, MD: Rowman & Littlefield.
Tierney, W. G. (2000). Undaunted courage: Life history and the postmodern challenge. In N. K. Denzin & Y. S. Lincoln (Eds.), *Handbook of qualitative research* (2nd ed.). London; Thousand Oaks; New Delhi: Sage.
Tobias, S. (1985). Test anxiety: Interference, defective skills, and cognitive capacity. *Educational Psychologist*, *20*(3), 135–142.
Torgerson, C. J., & Torgerson, D. J. (2001). The need for randomised controlled trials in educational research. *British Journal of Educational Studies*, *49*(3), 316–328.
UN. (2013). Millennium development goals. Retrieved from www.un.org/millenniumgoals/
UNESCO. (2000). *World education report 2000: The right to education: Towards education for all throughout life*. Paris: UNESCO publishing.
Valero, P. (2002). *The myth of the active learner: From cognitive to socio-political interpretations of students in mathematics classrooms*. Paper presented at the mathematics Education and Society, Helsingør, Denmark.
Van Sant, G. (Writer) (1997). *Good will hunting*. New York: Miramax Films.
Van Zoest, L. R., & Bohl, J. V. (2002). The role of reform curricular materials in an internship: The case of Alice and Gregory. *Journal of mathematics Teacher Education*, *5*(3), 265–288.
Vaughan. (2015, September 21). Education reformers' call for more tests and stronger discipline. Retrieved September 2016, from www.tes.com/news/school-news/breaking-news/education-reformers-call-more-tests-and-stronger-discipline
Von Glasersfeld, E. (1991). *Radical constructivism in mathematics education*. Dordrecht: Kluwer.
Vorderman, C., Budd, C., Dunne, R., Hart, M., & Porkess, R. (2011). *A world class mathematics education for all our young people*. London: The Conservative Party. Retrieved from www.tsm-resources.com/pdf/VordermanMathsReport.pdf
Vygotsky, L. (1981). The genesis of higher mental functions. In J. V. Wertsch (Ed.), *The concept of activity in social psychology* (pp. 144–188). New York: Sharpe.
Wacquant, L. J. (1991). Making class: The middle-class(es) in social theory and social structure. In S. G. McNall, R. F. Levine, & R. Fantasia (Eds.), *Bringing class back in contemporary historical perspectives* (pp. 39–64). Boulder, CO: Westview Press.
Walkerdine, V. (1988). *The mastery of reason*. London; New York: Routledge.
Walkerdine, V. (1989). *Counting girls out*. London: Virago Press.
Walkerdine, V. (1990). *Schoolgirl fictions*. London: Verso.
Walkerdine, V. (1997). Redefining the subject in situated cognition theory. In D. Kirshner & J. A. Whitson (Eds.), *Situated cognition: Social, semiotic, and psychological perspectives* (pp. 57–70). Mahwah, NJ: Lawrence Erlbaum.
Walkerdine, V. (1998a). *Counting girls out: Girls and mathematics* (2nd ed.). Abingdon: RoutledgeFalmer.
Walkerdine, V. (1998b). Developmental psychology and the child-centred pedagogy: The insertion of Piaget into early education. In J. Henriques, W. Hollway,

C. Urwin, C. Venn, & V. Walkerdine (Eds.), *Changing the subject: Psychology, social regulation and subjectivity* (pp. 153–202). London; New York: Routledge.

Walkerdine, V. (1999). Violent boys and precocious girls. *Contemporary Issues in Early Childhood, 1*(1), 3–23.

Walkerdine, V., & Lucey, H. (1989). *Democracy in the kitchen*. London: Virago.

Walshaw, M. (2004). The pedagogical relation in postmodern times: Learning with Lacan. In M. Walshaw (Ed.), mathematics *education within the postmodern* (pp. 121–139). Greenwich, CT: Information Age Publishing.

Walshaw, M. (2007). *Working with Foucault in education*. Rotterdam: Sense Publishers.

Watson, A. (2009). *Key understandings in mathematics learning: Paper 6: Algebraic reasoning*. London: University of Oxford.

Watson, A. (2010). Key understandings in learning mathematics. *Scottish Mathematical Council Journal.* 40, 14-15

Watson, J. B. (1913). Psychology as the behaviorist views it. *Psychological Review, 20*(2), 158–177.

Watt, H. M. (2005). Attitudes to the use of alternative assessment methods in mathematics: A study with secondary mathematics teachers in Sydney, Australia. *Educational Studies in mathematics, 58*(1), 21–44.

Weedon, C. (1997). *Feminist practice and poststructuralist theory*. Malden: Blackwell.

Wells, K. (2015). *Childhood in a global perspective* (2nd ed.) Cambridge: Polity Press.

Whitty, G., Power, S., & Halpin, D. (1998). *Devolution and choice in education: The school, the state and the market*. Philadelphia: Open University Press.

Wilchins, R. A. (2004). *Queer theory, gender theory: An instant primer*. New York: Alyson Books.

Williams, P. (2008). *Independent review of mathematics teaching in early years setting and primary schools*. London: DCSF

Willis, S. (1990). The power of mathematics: For whom? In J. Kenway & S. Willis (Eds.), *Hearts and minds: Self-esteem and the schooling of girls* (pp. 191–211). Lewes: Falmer Press.

Winn, M. (1983). *Children without childhood*. New York: Pantheon Books.

Wood, D. (1998). *How children think and learn* (2nd ed.). Oxford: Blackwell.

Woods, P., & Jeffrey, B. (1996). *Teachable moments: The art of teaching in primary schools*. Buckingham: Open University Press.

Woods, P., & Jeffrey, B. (2002). The reconstruction of primary teachers' identities. *British Journal of Sociology of Education, 23*(1), 89–106.

Wyness, M. (2012). *Childhood and society: An introduction to the sociology of childhood* (2nd ed.). Basingstoke: Palgrave Macmillan.

Zembylas, M. (2003). Emotions and teacher identity: A poststructural perspective. *Teachers and Teaching: Theory and Practice, 9*(3), 213–238.

Zevenbergen, R. (2003). Ability grouping in mathematics classrooms: A Bourdieuian analysis. *For the Learning of mathematics, 23*(3), 5–10.

Index

'ability': in education policy 78–81; in mathematics education research 98–104; pre-service teachers and 119–123; see also 'natural mathematical ability'
absolutist paradigm in mathematics 14–15, 56
accountability of schools 5, 123
achievement, as fixed state 113
'active' school students/learners 4, 91–92, 95, 103, 105
advert linking understanding with confidence 74–75, 78
age: of adulthood 40; of criminal responsibility 41; school class and 44
agency of child 45–46, 57
already-assigned able mathematical child 119–123
appeal of childhood 37–40
archaeology 33–35
Ariès, P. 41, 44, 46
assumptions of mathematics education 87
autonomy 52–53

Bennett, Tom 125
binary oppositions and deconstruction 34–35
biopower 33, 36, 69
Blair, Tony 65–66, 87; see also New Labour government
blaming: pupils 109; teachers 110
Boaler, Jo 92–95, 97, 111

case studies, poststructural 107
certainty, security of 14–15
child: agency of 45–46, 57; consumerism for 20; as discursive construct 26–27; (post)modern consumer 45–47; natural, of Rousseau 47–49; normal, of Piaget 49–51; psychological developmental, favouring of 22, 29; see also functional mathematical child; romantic child of mathematics education research
childhood: Age of Enlightenment and 16, 47; (de)constructing 37–40; (de)constructing in mathematics education 51–52; defining 40–42; education as shaping 42–45; as governed, in UK 38; as universal 39–40, 50–51
China, education system in 4
citation 13, 90
classrooms: girls in 93–94; mathematics pedagogy in 59–63; 'open' 92–93; productions of mathematical child in 129–130
Cockcroft Report 62–63
communities of practice 93
competence and confidence, conflation of 76–77, 97–98, 118–119, 131
compulsory education, timescale of 40, 43
confidence: 'ability' and 98–99; 'can-do' approach and 118–119; competence conflated with 76–77, 97–98, 119, 131; in mathematics education research 95–98; natural ability and 117; as performative 74–77, 78; of pre-service teachers 113; questioning discourse of 130; victim blaming and 77–78
Conservative government, education policy under 81–87, 123
constructivism 54–55
consumer culture and childhood 20, 45–47
Continued Professional Development 123

critical theory 15
critique, Foucault interpretation of 18–19
cultural history of childhood 41–42

deconstruction 33–35
defective, pupils seen as 109
defining childhood 40–42
Derrida, Jacques 34–35
developmental psychology: childhood and 46–47, 49–51; in mathematics education 52–53, 91–92; in mathematics education research 99–101
discipline, education as form of 43
discourses: of childhood 37–40; of derision 59–60, 63, 82; of dichotomy in education 53; of education 69; interruption and questioning of 130–131; overview 20–23; power and 25–26; of primary teaching 60–61; romantic and functional 112; of usefulness of mathematics 21–22, 90; *see also* 'ability'; confidence; progress, expectations of; understanding

education: as form of governance and discipline 43; improvement, need for, as omnipresent in 3, 22; neoliberal culture and 5–6; Piaget on 50; progressive 53–55, 58–59, 61–62, 63–64; Rousseau on 47–49; as shaping childhood 42–45; as site of normative practice 28–31; traditional 53, 55–59, 61, 63–64; *see also* norms of mathematics education
educational research, theory in 11–16
education policy: 'ability' in 78–81; 'confidence' in 74–78; under Conservative government 81–87; New Labour 66–68; overview 65–66; productions of mathematical child in 128–129; progress, expectations of 69–71, 73; 'understanding' in 73–74
Emile, or on Education (Rousseau) 48
Enlightenment 16, 47
essentialism: of Boaler 94; of pre-service teachers 122
evidence-based trends of neoliberalism 104

#FEAS 13
fictions and truth 19–20
Foucault, Michel: on discourses 20–23; poststructuralism and 16; on power 23–26; on production of truth 128; on truth and fictions 19–20; work of 17–19
Framework for Teaching mathematics 68
freedom, illusion of 48, 52
functional automaton: construction of mathematical child as 107–109; frustration of mathematical child as 110–111; production of mathematical child as 128–129
functional mathematical child: of New Labour 68–69, 71, 81; pre-service teacher as 119–120

gender and confidence 77–78, 96–97, 117
gendered binary of Western thinking 49
genealogy 33–35
General Certificate of Secondary Education 59, 83
'gifted and talented' pupils 79–80, 103
girls: confidence and 77–78; in mathematics classrooms 93–94
Gove, Michael 83, 84, 85, 86–87
governance, education as form of 43
governmentality 31–33, 36, 52, 75
Greening, Justine 6
grouping by 'ability' 103–104

Hammond, Philip 2
hermeneutic model of childhood 46
heterotopias 124

identity, formation of 35
Imafidon, Anne-Marie 122
improvement, need for, as omnipresent in education 3, 22
Increasing Pupils' Rates of Progress in mathematics (DfES) 71
individuality, promise of 69
innocent, childhood as 39–40
instrumental approach to education 13

knowledge and power 23–26

loss of childhood 38–39, 45

Making Good Progress publications (DCFS) 71–72, 77, 81
Man, as discursive construct 27
manufacturing mathematical child 29
mathematics Counts: The Cockcroft Report 62–63
mathematics education research: 'ability' in 98–104; comparative

approaches to 94–95; confidence in 95–98; large data sets and 89–90; overview 89; as privileging active mathematical child 91–92, 95; as (re)producing hierarchies and privilege 90; productions of mathematical child in 128–129; progress and 90–91; romantic child of 89, 96, 99, 104–105, 117, 119, 129
mathematics specialist schools 2
mathematics teachers 1
McGill, Ross 125
measurability and accountability, system of, in education 5
mobilising language for lower 'ability' pupils 80–81
(post)modern consumer child 45–47
Morgan, Nicky 82, 83

National Numeracy Strategy 66, 67, 68, 70
'natural' child: of Piaget 49–51; of Rousseau 47–49
'natural mathematical ability' 98–104, 116–117, 119–123
neo-conservative ideology 62
neoliberalism: confidence and 74–77; consumer culture, childhood, and 45–47; evidence-based trends of 104; functional child and 87; governmentality and 52; individual and 27; New Labour's version of 33, 66; normalisation and 30–31; in UK 5–7
neutrality, assumption of 91
New Labour government: education policy under 66–68; equity under 87; National Numeracy Strategy 63; neoliberalism of 33, 66; pre-service teachers of 107
normalisation 29–31, 36, 75, 130
norms of mathematics education: overview 1–5; pedagogies, mathematical child, and 52–59; in UK classrooms 59–63
NRICH website 102

'open' classrooms 92–93
Other and deconstruction 34

pedagogies: mathematics, mathematical child, and 52–59; in UK classrooms 59–63
performativity as method of legitimising education 66–67
Piaget, J. 46, 49–51, 53, 60

PISA (Programme for International Student Assessment) 2, 85
Plato 14–15, 42
'Plowden report' 60
political, educational research as 14
poststructuralism 16–17
'potential' 80–81
power: Foucault on 23–26; shifting of, through Twitter 125–127
power relations within systems 36
primary teaching, discourse of 60–61
privatisation of public sector 6, 67, 82
privilege: mathematics education research as (re)producing 90; querying 13
privileging: of active mathematical child 91–92, 95; of Randomised Control Trials 11–12, 13, 104; of skills within curriculum and documentation 68–69, 73; of STEM 83
problem-solving, 'real' mathematics as achieved through 96–97, 99–100, 103
Programme for International Student Assessment (PISA) 2, 85
progress, expectations of 69–71, 73, 107–111, 130
progressive pedagogy 53–55, 58–59, 61–62, 63–64
psychological developmental child, favouring of 22, 29

querying privilege 13
'quest for understanding' 111–112

Randomised Control Trials (RCTs), privileging of 11–12, 13, 104
ResearchEd 125
romantic child of mathematics education research 89, 96, 99, 104–105, 117, 119, 129
rote learning, understanding positioned against 111, 114–115, 116
Rousseau, J. 42, 47–49, 53

school class, construction of 44
Science, education as 12; *see also* STEM
self: within neoliberalism 67; poststructural 26–28, 58–59
sexuality and childhood 40–41
Shanghai mastery mathematics 4, 85, 86
situated cognition 93
skills, privileging of, within curriculum and documentation 68–69, 73

social media and interaction of teachers 123–127
social theory 15
sociology, childhood studies in 46
specialness 99–100
Spielman, Amanda 6
STEM (Science, Technology, Engineering and mathematics): funding for 12; privileging of 83; in US 2
structuralism 16
subject and subjectivity 26–28
success, reports of 72
surveillance in education system 30
symbol, child as 37–40

teachers: ability and 114–115, 119–123; construction of mathematical child and 107–109; discourses of mathematical child and 106–107, 129–130; earnings of 1; 'expertise' of 123–127; frustration of mathematical child and 110–111; as identifying as mathematical 115–117; neoliberal 'can-do' approach to mathematics and 118–119; social media and 123–127; on understanding 111–115

teachmeets 123
TEF (Teacher Excellence and Students Outcome Framework) 7
Thatcher, Margaret 61–62
theory in educational research 11–16
TIMMS (Trends in International mathematics and Science Study) 2, 85
traditional pedagogy 53, 55–59, 61, 63–64
truth and fictions 19–20
Twitter, shifting of power through 125–127

understanding: functional meaning of 73–74, 84, 111–112; pre-service teachers on 111–113, 119; quest for; questioning discourse of 130; as reserved for most able 114–115, 116–117
universal, childhood as 39–40, 50–51
usefulness of mathematics, discourse of 21–22, 90

Vorderman et al. report 84–85

Web 2.0 technologies 124